Hands-On Reactive Programming with Python

Event-driven development unraveled with RxPY

Romain Picard

BIRMINGHAM - MUMBAI

Hands-On Reactive Programming with Python

Commissioning Editor: Richa Tripathi
Acquisition Editor: Shriram Shekhar
Content Development Editor: Zeeyan Pinheiro
Technical Editor: Romy Dias
Copy Editor: Safis Editing
Project Coordinator: Vaidehi Sawant
Proofreader: Safis Editing
Indexer: Rekha Nair
Graphics: Alishon Mendonsa
Production Coordinator: Deepika Naik

First published: October 2018

Production reference: 2091118

Published by Packt Publishing Ltd.
Livery Place
35 Livery Street
Birmingham
B3 2PB, UK.

ISBN 978-1-78913-872-6

www.packtpub.com

To my family

– Romain Picard

If you can't explain it simply, you don't understand it well enough

– Albert Einstein

`mapt.io`

Mapt is an online digital library that gives you full access to over 5,000 books and videos, as well as industry leading tools to help you plan your personal development and advance your career. For more information, please visit our website.

Why subscribe?

- Spend less time learning and more time coding with practical eBooks and videos from over 4,000 industry professionals

- Improve your learning with Skill Plans built especially for you

- Get a free eBook or video every month

- Mapt is fully searchable

- Copy and paste, print, and bookmark content

Packt.com

Did you know that Packt offers eBook versions of every book published, with PDF and ePub files available? You can upgrade to the eBook version at `www.packt.com` and as a print book customer, you are entitled to a discount on the eBook copy. Get in touch with us at `customercare@packtpub.com` for more details.

At `www.packt.com`, you can also read a collection of free technical articles, sign up for a range of free newsletters, and receive exclusive discounts and offers on Packt books and eBooks.

Contributors

About the author

Romain Picard is currently a data science engineer. He has been working in the digital TV and telecommunications industry for 20 years. His daily work consists of data manipulation, machine learning model training, and model deployment. Almost all of these tasks are based on Python code, and he uses reactive programming whenever it's applicable. He was previously a media software architect and a software developer. In these previous positions, he designed and developed TV and OTT players that have been used in tens of millions of set top boxes. Romain is especially interested in algorithms, looking for the most suitable algorithm for each use case.

André Staltz, you have been a great source of inspiration these last few years. I discovered functional and reactive programming thanks to CycleJS. This book would not exist without your work.

Thank you to my fellows, you know who you are. We had some hard times, we achieved incredible things. I will remember the best of these moments forever.

Last but not least, thank you very much to Anne, Claire, and Nicolas for your unconditional love. You are all I need.

About the reviewer

Ricardo Bánffy is a hardware engineer by training and software engineer at heart. He has been writing executable poetry since the late 1980s in all types of languages for all kinds of computers, from GUI tools for Apple II+ computers and business software for mainframes to hardware provisioning and monitoring tools for massive Linux clusters. A passionate Python advocate since the late 1990s, he is often busy attending or speaking at conferences and local meetups. His most recent work involves orchestration tools for transforming large datasets using Python and lots of clever tricks.

Packt is searching for authors like you

If you're interested in becoming an author for Packt, please visit `authors.packtpub.com` and apply today. We have worked with thousands of developers and tech professionals, just like you, to help them share their insight with the global tech community. You can make a general application, apply for a specific hot topic that we are recruiting an author for, or submit your own idea.

Table of Contents

Preface

Welcome to *Hands-On Reactive Programming with Python*! This book is a step-by-step journey into event-driven programming and, more specifically, reactive programming. The resources available on this topic are still rather sparse, especially for Python. I hope that this book will help to fill a part of that gap, and that it will give you the knowledge and will to write code in a functional and reactive way.

Magic is rarely something good in computer science. In my career, I have met quite a number of developers who were happy when a development started to work magically or when a bug was fixed magically (usually with some help of a delay). Any programmer can be lazy, but certainly not in this way! Fortunately, I've also had the chance to meet a lot of developers with the good laziness skill: understanding everything you do to ensure that you will not have to do it twice. I firmly believe that to use any framework correctly, you have to understand how it works under the hood. This is why this book is structured this way, with explanations of the principles that make reactive and asynchronous programming work the way they do.

Writing this book has been incredibly rewarding, and worth the effort. As I write this preface, there is no online documentation for the Python implementation of ReactiveX, and it is still difficult to find code examples of the operators for the other programming languages' implementations. This is why I have taken care to provide working examples for all operators that are documented in this book. I have carefully read the implementation of each of them to ensure that they are documented exactly as they behave.

However, documenting the RxPY operators is not the main aim of this book. The practical examples provided chapter after chapter should gradually help you to become confident with ReactiveX and asynchronous programming, including rather advanced topics such as observable multiplexing.

I have worked hard to make this book as didactic as possible and as accurate as possible. However, if you find any mistakes or if you feel that some parts are missing explanations, feel free to tell me about it.

Who this book is for

This book is intended for software developers who are already at ease with Python and have heard about reactive programming but have not had a chance to work with it yet. However, no expertise is needed beyond that. Each chapter of the book describes new notions step by step so that the reader can gradually gain the necessary knowledge to understand the chapters that follow.

Hopefully, this will not be a *read once and put on the shelf* book. The operators documentation and descriptions of ways to tackle common problems should make this book regularly handy, even after being fully read.

What this book covers

Chapter 1, *An Introduction to Reactive Programming*, gives an overview of event-driven programming and reactive programming.

Chapter 2, *Asynchronous Programming in Python*, presents the foundations of asynchronous programming and the different ways to deal with input/output. It provides an initial introduction to AsyncIO.

Chapter 3, *Functional Programming with ReactiveX*, provides insights on how to structure the code of an application with ReactiveX, and how to use functional programming in particular.

Chapter 4, *Exploring Observables and Observers*, goes into the details of observables and observers, and all the possible ways to create observables.

Chapter 5, *Concurrency and Parallelism in RxPY*, explains how RxPY manages CPU concurrency via schedulers.

Chapter 6, *Implementation of an Audio Transcoding Server*, goes through the initial implementation of a realistic reactive and functional application.

Chapter 7, *Using Third-Party Services*, is a continuation of the previous chapter, explaining how to integrate an existing SDK with AsyncIO and RxPY. It also introduces Docker, a container-management platform.

Chapter 8, *Dynamic Reconfiguration and Error Management*, goes into functionalities and robustness in more depth, explaining how ReactiveX makes it simple to manage dynamic changes.

Chapter 9, *Operators in RxPY*, runs through a detailed documentation of 40 widely used operators that have not been covered in the book so far.

Chapter 10, *Testing and Debugging*, explains how to test reactive code, and how to debug it.

Chapter 11, *Deploying and Scaling Your Application*, shows how to deploy a Python application on the cloud and how to scale it, thanks to Docker, Docker Compose, and Traefik.

Chapter 12, *Reactive Streams for Remote Communication*, covers a rather advanced topic. It paves the way to reactive systems, and the global use of observables to communicate between applications.

Chapter 13, *A Checklist On Best Practices*, contains some final notes on things that are easy to forget when starting to code reactive applications.

To get the most out of this book

This book is about Python programming, but it is not an introduction to Python programming. It supposes that the reader is already familiar with the Python programming language. Moreover, asynchronous programming is not easy to comprehend at first. For this, some knowledge on computer science can help but is not mandatory. This book contains a lot of code samples and diagrams. In order to test these code samples, a computer with the following software is needed:

- A personal computer with either a Linux distribution, macOS X, or Windows
- Python already installed, at least Python 3.6
- A code editor or an IDE to view and modify the code provided

Download the example code files

You can download the example code files for this book from your account at www.packt.com. If you purchased this book elsewhere, you can visit www.packt.com/support and register to have the files emailed directly to you.

You can download the code files by following these steps:

1. Log in or register at `www.packt.com`.
2. Select the **SUPPORT** tab.
3. Click on **Code Downloads & Errata**.
4. Enter the name of the book in the **Search** box and follow the onscreen instructions.

Once the file is downloaded, please make sure that you unzip or extract the folder using the latest version of:

- WinRAR/7-Zip for Windows
- Zipeg/iZip/UnRarX for Mac
- 7-Zip/PeaZip for Linux

The code bundle for the book is also hosted on GitHub at `https://github.com/PacktPublishing/Hands-On-Reactive-Programming-with-Python`. In case there's an update to the code, it will be updated on the existing GitHub repository.

We also have other code bundles from our rich catalog of books and videos available at `https://github.com/PacktPublishing/`. Check them out!

Conventions used

There are a number of text conventions used throughout this book.

`CodeInText`: Indicates code words in text, database table names, folder names, filenames, file extensions, pathnames, dummy URLs, user input, and Twitter handles. Here is an example: "In the RxPY implementation, operators are methods of the `Observable` class."

A block of code is set as follows:

```
Observable.from_(...)
  .filter()
  .distinct()
  .take(20)
  .map(...)
```

When we wish to draw your attention to a particular part of a code block, the relevant lines or items are set in bold:

```
argv.subscribe(
    on_next=lambda i: print("on_next: {}".format(i)),
    on_error=lambda e: print("on_error: {}".format(e)),
    on_completed=lambda: print("on_completed"))
```

Any command-line input or output is written as follows:

```
$ source venv-rx/bin/activate
(venv-rx)$ pip install rx
```

Bold: Indicates a new term, an important word, or words that you see onscreen. For example, words in menus or dialog boxes appear in the text like this. Here is an example: "By definition, any program has to deal with external events through **inputs/outputs (I/O)**."

Warnings or important notes appear like this.

Tips and tricks appear like this.

Get in touch

Feedback from our readers is always welcome.

General feedback: If you have questions about any aspect of this book, mention the book title in the subject of your message and email us at customercare@packtpub.com.

Errata: Although we have taken every care to ensure the accuracy of our content, mistakes do happen. If you have found a mistake in this book, we would be grateful if you would report this to us. Please visit www.packt.com/submit-errata, selecting your book, clicking on the Errata Submission Form link, and entering the details.

Piracy: If you come across any illegal copies of our works in any form on the Internet, we would be grateful if you would provide us with the location address or website name. Please contact us at copyright@packt.com with a link to the material.

If you are interested in becoming an author: If there is a topic that you have expertise in and you are interested in either writing or contributing to a book, please visit authors.packtpub.com.

Reviews

Please leave a review. Once you have read and used this book, why not leave a review on the site that you purchased it from? Potential readers can then see and use your unbiased opinion to make purchase decisions, we at Packt can understand what you think about our products, and our authors can see your feedback on their book. Thank you!

For more information about Packt, please visit packt.com.

1
An Introduction to Reactive Programming

This first chapter covers the principles of reactive programming and ReactiveX. It is composed of three parts. The first part explains what reactive programming is and how it compares to other concepts and paradigms that are often used in event-driven programming. The second part explains the foundations of ReactiveX and RxPY, its Python implementation. This exploration of RxPY is explained with a simple example that allows us to understand the basics of ReactiveX. Finally, the last part is dedicated to the documentation of the ReactiveX project and the documentation of your projects. By the end of this chapter, you will be able to write some ReactiveX code and understand existing code.

The following topics will be covered in this chapter:

- What is reactive programming?
- An introduction to ReactiveX and RxPY
- A reactive echo application
- Marble diagrams
- Flow diagrams

What is reactive programming?

Reactive programming has gained a lot of popularity since 2010. Although its concepts and usage date from the early days of computing, this recent popularity is mainly due to the publication of the ReactiveX project. This might seem surprising for developers who had rarely used event-driven programming before. However, for people who faced tremendous state machines or callback hell, this seems more of an inevitable fact.

Before playing with ReactiveX and RxPY, this first part describes the principles being used in reactive programming and how they are used in asynchronous frameworks. This initial study of low-level features is not strictly necessary when using ReactiveX and asynchronous frameworks, but it helps a lot to understand how they work, which thus helps us to use them correctly.

Event-driven programming

What is the common connection between state machines, Petri net, **Kahn Process Networks (KPN)**, the observer design pattern, callbacks, pipes, publish/subscribe, futures, promises and streams? Event-driven programming!

By definition, any program has to deal with external events through **inputs/outputs (I/O)**. I/O and event management are the foundations of any computer system: reading or writing from storage, handling touch events, drawing on a screen, sending or receiving information on a network link, and so on. Nothing useful can be done without interacting with I/O, and I/O are almost always managed through events. However, 50 years after the creation of the first microprocessor, event-driven programming is still a very active topic with new technologies appearing almost every year.

The main purpose of this important activity is that, despite the fact that event-driven programming has existed since the beginning of computer science, it is still hard to use correctly. More than writing event-driven code, the real challenge lies in writing readable, maintainable, reusable, and testable code. Event-driven programming is more difficult to implement and read than sequential programming because it often means writing code that is not natural to read for human beings—instead of a sequence of actions that execute one after the other until the task to execute is completed, the beginning of an action starts when an event occurs, and then the actions that are triggered are often dispersed within the program. When such a code flow becomes complex—and this starts only after few indirect paths in a code—then it becomes more and more difficult to understand what is happening. This is what is often called the **callback hell**. One has to follow callbacks calling callbacks, which call further callbacks, and so on.

During the late nineties, event-driven programming became quite popular with the advent of **graphical user interfaces (GUIs)**. At that time, developers had the following options to write GUI applications:

- Objective-C on NextStep and macOS
- C++ on Windows

- C or eventually C++ on Unix (with X11)
- Java, with the hope of writing the same application for all these systems

All these environments were based on callbacks and it stayed that way for a very long time, until programming languages included features to improve the readability of event-driven code.

So event-driven code is often more difficult to read than sequential code because the code logic can be difficult to follow, depending on the programming language and the frameworks being used. Reactive programming, and more specifically ReactiveX, aims at solving some of these challenges. Python and its relatively recent support of async/await syntax also aims to make event-driven programming easier.

It is important to understand that reactive programming and event-driven programming are not programming paradigms, such as imperative or object-oriented programming, but are orthogonal to them. Event-driven programming is implemented within an existing paradigm. So, one can use event-driven programming with an object-oriented language or a functional language. Reactive programming is a specific case of event-driven programming. This can be seen in the following figure:

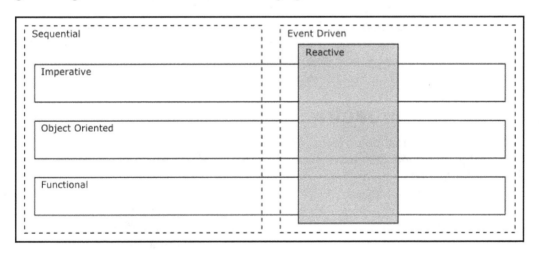

Figure 1.1: Event-driven programming and programming paradigms

Reactive versus proactive

So what is reactive programming?

An easy way to get the idea behind it is to use an analogy with people's behavior: someone who is proactive is somebody who takes initiatives. A proactive person will propose ideas or test things before somebody asks him to do so. On the other hand, a reactive person is somebody who waits for information before doing something. So, a proactive person acts on his own while a reactive person reacts to external changes. There are pros and cons to each behavior: a proactive person proposing solutions ahead of time is great, but may have difficulties dealing with unexpected changes. On the other hand, a reactive person may be very efficient in dealing with very dynamic environments.

Reactive programming can be considered as implementing a behavior in a similar way to a reactive person. A reactive system reacts on external events and provides a result that depends only on the event it has received. So why would reactive programming be better than sequential programming? Better is always a matter of preferences and context, so reactive programming may not be the solution most adapted to all the problems you will encounter. However, as you will see through this book, reactive programming shines at implementing event-driven code.

Reactive programming is inherently asynchronous. So it makes it easier to deal efficiently with inputs and outputs than with synchronous paradigms. Reactive programming favors composition. Each component is completely independent from another and can be plugged in with other components. This also makes testing quite easy and, as a consequence, it also helps to refactor existing code. Moreover, it is quite engaging, and with experience you will see that almost everything is a flow of events.

Reactor and proactor

When looking for information on event-driven programming concepts, two other similar terms are often mentioned: the reactor and the proactor. These are notions that are not really important when using high-level libraries such as ReactiveX and AsyncIO. Still, it is interesting to know what they are so that you can better understand what is going on under the hood. They are two kinds of low-level APIs that allow us to implement an event-driven library. For example, AsyncIO, which is the Python asynchronous API which can use a reactor or a proactor to expose the same APIs. Using a reactor or a proactor as the foundation of a framework is driven by the support, or not, of the proactor on the operating system. All operating systems support a reactor via the POSIX `select` system call or one of its derivatives. Some operating systems such as Windows implement proactor system calls. The difference between these two design patterns is the way I/O are managed.

Figure 1.2 shows a sequence diagram of how a reactor works. The three main components involved in this pattern are as follows:

- Reactor
- Event handler
- Event demultiplexer

When the **Main Program** needs to execute an asynchronous operation, it starts by telling it to the **Reactor**, with the identification of the **Concrete Event Handler** that will be notified when an event occurs. This is the call to the `register_handler`. Then the **Reactor** creates a new instance of this **Concrete Event Handler** and adds it to its handler list. After that, the **Main Program** calls `handle_events`, which is a function that blocks until an event is received. The **Reactor** then calls the **Event Demultiplexer** to wait until an event happens. The Event Demultiplexer is usually implemented through the select system call or one of its alternatives, such as `poll`, `epoll`, or `kqueue`. `select` is called with the list of **handles** to monitor. These handles are associated with the handlers that were registered before. When an event that corresponds to one of the handles occurs, the Event Demultiplexer returns the list of handles that correspond to the event that happened. The **Reactor** then calls the associated event handlers, and the event handlers implement the actual service logic. The following diagram demonstrates this:

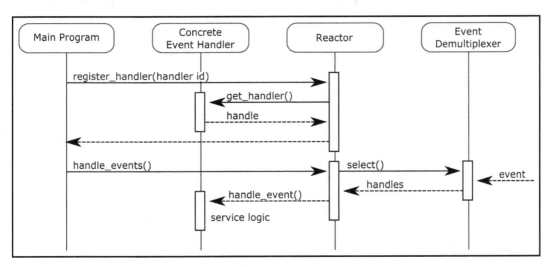

Figure 1.2: The reactor design pattern principles

Figure 1.3 shows a sequence diagram of how a **Proactor** works. On a Proactor system, asynchronous operations can be executed by an **Asynchronous Operation** processor. This is an entity which is provided by the operating system, and not all operating systems have support for it. There are more components involved in a Proactor than in a reactor. First, an **Initiator** asks the Asynchronous Operation processor to execute and operate. With this request, the Initiator provides the information about the operation to execute, as well as the instance of the **Completion Handler** and **Completion Event Queue** associated to the operation. Then the Asynchronous Operation processor creates an operation object that corresponds to the request of the Initiator. After that, the Initiator asks the Proactor to execute all pending operations. When an event associated with one of the operations happens, the operation notifies the Asynchronous Operation processor about it. The Asynchronous Operation processor then pushes this result to a Completion Event Queue. At that point, the Completion Event Queue notifies the Proactor that something happens. The Proactor then pops the next event from the Completion Event Queue and notifies the **Completion Handler** about this result. The Completion Handler finally implements the actual service logic.

On a Proactor, the Initiator and the Completion Handler may be implemented in the same component. Moreover, this chain of actions can be repeated indefinitely. The implementation of the Completion Handler can be an Initiator that starts the execution of another Asynchronous Operation. This is used to chain the execution of asynchronous operations:

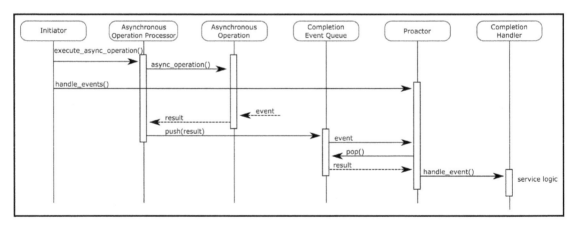

Figure 1.3: The proactor design pattern principles

As you can see, both patterns are somehow similar. They are both used to execute asynchronous operations. The main difference is in the way operations can be chained. On a reactor, asynchronous operations can be chained only by the main program once the blocking call to the event demultiplexer has been completed. On the other hand, a proactor allows the completion handlers to be initiators and so execute themselves new asynchronous operations.

Being aware of this is important because it allows us to understand what is going on behind the scenes. However, this is completely invisible with all the recent asynchronous frameworks. They all expose APIs whose behavior is similar to the proactor pattern because they allow us to easily chain asynchronous operations while others are still pending. However, they will still use a proactor depending on the operating system that you use. On some frameworks, when both the reactor and proactors are available, it is possible to select what pattern to use via configuration APIs.

Reactive systems

This book will cover many aspects on reactive programming. But an important thing to be aware of is that using reactive programming does not mean implementing a reactive system. A reactive system is much more than implementing a component with asynchronous and reactive programming. These are two notions that may be easily mingled due to the similarities in the way they are named, but they are completely different. As already explained, reactive programming is a way to code. On the other hand, a reactive system is an architecture pattern that allows us to write robust systems; that is, applications that are made of many components communicating via network channels, and with instances running on several (many?) servers, virtual machines, or containers. This architecture pattern is described in the reactive manifesto (`https://www.reactivemanifesto.org/`).

The four pillars of the reactive system are shown in the following figure:

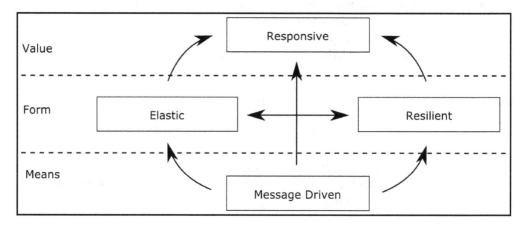

Figure 1.4: A reactive system

These four pillars are interdependent. The value of a reactive system is being reactive thanks to an elastic and resilient design. A reactive system relies on a message-driven communication between the components of the system. More specifically:

- **A reactive system is responsive**: It responds to events and user interactions rapidly and consistently. Responsiveness ensures that the application stays usable, and that, in case of a problem, these problems can be detected very quickly and thus handled correctly. Responsiveness is achieved thanks to the three other pillars of a reactive system.
- **A reactive system is resilient**: The system stays responsive even in the event of failure. Resilience can be achieved in several ways, such as replication and isolation. Failures are handled and contained in each component. Other components are dedicated to recover the components that failed and replication allows it to provide high-availability.
- **A reactive system is elastic**: The system stays responsive when the workload varies. The system can adapt to workloads that increase or decrease so that the allocated resources of the system are not oversized or undersized. In order to provide elasticity, the design must be vertically and horizontally scalable, with no performance bottleneck.
- **A reactive system is message-driven**: The different components of the system communicate via asynchronous message channels. Communication via messages allows us to isolate components. Saturation is controlled via back-pressure.

As you can see, reactive programming does not provide these four pillars in itself. Reactive programming is one of the tools that can be used to implement a reactive system, but it is not sufficient. Many other tools, such as message brokers, containers, orchestrations, or monitoring tools are needed to build a reactive system.

Introduction to ReactiveX and RxPY

ReactiveX is a library which aims to make asynchronous programming easy. As the header of the project's website says, it is: *The Observer pattern done right*. ReactiveX is a library based on the idea of observable streams. A stream is an entity that emits zero, one, or several items, over a period of time. This stream of items can be observed by other entities that are interested in receiving these items and manipulated by them. This simple idea is the basis of what has become an incredibly successful way of doing asynchronous programming.

As said in the very first paragraph of this book, asynchronous programming is a very active field. ReactiveX is a typical example of technologies that did not exist a few years ago but that are now heavily used. It was originally one of the components of the Volta project at Microsoft. This project consisted of a set of developer tools to help with developing client and server parts of web applications. The Volta project was suspended in 2008 but ReactiveX continued to be developed, up to the point when it was publicly released for the .NET platform in 2010. The library was very successful, with a community starting to grow up and big companies such as Netflix and GitHub using it. In 2012, implementations for .NET, JavaScript, and C++ were published as open source projects. Since that time, ReactiveX has even impacted the standardization of some programming languages. ReactiveX now has official implementations for almost 20 programming languages and was the foundation of the Java reactive streams (http://www.reactive-streams.org) standard and the EcmaScript observable (https://github.com/tc39/proposal-observable) API. Nowadays, many other libraries, heavily inspired by ReactiveX, are available for virtually any programming language.

All of this is based on concepts that have already existed for many years, such as the observer design pattern, the iterator design pattern, and some principles from functional programming. The ingenuity came from combining them in such a way that it avoids the callback hell. Even better, it is equally suited for frontend applications that deal with user events and GUI widgets, and backend applications that work with network and database requests.

ReactiveX principles

ReactiveX is based on two entities: observables and observers. These are the only things that one needs to understand to be able to start writing code. Everything else is based on the behavior of one of these two entities.

Observables represent a source of events. An observable is an entity that can emit zero or one of several items. An observable has an explicit lifetime with a start and an end. When an observable completes or faces an error, it cannot send items anymore; its lifetime has ended. An observable may never end. In this case, it is an infinite source of events. Observables are a way to manage sequences of items in an asynchronous way. Table 1.1, which follows, shows a comparison between how to access items in a synchronous or asynchronous way. As you can see, observables fill a gap and are allowed to operate on multiple items in an asynchronous way.

	Single item	Multiple items
Synchronous	Getter	Iterable
Asynchronous	Future	Observable

Table 1.1: Accessing an asynchronous sequence of items if possible

Observables work in push mode, as opposed to the pull mode of an iterable. Each time a new item is available, the observable pushes it to its observer. Table 1.2 shows the difference between the pull mode of an iterator and the push mode of an observable. This is what makes the behavior reactive and easy to handle with asynchronous code: whether items are emitted immediately or later is not important to the observer receiving it, and the code semantic is very similar to the one used in synchronous code:

Event	Iterable (pull)	Observable (push)
Retrieve data	For i in collection	on_next
Error	Exception is raised	on_error
Complete	End of loop	on_completed

Table 1.2 : Observables are push based

Observers are the receiving part of the items. An observer subscribes to an observable so that it can receive items emitted by this observable. Just as the observable emits items one after another, an observer receives them one after another. The observable informs the observer of the end of the sequence, either by indicating that the observable has completed (successfully) or by indicating that an error has occurred. These two kinds of completion are notified in a similar way, and so can be handled in a similar way. With ReactiveX, the error management is not a special case, but on a par with the items and completion management. In contrast to iterables that use exceptions, there is no radically different way of handling success from failure.

The implementation of RxPY (as well as all other implementations of ReactiveX) involves two other entities: a subscription function and a disposable object. Figure 1.5 shows a simplified representation of these entities. The AnonymousObservable class is the class that is almost always used to create an observable (directly or via another subclass). This class contains two methods to manage the lifetime of the observable and its observer. The first one, init, is not even a method but the constructor of the class. It takes a subscription function as an input argument. This subscription function will be called when an observer subscribes to this observable. The observable constructor returns a disposable function that can be called to free all resources used by the observable and observer. The second method of the AnonymousObservable class is subscribe. This is the method that is used to attach an observer to an observable and start the observable; that is, to make it start emitting items. The AnonymousObservable class can be used directly, but there are many cases where using an existing RxPY AnonymousObservable subclass is easier. This is typically the case when you need to create an observable from an iterable object or a single object.

The Observer class is a base class that contains three methods. They correspond to the behavior explained previously. This class must be subclassed to implement these three methods. The method on_next is called each time an item is emitted by the observable. The method on_completed is called when the observable completes successfully. Finally, the method on_error is called when the observable completes because of an error. The on_item method will never be called after the on_completed or the on_error methods.

The subscription entity is a function that takes an observer as input parameter. This function is called when the subscribe method of the observable is called. This is where the emission of items is implemented. The emission of these items can be either synchronous or asynchronous. Items are emitted in a synchronous way if the subscription function directly calls the on_items methods of the observable. But items can also be emitted asynchronously if the observer instance is saved and used later (after the subscription function returns). The subscription function can return a Disposable object or function. This Disposable object will be called when the observable is being disposed.

Finally, the Disposable class and its associated dispose function are used to clean up any resources used by an Observer or a subscription. In the case of an asynchronous observable, this is how the subscription function is notified that it must stop emitting items, because Observer is no more valid after that. The following figure shows these components:

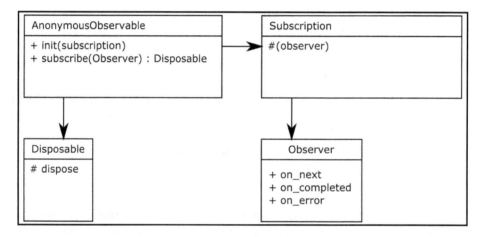

Figure 1.5: RxPY components

Let's try to make more sense of all these definitions. The following figure shows a sequence diagram of how these calls are organized when an observable is created, subscribed, and finally disposed:

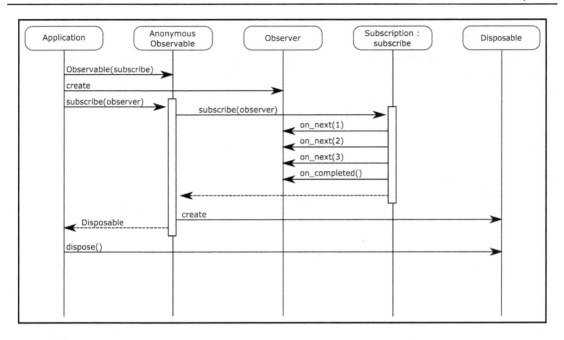

Figure 1.6: RxPY dynamics. An example of the creation of a synchronous observable and its subscription and disposal

First the application creates an `AnonymousObservable` and provides the `subscription` function associated to this observable. It then creates an `observer` object (actually a subclass of `Observer`). After that, the observable is subscribed, with reference to the `observer` object provided as an input parameter. During the call to `subscribe`, the `subscription` function is called. In this example, the `subscription` function is synchronous: it emits three items (the integers 1, 2, and 3), and completes the observable. When the `subscription` function returns, the observable is already completed. At that point, the `subscribe` method of `AnonymousObservable` returns the `Disposable` function to the application. The application finally calls this `dispose` function to clean up any resource still used by `subscription` and `observer`.

Operators

Now the principles of observables and observers should start to be more clear. However, you may wonder: how can this make development of asynchronous code easier? After all, what was described in the previous section is almost exactly the description of the observer design pattern, with additions for the management of completion and errors. The answer is that this is not the whole story, but the foundation of an extensible framework. What made ReactiveX different from other frameworks is its inspiration from functional programming, with the availability of many operators that can be chained in a pipeline. In the RxPY implementation, operators are methods of the `Observable` class. On some implementations of ReactiveX, they are implemented as functions which allow us to add new operators very easily. Look at the following example of pseudo-code:

```
Observable.from_(...)
      .filter()
      .distinct()
      .take(20)
      .map(...)
```

This is what a ReactiveX code looks like. It is a succession of operators that modify the items flowing through them. An operator can be seen as a monad: a construction that encapsulates program logic instead of data. (I apologize to functional programmers for this very simplistic definition.) An operator takes an observable as input and returns another observable. So, we can consider the observable data type as an abstract type that is used to compose functions together. Some operators accept other input parameters to provide additional program logic that will be executed on each item received on the operator. For example, the `map` operator that will be used later takes a function as a parameter. This function contains the code logic that will be executed on each item sent on the input observable.

Operators are not limited to the code logic of items. Since they work on the observable data type, they can also be used to manage observables' completion and errors. For example, some operators use completion events to chain observables one after another. Other operators use error events to gracefully manage these errors.

The RxPY implementation contains about 140 operators. We will cover the most used, which is about half of them. As you will be writing RxPY code, you will also be writing your own operators, even if they will not be directly usable in the kind of pipeline that we saw earlier. As we will see, writing a custom operator is the way to factorize code and make functions simpler when using ReactiveX.

Installating RxPY

RxPY is available as a Python package published on PyPI (`https://pypi.org/`), so it can be installed with `pip`. Depending on your operating system, you may already have `pip` installed. Otherwise refer to the `pip` installation documentation (`https://pip.pypa.io/en/stable/installing/`).

By following the examples in this book, you will install several libraries and sample packages that you may not want to keep on your system. In order to avoid cluttering your environment, you should run all these examples in a `virtualenv`. `virtualenv` is a tool that allows you to create isolated Python environments. With it you can create many different Python environments, potentially using different Python interpreters that are independent from each other. This is a great tool when developing in Python because it allows you to:

- Test libraries without installing them on your system
- Test some code with different versions of Python interpreters
- Test some code with different versions of dependency packages
- Have one independent and reproducible execution environment per project

If you are not already familiar with it, I encourage you to use it when running the example code that we will use. The installation of `virtualenv` is very easy via PyPI, using the following command:

```
pip3 install virtualenv
```

Creating a new virtual environment is also quite easy, in a single line with three parameters, using the following line of code:

```
virtualenv --system-site-packages -p /usr/local/bin/python3 venv-rx
```

The `--system-site-packages` option indicates that we want to use system packages when they are already installed. If you omit this parameter you will create a complete Python environment from scratch. This would be better for isolation but requires much more space because each dependency will be reinstalled in `virtualenv`. In our case, we do not need a strict isolation from the system; we only want to avoid installing new packages in our system. The `-p` option indicates what the Python interpreter will use. You should adapt it to your environment. The `/usr/local/bin` value corresponds to a macOS system. On Linux, the `cpython` interpreter is usually located at `/usr/bin`. Finally the `venv-rx` parameter is the name of `virtualenv` created. After running this command you will see a new directory named `venv-rx`.

Once `virtualenv` is created, you can enter it and leave it. Once you have entered `virtualenv`, all actions done by the Python interpreter are done in this isolated environment. Entering into `virtualenv` is done by sourcing a script in its `bin` directory, as can be seen in the following code:

```
source venv-rx/bin/activate
(venv-rx) $
```

When you are inside `virtualenv`, the name of `virtualenv` is printed in parentheses before the shell prompt. This is how you know if you are inside an isolated environment or on your system environment. Leaving `virtualenv` is done by executing the `deactivate` function, as can be seen in the following code:

```
(venv-rx) $ deactivate
$
```

From that point, the `rx` package can be installed via the `pip` tool, as can be seen in the following code:

```
$ source venv-rx/bin/activate
(venv-rx) $ pip install rx
```

If you want to install the latest development version, you can also install it directly from the GitHub sources. First clone the repository, and then install RxPY from the local sources, as demonstrated in the following code:

```
(venv-rx) $ git clone https://github.com/ReactiveX/RxPY.git
(venv-rx) $ cd RxPy.git
(venv-rx) $ python3 setup.py install
```

A reactive echo application

After this short introduction to ReactiveX and RxPY, the time has come to see some concrete code and write a first example. This first RxPY application is a **command line interface (CLI)** program that echoes the parameters that are provided as input. Save the following code in a file called echo1.py, or use the echo1.py script from the Git repository of this book, as shown in the following code:

```
import sys
from rx import Observable

argv = Observable.from_(sys.argv[1:])

argv.subscribe(
```

```
        on_next=lambda i: print("on_next: {}".format(i)),
        on_error=lambda e: print("on_error: {}".format(e)),
        on_completed=lambda: print("on_completed"))
```

Ensure that you are running in `virutalenv`, as shown in the following code:

```
$ source venv-rx/bin/activate
```

And when you run it, you should see the following output:

```
(venv-rx)$ python3 echo1.py hello world !
on_next: hello
on_next: world
on_next: !
on_completed
```

We ran the program with three parameters (`hello`, `world`, and `!`), and it printed these three parameters as well as information on the end of `Observable`. Let's detail each line of this program. We will start by importing the modules that we will use, as in the following code:

```
import sys
from rx import Observable
```

The `sys` module allows us to access the command line arguments. The `rx` module is the name of the RxPY package, which we installed from `pip`. We do not import the complete `rx` module, but just the `Observable` class. In many cases we will only need this class, or a few other ones. Then we can create an observable from the command line arguments, as in the following example:

```
argv = Observable.from_(sys.argv[1:])
```

`sys.argv` is a list containing the command line arguments that were used to run the program. The first argument is the name of the script being executed. In this case its value is `echo1.py`. Since we do not want to use this argument we omit it with a slice, using the second up to the last argument of the list. An observable is created from this list with the `from_` creation operator. This operator creates an observable from a Python iterable object, which is the case of our argument list. We affect the reference of this observable to the `argv` variable. So, `argv` is a reference to an observable that will emit items containing the arguments provided on the command line, one item per argument. After this affectation the observable is created, but does not emit any item yet; items are emitted only once the observable is subscribed. On the last part of the program, we subscribe to this observable and print text depending on the event being received, as can be seen in the following code:

```
argv.subscribe(
```

```
on_next=lambda i: print("on_next: {}".format(i)),
on_error=lambda e: print("on_error: {}".format(e)),
on_completed=lambda: print("on_completed"))
```

Three callback arguments are provided to the subscribe method: on_next, on_error, and on_completed. They are all optional, and they correspond to the reception of the associated events. As already explained, the on_next callback will be called zero or more times, and the on_error and on_completed callbacks can be called once at the most (and never if the observable never ends, which is not the case here). The call to the subscribe method is the one that makes the argv observable start emitting items. In this simple application, the code of each callback is very simple, so we use lambda instead of functions.

Lambdas are anonymous functions; that is, functions that can be referenced only from where they are defined, because they have no name. However, lambdas have restrictions over functions, which makes them only suitable when simple manipulations are done with the data:

- Lambdas can use only expressions, not statements
- Lambdas contain only one expression
- Lambdas cannot declare or use local variables

So, lambdas are very useful when you need to do an action on one or several input parameters. For more complex logic, writing a function is mandatory. Lambdas are used a lot when developing RxPY code because many operators take functions as input. So, such operators are functions that accept functions as input parameters. Functions that accept functions as input are called higher order functions in functional programming and this is another aspect of functional programming used a lot in ReactiveX.

As you can see, the on_next callback is called once for each argument provided on the command line, and the on_completed callback is called right after. In this example application, we use a synchronous Observable. In practice, this means that all items are emitted in the context of the subscribe call. To confirm this, add another print statement after the subscribe call:

```
argv.subscribe(
    on_next=lambda i: print("on_next: {}".format(i)),
    on_error=lambda e: print("on_error: {}".format(e)),
    on_completed=lambda: print("on_completed"))
print("done")
```

Then run the program again. You should see the following output:

```
(venv-rx) $ python3 ch1/echo1.py hello world !
on_next: hello
```

```
on_next: world
on_next: !
on_completed
done
```

As you can see, the `done` print is displayed after the observable completes because the observable emits all its items during the call to `subscribe`.

We will now add some functionality to this echo application. Instead of simply printing each argument, we will print them with the first letter in uppercase. This is the typical case of an action that must be applied to each item of an observable. In the current code, there are two possible locations to do it:

- Either by using an operator on the `argv` observable
- By modifying the `on_next` callback in the `subscribe` call

In a real application, there will usually be only a single place where the action must be applied, depending on whether the action must be done in the observer or on the observable directly. Implementing the action in the observer allows you to isolate the change to this single observer. The other way of implementing the action on the observable allows you to share this behavior with several observers. Here we will implement the action on the observable with the `map` operator. Modify the code as in the following example, or use the `echo2.py` script from the GitHub repository (`https://github.com/PacktPublishing/Hands-On-Reactive-Programming-with-Python`) of the book:

```
argv = Observable.from_(sys.argv[1:]) \
    .map(lambda i: i.capitalize())
```

The `map` operator takes an observable as input, applies a transformation function on each item of this observable, and returns an observable which contains all input items, with the transformation applied to them. Here we have used `lambda` that returns the item (a string) capitalized; that is, with its first letter in uppercase. If you run this new code you should get the following output:

```
(venv-rx)$ python3 ch1/echo2.py hello world !
on_next: Hello
on_next: World
on_next: !
on_completed
done
```

As you can see, the output is the same, but with capitalized names. Congratulations; you have just written your first reactive application!

Marble diagrams

The ReactiveX project is composed of several hundreds of operators, and the Python implementation contains about 140 of them. When writing ReactiveX code, especially in the early days, you should regularly refer to the operator's documentation. Do not hesitate to read through it to find the most adapted operator for your needs. This is a good way to discover operators that you may use later, and you may find an operator doing exactly what you want to implement.

Unfortunately, this documentation is often difficult to understand. A representative of this situation is the `FlatMap` (`http://reactivex.io/documentation/operators/flatmap.html`) operator description:

> *"Transform the items emitted by an Observable into Observables, then flatten the emissions from those into a single Observable"*

This simple description is—obviously—correct, but may not be easy to comprehend. This is why there is also a more detailed explanation on how the operator works. In the case of the `flat_map` operator, the behavior is to take an observable as input and apply a transformation on each item of this observable. The transformation is done by a function also provided as an input of the operator. This function is called for each item emitted by the input observable and returns an observable at each execution (that is, for each item). Finally, `flat_map` merges all the observables returned by the transformation function in a single output observable.

This is a very detailed description of how the operator works, but even when you are used to the ReactiveX terminology, you need to spend some time carefully reading each word of the documentation to understand what it means. Marble diagrams are a clever application of the *a figure is worth a thousand words* idiom. They represent graphically an example of the behavior of an operator. All operators are documented with their descriptions, and a marble diagram. Most of the time, the marble diagram allows you to understand the behavior of the operator without even having to read the documentation.

Figure 1.7 shows the structure of a marble diagram. A marble diagram is composed of three parts: input timelines, a transformation description, and output timelines:

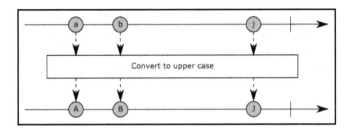

Figure 1.7: Marble diagram

A timeline represents an observable state according to the time that goes on. It is drawn as an arrow going from left to right. Each item emitted on the observable is drawn as a circle. The official documentation uses different shapes and colors to represent items. In this book, we will only use circles with labels. Depending on the operator, there may be one or several input timelines.

Below the input timeline is the transformation description drawn as a rectangle. Some brief information about the transformation being performed is printed inside this rectangle. There are dashed arrows between the input timeline items and the transformation description each time the transformation is applied to an item or some items.

Finally, below the transformation description are the output timelines. They represent the result observables of the operator. In the example of Figure 1.7 each input letter is transformed to uppercase, so a becomes A, b becomes B, and j becomes J. Just like input timelines, most of the time there is only one output timeline. But some operators may return several observables, and some return observables of observables. This is shown in the following figure, in which for each item a new observable is generated, emitting the next three letters:

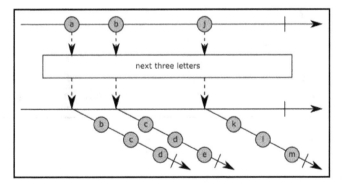

Figure 1.8: Observable of observable

An observable of observables is an observable that emits items that are themselves observables. While this may surprise at first, this is just one level of composition; an observable can convey items of any type, including observables. So, at some point you may work with several layers of observables being composed this way. Such observables are called higher order observables in this book, borrowing the naming convention used for higher order functions.

The last thing to understand in marble diagrams is the way timelines can end. An observable lifetime ends either on completion (that is, on success) or on error. These are respectively represented as a vertical line and as a cross, as shown in the following figure:

Figure 1.9: The end of an observable. On the left an observable that completes successfully and on the right an Observable that terminates in an error

The map operator

Let's see a real example with the map operator. This operator takes a source observable as input and returns an observable as output. It applies a function to each item of the source observable, and emits the result of this function on the output observable. Hopefully, its marble diagram, shown in the following figure, should make the description much more clear:

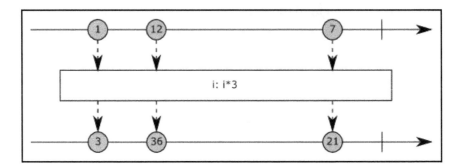

Figure 1.10: The map operator

The marble diagram shows an input timeline with three integer items: 1, 12, and 7. The transformation is described with syntax similar to that of the Python lambda. Note that the official ReactiveX documentation uses the JavaScript arrow function notation, because it uses marble diagrams from the JavaScript implementation. In this example, the transformation is a multiplication by 3 of the source item. The output timeline contains also three items, corresponding to the input items values multiplied by 3.

The prototype of this operator is the following one:

```
Observable.map(self, selector)
```

The `selector` parameter is the function that will be executed on all items of the input observable.

The from_ operator

The `from_` operator is the operator that was used in the previous example to create an observable from a list. The marble diagram of this operator is shown in the following figure:

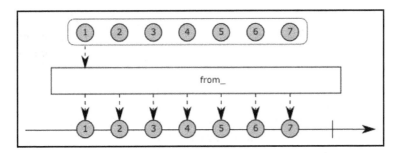

Figure 1.11: The from_ operator

 The name of this operator is strange because it ends with an underscore. The reason for this underscore is that `from` is a reserved keyword in Python, so it was not possible to name this operator as it should be; that is, `from`. If you dislike this notation, there is an alias named `from_list`. You can use it for a more Pythonic code at the expense of a longer name.

The prototype of this operator is the following one:

```
Observable.from_(iterable, scheduler=None)
```

The first parameter accepts any iterable object. This includes lists, tuples, dictionaries, and any class that implements the iterator methods __iter__ and next. The second parameter is used to provide a scheduler that will be used to emit the items of the observable. This parameter is present on all creation operators. It is useful when running in an asynchronous environment or an environment with concurrency. We will study schedulers in detail in Chapter 5, *Concurrency and Paralellism in RxPY*.

The from_ operator creates an observable that emits one item per entry in the iterable. It then completes the observable. Here are some examples of usage which show the items that they return:

```
Observable.from_(sys.argv) # argv[0], argv[1], argv[2]..., completed
Observable.from_([1, 2, 3, 4]) # 1, 2, 3, 4, completed
Observable.from_({'foo': 'fooz', 'bar': 'barz'}) # 'foo', 'bar', completed
```

Note that when using a dictionary, the observable contains the keys of the dictionary and not the values. This is the same behavior as a classic Python iteration on a dictionary using a for loop.

Flow diagrams

Marble diagrams are a great way to explain how an operator works. However, they are not suited to describe how a program, a function, or a component works. Marble diagrams can show from example how a transformation on one observable is applied, but they cannot be used to describe how operators are combined to achieve a more complex operation on the data. We need a kind of diagram that shows the complete transformations applied on observables without the details of each operator being used. We need a diagram in which one considers that the operators are known by the reader but the overall behavior of a component must be described.

Reactivity diagrams

Fortunately, we can use diagrams inspired from a tool used in sequential programming: UML **activity diagrams**. An activity diagram is the UML name of something you may know as a flowchart. These diagrams are used to describe the sequences of actions which are performed by a program, but they can also express repetitions, alternatives, joins, merges and so on. Activity diagrams with only few tweaks are a great way to represent the behavior of an RX component. We will call them **reactivity diagrams**.

The main difference between an activity and a reactivity diagram is that an activity diagram represents actions that are performed when the component is called, while a reactivity diagram represents actions which are performed each time an item is emitted on one of the source observables. Other than that, the elements defined by UML are used in almost the same way. Let's detail this with the example shown in the following figure:

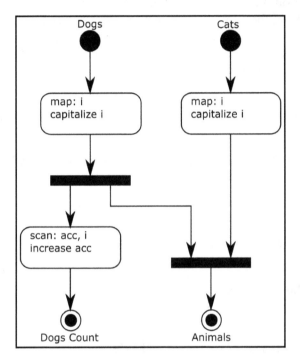

Figure 1.12: A reactivity diagram

This is an example of a function which takes two observables as input and provides two observables as output. This function counts the number of dogs emitted on the Dogs input observable and sends back the name of all animals emitted on both the Dogs and Cats input observables. Input observables are observables that the component observes. They emit the items that will be transformed by the component. Input observables are represented as black circles. Output observables are observables that are the result of the transformation of the component. Output observables are represented as encircled black circles.

The previous example shows an important point in RX programming: from now on—almost—everything that you will write will deal with observables. It means that almost all components are written as functions that take observables as input and return observables. This is the way reusability is achieved via composition.

The same transformation is applied to the items of both input observables: capitalize the name of the animal. Then the capitalized dog name items are being shared; that is, they are being emitted on two observables. Finally, the capitalized dog name items are counted and the value of this count is emitted in the dogs count observable. On the right side, the dog and cat name observables are merged to an observable that emits the capitalized names of all animals.

So, if such a component is used with the following observables, it will be shown as in the following example:

```
dogs = Observable.from_(["sam", "max", "maggie", "buddy"])
cats = Observable.from_(["luna", "kitty", "jack")
```

It will emit the following items on the output observables:

```
dog_count: 1, 2, 3, 4
animals: sam, luna, max, maggie, buddy, kitty, jack
```

The actual ordering of the items emitted on the `animals` observable will depend on when they are emitted on the input observable.

Reactivity diagram elements

Reactivity diagrams can be constructed from the following elements:

- **Circles:** Observables are represented as circles. An input observable is represented as a black circle. An output observable is represented as an encircled black circle. Two other notations allow us to indicate when actions are done: when an observable terminates on completion or on error. This notation is similar to the marble diagrams; an observable error event is represented as a circle with a cross in it, and an observable completion event is represented as a circle with a bar in it. This is shown in the following figure:

Figure 1.13: Observable notations. From left to right: input, output, error, completion

- **Rectangles:** Operators are represented as rounded rectangles. The text inside the rectangle describes the actions being performed. The first line contains the name of the operator and its parameters. The following lines contain the description of the action. This notation can also be used for components being used in the current component. This notation can also be used as a merge point for operators that combine several observables. This is shown in the following figure:

Figure 1.14: Operators notation

- **Flow:** Items flows are represented as arrows. The type of items emitted on the observable is written near the arrow. Item flows show how operators and other elements are linked together. This is shown in the following figure:

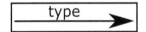

Figure 1.15: Items flows notation

- **Diamond:** Decisions are represented as a diamond. The decision notation is used only for operators that take an observable as input and split it into two or more observables, the split being based on a segmentation logic described in the diamond. The text inside the diamonds describes the segmentation logic in the same way as the operator's notation. This is seen in following figure:

Figure 1.16: Decisions notation

- **Horizontal or vertical black bar:** Share and merge are represented as a horizontal or vertical black bar. An observable is shared when there is one incoming observable and several outgoing observables on the bar. Observables are merged when there are several incoming observables and one outgoing observable on the bar.

- This is demonstrated in the following figure:

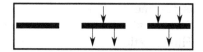

Figure 1.17: Share and merge notation: share (center), merge (right)

- **Rectangle with the upper-right corner bent**: Out of monad actions are represented as a rectangle with the upper-right corner bent. Out of monad actions are the actions that are not done via an operator or a component operating on observables. The typical usecase is the code of the subscription associated to an observer. The text in the rectangle describes briefly the actions being done. This can be seen in the following figure:

Figure 1.18: Out of monad notation

Reactivity diagrams of an echo example

We will complete this tour of the reactivity diagrams by writing the echo example. Its diagram is shown in the following figure:

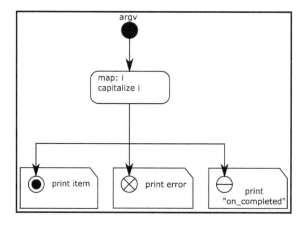

Figure 1.19: The echo app reactivity diagram

This simple diagram should allow any developer to understand what is going on, provided that he knows that it applies to each item emitted on the `argv` input observable. First, the input observable is created from the `argv` variable. Then each item is capitalized with the `map` operator. Finally, each event type (item, completion, or error) is printed. Note that the content of each element is not a copy of the code, but a small description of what it does. The echo example was quite simple, but in a real application you want to document the behavior with reactivity diagrams, not duplicate the code on a diagram.

Summary

You should now understand what event-driven programming is, what reactive programming is, and what are the common points and differences between them. It is important to remember that event-driven programming is not a programming paradigm, but a way to structure the code flow. Knowing the basics of the reactor and proactor design patterns is also important to better understand how the frameworks that will be used in the next chapters work.

From now, you can start writing reactive code for tasks that you may have written in a sequential way. This kind of exercise, even for very simple algorithms, is good training in how to structure your code as a data-flow instead of a code-flow. Switching from a code-flow design to a data-flow design is the key point in writing ReactiveX applications.

Last but not least, you should now be able to navigate easily in the ReactiveX documentation and understand more easily the behavior of each operator, thanks to marble diagrams. Never hesitate to use them when you need to write your own operator or component. This is always a good way to show what you want to achieve. For a more dynamic view, reactivity diagrams will help you design bigger components or document how they are composed together.

The next chapter will introduce how asynchronous programming is done in Python, and, more specifically, with its dedicated module of the standard library, AsyncIO. But before that, detailed explanations of the underlying principles of asynchronous functions will be provided so that you can understand what's going on under the hood.

Questions

- Is event-driven programming possible only with some programming languages?
- What are the differences between reactive programming and reactive systems?
- What is an observable?
- What is an observer?
- Are observables pull-based or push-based?
- What makes reactivity diagrams different from activity diagrams?
- How do you create observable emitting integers from 0 to 10,000?
- How do you create an observable from another observable where all items are multiplied by 3?

Further reading

The description of the observer design pattern was originally documented in the book *Design Patterns: Elements of Reusable Object-Oriented Software*. You can read it to understand one of the foundations of ReactiveX. This book contains the description of all base design patterns used in object-oriented programming.

A detailed description of the reactor and proactor design patterns is available in the book *Pattern-Oriented Software Architecture, Patterns for Concurrent and Networked Objects, Volume 2*. This book contains information on concurrency, synchronization, and event handling.

The ReactiveX documentation is available online here: `http://reactivex.io/documentation/operators.html`. This documentation is generic to all programming languages, featuring marble diagrams of each operator. Refer to this documentation when looking for an operator. For each operator, it contains links to the specificity of each implementation.

The Reactive Manifesto is a great source of information to understand what is a reactive system and how to implement such a system: `https://www.reactivemanifesto.org/`.

You must read and learn *The Observable Contract* available here: `http://reactivex.io/documentation/contract.html`. It describes in a few words the rules that govern observables and observers. Once you are at ease with these concepts, you will be able to write and read ReactiveX code in an efficient way.

2
Asynchronous Programming in Python

his chapter covers the principles of asynchronous programming and the AsyncIO library. It is composed of three parts. The first one explains what asynchronous programming is, how it is different from synchronous programming, and why and when it is more efficient than synchronous programming. This first part also goes through the history of asynchronous programming in Python to allow you to better understand the current state of Python in this domain. The second part is dedicated to the AsyncIO library. AsyncIO, the official Python asynchronous library, contains all features needed to implement readable asynchronous code. The last part explains how to implement a real application and, more specifically, an HTTP server. By the end of this chapter, you will be able to write an asynchronous network service with AsyncIO.

The following topics will be covered in this chapter:

- Asynchronous programming
- The history of asynchronous programming in Python
- An introduction to AsyncIO
- Reactive HTTP echo servers

What is asynchronous programming?

Chapter 1, *An Introduction to Reactive Programming*, discussed in detail the principles of event-driven programming and reactive programming. As explained in the previous chapter, event-driven programming can be implemented in many ways: with different programming paradigms such as imperative or object-oriented, but also with different concurrency mechanisms. Asynchronous programming is one way to manage concurrency.

Concurrency is several tasks competing for the same resource at the same time. The definition of "at the same time" can be different depending on the resource being used. There are two main resources that a task may require: a **Central Processing Unit (CPU)** and I/O. In most cases, a task is either CPU bound or I/O bound; that is, either a task makes a lot of computations and is constrained by the available CPU resources, or a task takes a lot of I/O actions and is constrained by the available I/O resources. Depending on the type of task, different concurrency mechanisms can be used in Python: processes, threads, and async. The following table shows them and in what case they are the most adapted:

	Process	Thread	Async
CPU bound	Yes	Yes, with restrictions	No
I/O bound	Very limited	Limited	Yes

Table 2.1: The three ways to manage concurrency in Python and their efficiency in solving CPU and I/O concurrency

Processes and threads are well suited to handle concurrency on CPU-bound tasks because they allow several tasks to run at the same time on the different execution units of the CPU. This is the easiest way to use all the cores of a CPU instead of using only one, which is the default situation when writing a Python program. With processes, several instances of the Python interpreter run at the same time, and so each one can use one core of the CPU. When using threads, several cores of the CPU are used within the same process. The advantage (or drawback depending on the point of view) of threads over processes is that they share the same memory space. So threads can share memory more efficiently than processes. The latter need to copy data when communicating together. (It is possible to share memory between processes, but via APIs specific to each operating system.)

From the point of view of the operating system, processes and threads allow the same performance if the tasks are CPU-bound. Each task can run independently of each other. However, this is not the case in Python. The implementation of the CPython interpreter, which is the most used one, relies on a global lock, also known as the **Global Interpreter Lock (GIL)**. The GIL is a lock which prevents several executions of Python code occurring at the same time. This means that multithreading in Python is very limited because two threads will never run concurrently even when several cores are available on the CPU. This is why multithreading should be avoided in most cases when using Python because it does not allow you to fully benefit from multiple cores.

Processes can be used to manage I/O concurrency. But since each single-threaded process can execute only on one task at a time, it means that when a task is waiting for an I/O operation to complete, it blocks the whole process and no other task can run during that time. The following figure shows an example of what happens in such a case:

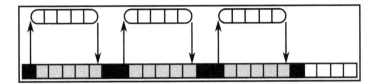

Figure 2.1: Blocking I/O operations running on a single process. The black blocks are cycles where the CPU is running and the gray blocks are cycles where the CPU is blocked

The task has three I/O operations to execute. Each I/O operation takes five cycles to complete. When an I/O operation completes, the task needs one cycle to handle its result. In this case, the CPU is active for six cycles (the black blocks) and blocked during 15 cycles. During these 15 cycles, no other code can run on the process. With such a design, I/O concurrency can be implemented by executing many processes. But this is not scalable because it will consume a lot of memory, and orchestrating all these processes can be difficult and inefficient.

Threads are a better way to handle I/O concurrency because they allow you to execute several operations at the same time in the same process. Compared to a single threaded process, this allows the main thread of the process to always be available when I/O operations are ongoing. This is shown in the following diagram:

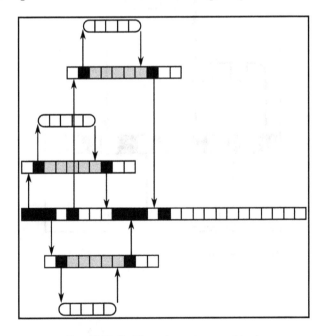

Figure 2.2: Blocking I/O operations running on several threads

There are four execution units here: the main thread of the process (the longest in the figure) and three other threads. Just as before, three I/O operations must be executed. In this case, one thread is used for the execution of each operation. As we can see, the main thread is never blocked, and so it can execute other tasks when I/O operations are ongoing. The other benefit is that the I/O operations can now execute concurrently. On the CPU cycle eight in *Figure 2.2*, the three I/O operations are ongoing. Each thread is still blocked when it executes its I/O operation, but it does not block the whole program.

Multiprocess and multithreaded designs are used in a lot of widely used projects that rely on I/O bound tasks. However, this design quickly hits limits in intensive use cases. These limits can be overcome by using more powerful systems (more CPU cores/more memory) but it has a cost. This is where asynchronous programming has a big advantage. Asynchronous programming allows you to handle I/O concurrency much more efficiently than other solutions.

The principle of asynchronous programming is that instead of waiting for blocking I/O operations on several execution units, a single execution unit multiplexes non-blocking I/O operations. The following figure shows this:

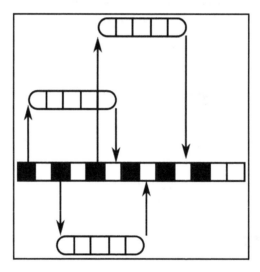

Figure 2.3: Non-blocking I/O operations running on a single thread/process

Notice how the figure is much simpler than the multithreaded design and much shorter (in terms of cycles being used) than the multiprocess one. This is a visual way to show that, system wise, asynchronous design is simpler than multithreading and more efficient than blocking I/O operations. In this case, once the first I/O operation is started then the execution unit is not blocked, so it can start the second and third I/O operations even though the previous one(s) is/are still ongoing. Once an operation has completed, the main thread is notified and can handle the result. So, the execution of the three I/O operations has been multiplexed on a single execution unit, and during their whole execution the CPU was never blocked.

Systems that are I/O bound such as network systems (proxies, servers, message brokers, and so on) are usually more efficient when they are programmed in an asynchronous way than with blocking calls. Since asynchronous programming requires fewer system resources to execute the same actions than blocking programming, it scales better and limits costs at the end. However, many programmers choose to start with multithreaded designs for I/O-bound tasks. As explained in Chapter 1, *An Introduction to Reactive Programming*, the main reason for this is that in a lot of cases, multithreaded seems easier at the beginning, especially when the programming language has no facility to deal with asynchronous programming. However, when all the tools are available to develop code asynchronously, then going asynchronous for I/O-bound tasks is probably a better choice in the long-term because real-time bugs in multithreaded code can be really hard to reproduce and fix, while asynchronous code is predictive and so easier to test.

The history of asynchronous programming in Python

Since the early days of Python, it has always been possible to do asynchronous programming, but in the *old* way; that is, by using callbacks. Chapter 1, *An Introduction to Reactive Programming*, already explained some of the evolution in the frameworks and programming languages that made asynchronous programming easier during the last few years. The Python language naturally followed that trend, and many incremental improvements have been made since the early 2000s. Figure 2.4 shows the history of the main changes that occurred in Python concerning asynchronous programming.

The evolution on the left side are the elements that are still part of Python. The evolution on the right side concerns asynchronous frameworks and one deprecated module of the standard library:

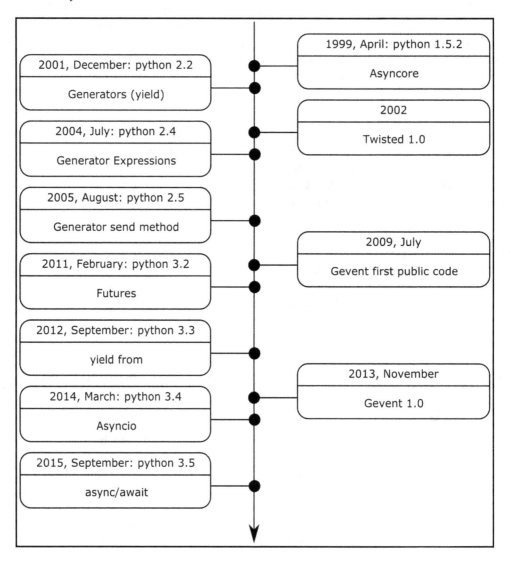

Figure 2.4: The main steps of asynchronous programming in Python

The first dedicated support for asynchronous programming appeared in 1999—five years after the release of Python 1.0. The `asyncore` module was added in the standard library with release 1.5.2. This module was designed to develop asynchronous socket handlers. It was based on callbacks for the implementation of the handlers, and either `select` or `poll` as a reactor (*Chapter 1, An Introduction to Reactive Programming*, contains more details on the reactor design pattern). This module has been tagged as deprecated in Python 3.6, since `asyncio` replaced it with the support of much more features.

Then, in 2001, the support of generators was added in Python 2.2. Generators allow you to implement a function which behaves like an iterator. The main benefit compared to an iterator is that the whole list does not need to be stored in memory, but instead it can be computed on-demand. So, generators allow you to generate very big (or even infinite) lists, without a need to store this whole list in memory. By themselves, generators have nothing to do with asynchronous programming. Most probably, the people who designed it never thought about asynchronous programming at the time. However, as we will detail later, generators have a property which makes them very useful in asynchronous programming. They are functions that can be interrupted at some chosen location and they can be resumed at a later time in that location with their execution context being restored.

The first framework that made use of generators to ease asynchronous programming was Twisted (`https://twistedmatrix.com`). Twisted is an asynchronous framework that also uses callbacks for handlers, which is similar to `asyncore`. However, the Twisted framework added two main improvements when its first release was published in 2002. The first one was the split between transport implementations and protocol implementations. The transport layer is in charge of the transporting of the messages, while the protocol layer is in charge of handling the messages. The second one was the use of generators to make asynchronous programming look like synchronous programming. Using generators instead of callbacks makes the code much more readable since the handling of a sequence of asynchronous operations is done in a single generator function instead of many callbacks.

The next two Python releases brought improvements on generators with the support of generator expressions in Python 2.4 and the addition of the send methods to generators in Python 2.5, published in 2004 and 2005, respectively. Generator expressions allow you to use generators with a syntax similar to list comprehension. The send method is a big improvement for asynchronous code because it allows you to give back a value to the generator each time it is resumed. This allows a generator and its caller to communicate. Before this, only the generator could provide data to its caller.

In July 2008, another asynchronous framework was published: Gevent (`http://www.gevent.org/`). Gevent is an alternative to Twisted. One main difference is that it uses the `libev` C library for the event loop implementation instead of a pure Python implementation in Twisted. Release 1.0 of Gevent was published in 2013.

In 2011, a final series of evolution dedicated to asynchronous programming added all the necessary features to make Python a state-of-the-art programming language concerning asynchronous programming. Futures were added in 2011 with the release of Python 3.2. A future is a way to represent a value that is not available yet, but that will be available at some point in the future. Delegation to a sub-generator was added in 2012 with the release of Python 2.3.

In 2014, the `asyncio` module was added to the standard library with the release of Python 3.4. This was a major addition that made Python async-ready without the need for third-party frameworks. The `asyncio` module took inspiration from existing frameworks and brought the best ideas directly available in Python. This was a major improvement compared with `asyncore`. The split between the transport layer and the protocol layer of Twisted was reused here. The event loop could run on a reactor or a proactor depending on the operating system, and coroutines (based on generators) were used to write asynchronous code that looked like synchronous code.

The last evolution was in 2015 with the addition of the `async/await` syntax in Python 3.5. One can consider `async/await` as syntactic sugar on top of the generator yield keyword. The two new keywords allow you to make asynchronous code and coroutines explicit, compared to the generator syntax, which can be used for other purposes than asynchronous programming. This last evolution made Python one of the first languages to support all features, allowing you to write asynchronous code almost as easily as synchronous code (or more objectively, easier to read than synchronous code).

The best way to understand why all these evolutions improved asynchronous programming in Python is to see the impact that they had by writing asynchronous code without these features and adding them one by one. We will go through these steps by implementing a simple state machine, driven by simulated asynchronous events. This same state machine will be implemented in different ways each time, using more recent features of Python. The state machine is the one shown in the following diagram:

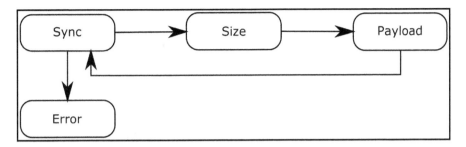

Figure 2.5: A length-based packet unframing state machine

This state machine unframes packets coming from a data channel. The structure of each frame is the following one:

- A `sync` word with a value of 42
- An integer indicating the size of the payload
- The payload, whose length must correspond to the value of the size field

For simplicity, the implementations will not care about the size and endianness of the words/integers (16, 32, or 64 bits, little or big-endian). We will simply use the Python integer type. Moreover, the channel is simulated. The aim here is to see how writing asynchronous code evolved, not to write real asynchronous code (but don't worry, this will come later). If a `sync` word other than 42 is received, then the state machines go into an error state.

Asynchronous handlers with callbacks

In the early days of Python, writing such a state machine would be based on callbacks or some class methods. An object-oriented implementation would be implemented via two classes: a `Channel` class and a `Parser` class. The `Channel` class reads data from a network link and notifies a listener when some data is available. Here is a simple implementation of this class:

```
class Channel(object):
    def set_data_callback(self, callback):
        self.callback = callback
    def notify(self, value):
        self.callback(value)
```

It contains two methods:

- The `set_data_callback` method allows you to register a callback (it is also often called a listener or an observer) which is called whenever some data is available
- The `notify` method is a hook that is used here to simulate incoming data

In a real implementation, the `Channel` class would wait for incoming data being available and then call the callback.

The `Parser` class is the implementation of the state machine. Its implementation is the following one:

```
class Parser(object):
    def __init__(self, transport):
        transport.set_data_callback(self.on_data)
        self.state = self.sync
        self.remaining_size = 0
    def on_data(self, data):
        self.state(data)
    def error(self, data):
        print("error: {}".format(data))
    def sync(self, data):
        if data == 42:
            self.state = self.size
        else:
            self.state = self.error
    def size(self, data):
        self.remaining_size = data
        self.state = self.payload
    def payload(self, data):
        if self.remaining_size > 0:
            print("payload: {}".format(data))
        self.remaining_size -= 1
        if self.remaining_size <= 0:
            self.state = self.sync
```

It is composed of five methods and the constructor. Four of these methods correspond to the four states of the state machine. The constructors has a `transport` input parameter. This parameter contains an object of type `Channel` or any other object that exposes the same API as the `Channel` class. In the constructor, the parser registers itself as a listener of the transport object.

Note that the `self.on_data` syntax registers a bound method as a listener. This means that when the `transport` object will call the callback, the `on_data` method of the object referenced by self will be called. This is a built-in feature of Python, but it is not the case for all programming languages. The C language will never support this, and C++ started to support it through function objects in C++11. Without such a feature, registering a listener is more complex. Either the registration method must have two parameters, one to provide the function to call and another one to give the context to the listener, or the `Parser` class must inherit from a `Listener` base class (as defined by the observer design pattern). So writing this kind of code with Python has always been easier than with some other programming languages.

The constructor then initializes the current state to `sync`, and then sets the size of the `payload` to 0. Bound methods are also used to store the current state as a reference to a method of the `Parser` object. This allows you to dispatch incoming data to the correct state with a single function call.

The `on_data` method is the data callback. Each time a new value is available on the `transport` object, then this method is being called. This method is just a trampoline that forwards the data to the current state handler.

Then each state is implemented as a method. The `error` state just prints an error. The `sync` state transits to the `size` or `error` state, depending on the value of the received data. The `size` state initializes the number of values to receive in the payload and transits to the `payload` state. Finally, the `payload` state prints the data of the payload and goes back to the `sync` state once all the payload data has been received.

This implementation can be tested with the following code:

```
s = Channel()
p = Parser(s)

s.notify(42)
s.notify(3)
s.notify(33)
s.notify(44)
s.notify(24)
s.notify(43)
s.notify(4)
```

Note that the `notify` method is here to simulate events that should be asynchronous. The following values should be printed:

```
payload: 33
payload: 44
payload: 24
error!
Done
```

The payload of the first packet is printed,but then the `sync` value of the second packet is not correct so an error is printed. This is an implementation of a very simple state machine, but following the code flow is not immediate. One has to read the code of each state handler to understand what will be the next active handler. When such code is used on big state machines or hierarchical state machines, it is hard to debug and evolve it. However, the benefit of such a design is that a state machine is deterministic, so one can test all its transitions with unit testing.

Asynchronous handlers with generators

The previous code works perfectly, but as it expands it becomes more and more difficult to maintain. The main reason is that the code flow is spread across multiple locations. Generators can solve this issue by writing asynchronous code that looks like synchronous code. Before rewriting the previous code with a generator, let's look at generators.

Understanding generators

Generators are special functions that can be interrupted at specific locations in their code and can be resumed at a later time with their execution context being restored. Generators are an easy way to create an iterator.

An iterator is created by an iterable object. An iterable is a class that implements the __iter__ method. When called, the __iter__ method must return an iterator object; that is, an object that implements the `next` method. In many cases, the implementations of the iterable and the iterator are in the same class, and the implementation of __iter__ just return `self`. The `next` method must return the next value of the iterator each time it is being called. With generators, all this is much easier. The implementation of the iterable and the iterator is just a function. This function yields values until the iterator completes. So, generators ease the implementation of iterators.

A function is a generator if it contains a yield expression. In this case, the function has a special behavior. When it is called, its content is not executed as it is for functions. Instead, a generator object is returned. Let's see an example:

```
def double(x, end):
    v = x
    while True:
        v = v*2
        if v > end:
            break
        yield v
    return
```

The `double` function is a generator because it contains a `yield` expression. This generator returns a series of values that are the doubles of their preceding value. The generator stops when the current value is bigger than the value provided in the `end` parameter. Let's see what happens when we create an instance of this generator:

```
g = double(3, 30)
g
<generator object double at 0x10de6fb48>
```

The `g` variable is a reference to a generator object. From that point, no code in the `double` function has be executed yet. Execution will start when a value is requested:

```
next(g)
6
```

On this first call, the generator was executed until the `yield` statement. The returned value is the initialization value (which is, 3 in our case) multiplied by 2. Each time a new value is requested, the generator takes another step in its loop:

```
next(g)
12
next(g)
24
next(g)
Traceback (most recent call last):
  File "<stdin>", line 1, in <module>
StopIteration
```

Two more values are returned by the generator. On the last call, an exception is returned. This is how a generator completes. The double function returned because the computed value was 24 * 2 = 48, which is bigger than 30. When a generator completes (and, more generally, when an iterator completes), a StopIteration exception is raised. So this exception must be caught by the caller for it to know when an iterator has completed.

Generators have an additional feature compared to iterators. They can receive values from the caller, so they are not limited to only sending values. Let's create another generator very similar to the previous one:

```
def double_from(x, end):
    v = x
    while True:
        v = v*2
        if v > end:
            break
        v = yield v
    return
```

The only difference is that the v value is set from the result of the yield expression. This is how a generator can receive a value from the caller of the generator. To provide this value, the caller must use the send method of the generator instead of the next function:

```
g = double_from(3, 30)
next(g)
6
g.send(4)
8
g.send(1)
2
g.send(9)
18
```

Using generators for asynchronous handlers

So how can generators help with writing asynchronous code? The twist comes from the fact that a generator can be interrupted where we want it to be and resumed later when something happens, such as when an asynchronous action is completed. This means that generators can be used to trigger asynchronous action executions with the yield expression, and they can be resumed when the action has completed.

Let's rewrite the state machine as a generator. The asynchronous operations are the read calls on the transport channel. So, each time the state machine needs to get some data, it has to yield so that more data can be read. Here is the new code of the state machine:

```
def parser(read_next):
    while True:
        sync = yield read_next
        if sync != 42:
            print("error!")
            return

        size = yield read_next

        while size > 0:
            data = yield read_next
            print("payload: {}".format(data))
            size -= 1
```

The main and very visible change is the fact that the whole code is much smaller. Instead of a class composed of four methods for each state, the implementation is now a single function with a code flow very similar to synchronous code. In order to understand what is going on, read the code as if the `yield read_next` expression was a call to a `read_next` function that would return the next integer in the transport channel. The function is an infinite loop composed of three parts:

1. The first part reads the `sync` word and returns an error if its value is not `42`
2. The second part reads the size of the payload
3. The last part reads all the words of the payload and prints them

Once this is done, the loop takes another step and reads the `sync` word of the next packet. Reading and writing this code is much more natural than reading/writing code based on a state machine for several reasons:

- The code flow follows the application logic. This helps you avoid mental headaches when trying to remember where the implementation of the previous n^{th} step was.
- All states are local variables. This also helps you to read the code with state variables being declared and initialized when needed instead of the constructor of the class that can be out of sight.

Now that the state machine is implemented, it must be fed data. Another generator is used to simulate the availability of data on the channel:

```
def socket():
    yield 42
    yield 3
    yield 33
    yield 44
    yield 24
    yield 43
    yield 4
```

This generator is much simpler and yields the same values as in the previous implementation. Here, the implementation is now a function instead of a class. The missing piece is a component that will orchestrate these two generators and feed the parser generator data returned from the socket generator. A first implementation attempt could look like this:

```
s = socket()
p = parser(s)

next(p)
word = next(s)
p.send(word)
word = next(s)
p.send(word)
word = next(s)
p.send(word)
word = next(s)
p.send(word)
word = next(s)
p.send(word)
word = next(s)
p.send(word)
```

First, the `socket` and `parser` generators are instantiated. Then the `parser` is initialized with a first call to the `next` function. After that, the first word is read on `socket` by calling the `next` function on the `socket` generator. Its result is stored in the `word` variable. This data is forwarded to the `parser` generator by calling its `send` method. Finally, this `next`/`send` sequence is repeated several times to alternatively read some data and feed the `parser` this data. If you run this whole code, you will get the following output:

```
payload: 33
payload: 44
payload: 24
error!
```

The good news is that it works! The bad news is that the code managing the generator is completely redundant; it does not use the yielded values of the parser and does not work if we change one of the generators. This part should work whenever the data being returned by the socket generator changes, and also if the definition of the state machine changes. So, let's reimplement it as a loop:

```
s = socket()
p = parser(s)

try:
    c = next(p)
    while True:
        data = next(c)
        c = p.send(data)
except StopIteration:
    print("Done")
```

When executed, it provides the following output:

```
payload: 33
payload: 44
payload: 24
error!
Done
```

This is much better. First, the completion of the generators is correctly handled by catching the StopIteration exception. Then, by replacing the next/send sequence with an infinite loop, the program still works if one of the generators changes.

By implementing these two generators and the loop managing them, we have basically implemented an asynchronous framework with an event loop. The only thing that is missing is a system call to select or poll after sending, so that the event loop will actually wait for data to be available on a real socket before iterating.

Introduction to AsyncIO

AsyncIO is the official asynchronous framework for Python. As explained in the previous section, this does not mean that it is the only one available. Twisted and Gevent are two other asynchronous frameworks that are very famous. However, since its release in Python 3.4, AsyncIO has become very popular rather quickly. There is no doubt that one reason for this success comes from the philosophy of Python: There should be only one obvious way to do something. Since AsyncIO is part of the standard library, it is the *de facto* way to do asynchronous programming in Python. Another reason is probably that it was released with the correct timing, when developers regained interest in asynchronous programming.

AsyncIO relies on three entities:

- **Futures**: They represent values that will be available later
- **Coroutines**: They allow you to execute asynchronous actions
- **Event loops**: They schedule the execution of the active tasks

These three entities are the classical ones in modern asynchronous programming. Let's look at each of them.

Futures

A **Future** is an object that is used to store a value that is not available when the future is created, but that will be available at a later time. This is an alternative to callbacks in the typical use case of executing an asynchronous action. An asynchronous function is called, so its return value is not available yet. One way to deal with this is to provide a callback that will be called when the action completes. Another option is to return a future in the asynchronous function and set the result of the action in future once the action has completed. The caller of the asynchronous function can then be notified when future is set.

The following figure shows how a **Future** object can be used:

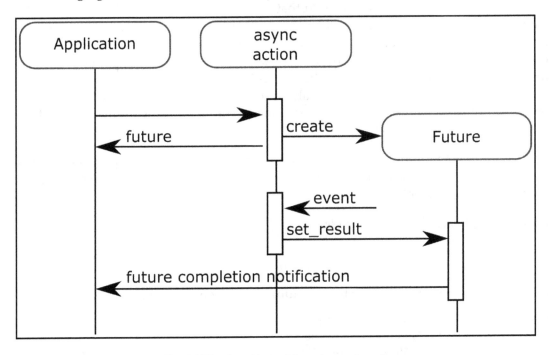

Figure 2.6: Using a Future object to wait for asynchronous action results

Let's look at an example. The following program simulates an asynchronous action whose result is 42. This result value is put into future, and the value of the future is printed on the console:

```
import asyncio
f = asyncio.Future()
print("Future is done: {}".format(f.done()))
f.set_result(42) # this is done asynchronously in a real code
print("Future is done: {}".format(f.done()))
print("result is: {}".format(f.result()))
```

Running this code prints the following output:

```
Future is done: False
Future is done: True
result is: 42
```

Let's see what happens here. First, the `asyncio` module is imported. Then a `Future` object is created and stored in the `f` variable. At that point, the `Future` object does not contain any value yet. This can be checked with the `done` method. The `done` method indicates whether future has completed or not. A future is completed if it has been set to a value or if it has been cancelled. The `print` statement confirms that the future is not completed yet. After that, the future value is set to `42` with the `set_result` method. The `set_result` method marks future as completed and sets its value. From that point, the future is completed, which is confirmed by the second `print` statement. The value of the future is then retrieved with the call to the `result` method.

The `result` method returns the value of future, but only if has been set previously with a call to `set_result`. If the future has no value set or if it has been canceled, then the `result` method raises an exception.

For example, look at the following code:

```
f = asyncio.Future()
print("result is: {}".format(f.result()))
```

It raises an `InvalidStateError` because future is not completed yet:

```
Traceback (most recent call last):
  File "<stdin>", line 1, in <module>
asyncio.base_futures.InvalidStateError: Result is not set.
```

Look at the following code:

```
f = asyncio.Future()
f.cancel()
print("result is: {}".format(f.result()))
```

It raises a `CancelledError` exception because the future has been canceled:

```
Traceback (most recent call last):
  File "<stdin>", line 1, in <module>
concurrent.futures._base.CancelledError
```

Canceling a future is done with the `cancel` method. There is no value associated with cancelation. Canceling a future is useful when an action has been started, but it must be interrupted before it completes. In this case, a future has no value, but any client waiting for it can be notified that it has been canceled.

It is also possible to put an exception into future with the `set_exception` method. If future contains an exception, the `result` method raises this exception when being called. The exception can also be retrieved with the `exception` getter method.

The last feature of future is the ability to attach callbacks for completion. The `add_done_callback` method associates a completion callback with future. This callback is called when future completes. The `remove_done_callback` method removes a callback previously associated with future. However, this feature is rarely needed when writing applicative code in AsyncIO.

Coroutines

Coroutines are another building block of AsyncIO. Coroutines were already covered in detail previously in this chapter. A coroutine is basically a generator with syntactic sugar. A coroutine is an asynchronous function that can be interrupted and resumed at specific locations. A coroutine is declared the same way as a function, but with the `async` keyword prefixed:

```
import datetime

async def wait(delay):
    now = datetime.datetime.now()
    print("wait for {} seconds at {}:{}:{}".format(
        delay, now.hour, now.minute, now.second))
    return True
```

This coroutine just returns `True` for now. The first big difference between a coroutine and a regular function is the fact that its code is not immediately executed when the coroutine is called. Instead, a coroutine object is returned:

```
wait(3)
<coroutine object wait at 0x10b807570>
```

The second difference between a coroutine and a function is the fact that a coroutine can call another coroutine, and so it can be interrupted and resumed at these code locations. Calling another coroutine, and asynchronously waiting for its result, is done with the `await` keyword. For example, the `wait` coroutine can wait for some time without blocking the whole program by using the `asyncio.sleep` coroutine:

```
import asyncio
import datetime

async def wait(delay):
```

```
now = datetime.datetime.now()
print("wait for {} seconds at {}:{}:{}".format(
    delay, now.hour, now.minute, now.second))
await asyncio.sleep(delay)
now = datetime.datetime.now()
print("waited for {} seconds at {}:{}:{}".format(
    delay, now.hour, now.minute, now.second))
return True
```

The await syntax indicates to the Python interpreter that when the sleep coroutine is called, then the execution of the wait coroutine must be interrupted. The execution of the wait coroutine resumes when the sleep coroutine completes. This means that the wait coroutine continues its execution after the await expression, with all its context (local variables and closures) being restored. So, let's try to run this wait coroutine. Executing a coroutine and retrieving its result is done with the await keyword, used before the call itself. But there is a catch; this works only inside of a coroutine. So, trying to use the await keyword outside of a coroutine does not work:

```
await wait(3)
  File "<stdin>", line 1
    await wait(3)
              ^
SyntaxError: invalid syntax
```

This is the typical chicken and egg issue. A coroutine can only be called by another coroutine. So how can someone bootstrap a first call to a coroutine? This is the role of the event loop.

Event loop

The event loop is the entity of AsyncIO and is in charge of scheduling all asynchronous actions that must executes concurrently. Fundamentally, it is just an infinite loop that waits for some events to happen and execute handlers associated with these events. In the case of AsyncIO, these handlers are coroutines.

An event loop is automatically created by asyncio when a process is started. A reference to this event loop can be retrieved with the get_event_loop function of the asyncio module. Event loops inherit from the BaseEventLoop abstract class.

This class contains several methods used to execute asynchronous code. One of them is the `run_until_complete` method. With these two methods, the `wait` coroutine of the previous part can now be executed:

```
loop = asyncio.get_event_loop()
loop.run_until_complete(wait(2))
loop.close()
```

This code is available in the `event_loop.py` script. When executed, it shows the following output:

```
wait for 2 seconds at 23:8:22
waited for 2 seconds at 23:8:24
```

The second `print` statement confirms that the execution lasted for 2 seconds, which is the expected behavior. The important point in this program is the fact that during these 2 seconds, other actions could run; the process was not blocked while sleeping. This is easy to test with only one change to this program. Instead of executing the `wait` coroutine once, let's run it twice at the same time:

```
loop = asyncio.get_event_loop()
loop.run_until_complete(asyncio.gather(
    wait(2),
    wait(1)))
loop.close()
```

The code is almost the same, but instead of providing a coroutine to the `run_until_complete` method, the result of the `gather` method is provided. The `gather` method returns a future that aggregates the result of the futures or coroutines being passed as arguments.

The coroutines are not used directly by the `run_until_complete` method. Several steps are needed before the coroutine can execute some code. This was already the case in the previous example. Let's now see what happens when `run_until_complete` is called. First, a `task` is created and the coroutine is associated with it. The `task` is an entity that tracks the current coroutine being executed and resumes it when needed. The future is created and added to the event loop.

A future allows the event loop to know when an action has completed, but it also allows it to cancel an ongoing action. The following figure shows all these steps:

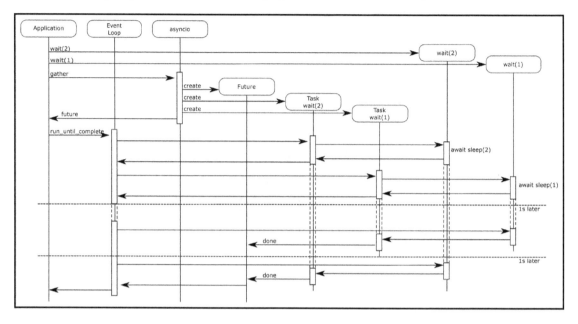

Figure 2.7: Execution of two concurrent coroutines in asyncio

The two first steps consist of creating the coroutine objects. Then the `gather` function creates one task per coroutine that must be executed and then wraps them in a single future. This future will complete once both tasks have completed. The future is returned to the application, and the application provides this future as a parameter to the `run_until_complete` method. From that point, the code of the coroutine starts being executed. First, the `wait(2)` coroutine calls an asynchronous sleep. This suspends the execution of the coroutine and its tasks. This allows the event loop to start executing the `wait(1)` coroutine, which also calls the asynchronous sleep, and so is suspended.

At that point, the event loop is suspended because there is no active task to execute. Should another task be active at that time, it could execute some code. About 1 second after that, the first sleep timer fires. This wakes up the `wait(1)` coroutine, which can complete. At that point, the event loop is suspended again. After another second, the second sleep timer fires. This wakes up the `wait(2)` coroutine that can complete its execution. Since the two tasks have now completed, the future also completes. This triggers the stopping of the event loop.

Take some time to fully understand this sequence diagram. These are all the steps that must be perfectly understood to write `asyncio` code.

It is also important to note two things in this code. First, even thought the `wait(2)` coroutine starts its execution first, the `wait(1)` coroutine completes before it. This happens in a single-process, single-threaded program. Such interleaving is not possible with blocking sleep calls. It would require two distinct threads.

Second, during all that time, the call to `run_until_complete` blocks its caller. This call is usually the end of an `asyncio` program, with only some cleanup after that. When the `run_until_complete` function returns, the event loop is stopped. It can then be closed to free up its internal resources. It is possible to restart an event loop that is stopped, but it is not possible to restart an event loop that is closed. So, this sequence is possible:

```
loop.run_until_complete(wait(2))
loop.run_until_complete(wait(1))
```

This one raises an error:

```
loop.run_until_complete(wait(2))
loop.close()
loop.run_until_complete(wait(1))
```

So now that the execution of this program is clear, you should be able to guess what it prints on the console:

```
wait for 1 seconds at 23:33:31
wait for 2 seconds at 23:33:31
waited for 1 seconds at 23:33:32
waited for 2 seconds at 23:33:33
```

Surprise! The `wait(1)` coroutine effectively lasted for 1 second and the `wait(2)` coroutine for two seconds. However, the `wait(1)` coroutine started its execution before the `wait(2)` coroutine, even though they were provided the other way to the `gather` call. This is normal behavior. The order of execution of the coroutines provided to `gather` is not guaranteed. This should not be an issue for any asynchronous code, but keep it in mind.

An HTTP echo server

This section details a simple but realistic implementation of an asynchronous network service: an echo HTTP server. The behavior is the same as in the reactive echo server implemented in Chapter 1, *An Introduction to Reactive Programming,* but instead of echoing the command-line arguments, the server sends back the requests it receives on an HTTP request.

aiohttp

The AsyncIO library does not contain an HTTP stack. In this example, as well as throughout this whole book, the aiohttp package will be used. The aiohttp package is a complete implementation of the HTTP 1.x protocol with the support of web sockets. It can be used to implement clients and servers. This is a great package to implement HTTP microservices. Its installation is very easy with pip:

```
(venv-rx)$ pip3 install aiohttp
```

Ensure that the package installation is done within virtualenv. Read Chapter 1, *An Introduction to Reactive Programming,* for more information on how to use virtualenv.

An AsyncIO HTTP server

The full implementation of the server is as follows, and it is also available in the GitHub repository (https://github.com/PacktPublishing/Hands-On-Reactive-Programming-with-Python) for this book in the http_echo.py script:

```python
import asyncio
from aiohttp import web

async def echo_handler(request):
    response = web.Response(text=request.match_info['what'])
    await response.prepare(request)
    return response

async def start_server(runner):
    await runner.setup()
    site = web.TCPSite(runner, 'localhost', 8080)
    await site.start()

app = web.Application()
app.router.add_route('GET', '/echo/{what}', echo_handler)
```

```
runner = web.AppRunner(app)

loop = asyncio.get_event_loop()
loop.create_task(start_server(runner))
loop.run_forever()
loop.close()
```

To test it, it must be executed from a terminal, and a client can be executed from another terminal. The `curl` tool is an easy way to test this server:

```
$ curl http://localhost:8080/echo/hello
hello
$ curl http://localhost:8080/echo/foo
foo
```

The whole code fits into less than 25 lines of code, despite not using the high-level APIs of `aiohttp`! The header of the script contains two imports: one for `asyncio`, and one for the web module of `aiohttp`. The `web` module contains all the APIs needed for this server.

Let's overlook the two coroutines for now and jump directly to the initialization of the server. The first part of the initialization consists of creating a web application. This is an object that is used to configure the HTTP routes of the application. Just after that, a route is created and added to the application. This route listens to HTTP GET requests on the path `/echo`. The remaining part of the path (`{what}`) is called a variable resource in `aiohttp`. This allows you to do pattern matching on the URI path. In this case, the last part of the URI path will be put in a variable named `what`. This is the value that will be returned by the server. The last line of this block creates a `runner` for this application. A `runner` is an object used to run an application.

The last block of the script retrieves the default event loop, creates a new task to start the server, and then runs forever. This program will never end unless it is interrupted manually (for example, by typing *Ctrl + C* on the terminal). The `create_task` method schedules the execution of a coroutine. It wraps the coroutine in future and returns a `task` object. This `task` object can be used to interrupt the action if needed, or to ensure that it is completed. In this implementation, the result of `create_task` is not used.

Let's now look at the implementation of the two coroutines:

- The first coroutine, `echo_handler`, is the implementation of the request handler. Remember that a coroutine is recognizable from its definition, which starts with the `async` keyword. It is called each time a new HTTP request is received. This coroutine first creates a response, and then fills the content of the response with some text. The content of the text is retrieved from the value of the `what` key of the `match_info` dictionary of the request. This value is the result of a parsing of the request path that was declared in the route. All variable resources declared in a route are accessible in the `match_info` dictionary of the requests. Then the response is prepared. This is a required step before returning it as the result of the coroutine. The response returned by the coroutine is used to construct the HTTP response of the associated request.
- The second coroutine, `start_server`, is the cone that starts the server. It first initializes the runner, passed as a parameter of the coroutine. Then an instance of the HTTP server is created, listening on `localhost` port `8080`. This is a `TCPSite` object in `aiohttp`. Finally, the server is started.

This whole implementation is fully non-blocking. Note that all functions of the `aiohttp` web module are in fact coroutines. They are all called with the `await` prefix. All these `await` instances are locations in which the coroutines can be interrupted and resumed later.

Summary

This chapter covered all the base concepts of asynchronous programming and how they work in Python. You should now understand what it means to `yield` or `await` a coroutine and know the differences between blocking and non-blocking designs. Hopefully, the short history of asynchronous programming in Python and the examples of asynchronous programming with callback also helped you understand why Python is one of the few languages with best-in-class support of asynchronous programming.

Moreover, you should also be familiar enough with the AsyncIO APIs to write your own asynchronous applications. This chapter only covered the basic usage of AsyncIO, but the features presented here are the most-used ones. Other more advanced features will be introduced in this book, as they are needed in other examples.

One last word on this chapter: Do not be fooled by the simplicity of the echo server implementation. As simple as it is, it is nevertheless a solid foundation to implement real microservices in Python in a fully asynchronous way. A bigger project would require more code, but it would be based on the same APIs that are already used in this small project: the creation of an application, the routing of requests, eventually with variable resources, and the implementation of handlers.

The next chapter continues this introduction of asynchronous and reactive programming with a way to structure your code. More specifically, it will show you how functional programming is well adapted for the implementation of asynchronous code with ReactiveX.

Questions

- Why is asynchronous programming more efficient than multiple processes/threads to handle I/O concurrency?
- Why is asynchronous programming not a solution to improve the performance of CPU-bound tasks?
- What is the reason why multithreading is not performing as well in Python as in other programming languages?
- What is the benefit of a generator compared to an iterator?
- Why does a generator help in writing asynchronous code?
- What is the difference between calling the `next` function and calling the `send` method of a generator object?
- How is a coroutine declared?
- How can a coroutine call another coroutine?
- What is the role of the event loop?

Further reading

The evolution of the Python language is documented in **Python Enhancement Proposals (PEPs)**. The three main evolution points of asynchronous programming in Python are described in detail in these dedicated PEPs:

- Generators are documented in PEP-255: `https://www.python.org/dev/peps/pep-0255/`
- Delegating to sub-generators (yield from) is documented in PEP-380: `https://www.python.org/dev/peps/pep-0380/`
- The `async/await` syntax is documented in PEP-492: `https://www.python.org/dev/peps/pep-0492/`

The documentation of the AsyncIO package is in the Python official documentation. Do not hesitate to read it to see all features available with event loops, futures, and coroutines: `https://docs.python.org/3/library/asyncio.html`.

The documentation of the `aiohttp` package is very detailed, and contains examples. This package will be used throughout this whole book to write microservices. Its documentation is available here: `https://aiohttp.readthedocs.io/en/stable/index.html`.

3
Functional Programming with ReactiveX

This chapter is dedicated to functional programming and how to use this paradigm with ReactiveX. It is composed of three parts. The first part is a rapid introduction to functional programming. The aim of this part is to introduce the few notions that are needed to start writing functional code in Python. The second part presents one of the main issues of real ReactiveX applications: observable cycles. This part describes when this problem occurs and several ways to solve it. In particular, it explains how to use functional programming to solve the issue while isolating side effects from pure code. The last part goes in detail about a new implementation of the echo server, but using ReactiveX and coded in a functional way.

The following topics will be covered in this chapter:

- Functional programming
- Observable cycles
- Structuring functional and reactive code
- The HTTP echo server with an HTTP driver

What is functional programming?

Functional programming is a programming paradigm that has gained a lot of popularity since 2010. In the last few years, many functional frameworks or libraries have appeared in many programming languages, and functional languages have seen a rise in interest. Functional programming is not a new programming paradigm, but getting into it from a theoretical perspective can be intimidating.

The world of functional programming is full of new terms (such as monoid, monad, currying, purity, and higher-order function) that can seem difficult to comprehend, and some of them come with different definitions depending on the source of the information. But functional programming has some very interesting benefits:

- Functional code is deterministic, with behavior that can (at least in theory) be proven
- Functional code can isolate side effects from the pure program logic
- Functional code makes testing easier

The good news is that one does not have to study functional programming in depth in order to benefit from this paradigm, nor to use a functional language. Many modern programming languages support some functional features and allow you to write functional code. So, it is possible to get the benefits of deterministic code and easier testing by only using some of the elements of functional programming.

Some base elements of functional programming

Many of the examples described in this book follow the functional programming paradigm. Since ReactiveX is already using several principals of functional programming, it is a natural way to structure such applications. However, only a subset of the functional programming principals will be used. The structure and separation of responsibilities that will be done in the code rely on the following:

- **Lambdas and closure**: These ease the readability of the code
- **Side effects and pure functions**: These allow you to write deterministic and testable code
- **Higher-order functions**: These are building blocks for many code constructs

Lambdas

Lambdas were introduced in the code sample of Chapter 1, *An Introduction to Reactive Programming*. They are heavily used with ReactiveX. More than that, the availability of lambdas is one of the key features that makes ReactiveX code easy to write and read. A lambda is a single-expression anonymous function. It behaves just like a function and must contain only one expression. A lambda is declared with the keyword lambda. Lambdas are very useful when a short function has to be provided to another function or a variable. In such cases, when the function to be provided is a one-liner, using lambda is easier because it avoids declaring many functions.

Here is a simple example of the usage of `lambda`:

```
def exec(f, value):
    f(value)

def title(value):
    print(value.title())
exec(title, "Hello world")
exec(lambda i: print(i.upper()), "Hello world")
exec(lambda i: print(i.lower()), "Hello world")
```

The `exec` function takes a function (`f`) and `value` as input parameters, and then executes the `f` function with `value` as a unique argument. In the example, the `exec` function is first called with a named function as an argument, the `title` function. The `title` function takes a string as a parameter and prints it in title case. This works perfectly, but it requires some boilerplate code just to print a statement.

The last two calls of the `exec` function use `lambda` instead of a function. The first call prints the string in upper case and the latter prints the string in lower case. In these two examples, there is no need to declare two other functions. The provided function object is declared inline as an input argument. There is less code to write, and reading the code is easier because the text follows the code logic. Run this example to get the following output:

```
Hello World
HELLO WORLD
hello world
```

With ReactiveX code, lambdas are heavily used because many small operations are chained together. Consider this other example:

```
from rx import Observable

a = Observable.from_(["Hello", "Goodbye"]) \
    .map(lambda i: i + " the") \
    .map(lambda i: i + " world") \
    .map(lambda i: i.upper())
a.subscribe(lambda i: print(i))
```

Here, three actions are done on each item of `Observable`:

- Appending the `the` word
- Appending the `world` word
- Converting the whole as upper case

These three actions are trivial, so writing a dedicated function for each of them is a waste of time, space, and readability. Also, since the subscription action is also trivial, `lambda` can also be used here. The result of this code sample is the following one:

```
HELLO THE WORLD
GOODBYE THE WORLD
```

Each item of `Observable` went through the three operations before being printed, and using `lambda` made the code smaller and easier to read.

Closures

Closures are another feature that are heavily used in functional programming. A closure is the fact that a function can capture the value of a variable in one of its parent scopes. Let's see what this means in the following example:

```
def action():
    print(value)

value = "hello"
action()
```

First, the `action` function is declared. This function prints the value of `value` even though `value` is neither a parameter nor a local variable. So how can this work? When the `action` function is being called and the `print` expression is executed, the interpreter searches for a reference of the `value` variable from the inner scope, up to the outermost scope. The interpreter searches in this order:

- Local variables
- Function arguments
- Global variables

There is no local variable or function argument that can be used here. However, when `action` is called, the global variable value exists and can be used. Running this snippet prints the `"hello"` string.

This example is not really useful but it provides you with an idea of how closures work. In real code, closures are mostly used to capture values in nested functions. A nested function is a function which is declared inside a function. Let's see this in the following example:

```
def act_on(what):
    def exec(f):
        f(what)
    return exec
```

```
run1 = act_on("Hello")
run2 = act_on("World")
run1(print)
run2(lambda i: print(i.upper()))
run2(print)
run1(lambda i: print(i.upper()))
```

The act_on function takes a value as an argument. The act_on function contains a nested function named exec and returns it. The exec function takes a function as an argument and calls it with what as an input. In this example, when the exec function is returned by the act_on function, then what is captured as a closure. It is not a local variable, and not an argument of exec but an argument of act_on. So, the value of what when act_on is being called is captured in the function object being returned.

This way of capturing values can be seen with the code that uses the act_on function. Two variables, run1 and run2, are created with different values in the what argument. Then they are called twice, with different actions, in an interleaved way:

- Display print on run1
- Print upper case on run2
- Print on run2
- Print upper case on run1

Running this code gives the following result:

```
Hello
WORLD
World
HELLO
```

We can see that the what values provided on the calls to act_on have been captured in the function that was returned. This captured value is correctly used in subsequent calls without having to provide it as a parameter.

Closures are used a lot in functional programming, and in Python generally. This allows you to capture behavior configuration directly in a function instead of storing this as a state in a class of another location.

Side effects and pure functions

Another concept that is important to understand is a side effect. A function has a side effect if it interacts with an external mutable state. A state in this definition can be any kind of store (such as a global variable) or an entity that is accessed via I/O operations (such as a database or a network connection). Side effects exist in several ways:

- A function without an input parameter is a side effect because its action depends on information that has not been provided as an input
- A function without an output parameter is a side effect because it means that it interacted with some external state
- A function that operates on I/O is a side effect because its result depends on an external state, which is either being read or written

The following functions contain side effects:

```python
def side_effect1(i):
    print(i)

def side_effect2():
    return random(1, 10)

store = 0
def side_effect3(a):
    store += a
    return store
```

From its prototype we have the following observations:

- The `side_effect1` function is a side effect because it does not return any value. This is confirmed by the fact that it prints a value; that is, does an I/O operation on the console.
- The `side_effect2` function can also be directly classified as a side effect from its prototype. It does not contain an input parameter, but returns a value. In this case, the side effect is reading a value from another entity. (By the way, it is also probably an I/O operation on the random device driver, depending on the operating system.)
- The `side_effect3` function is a side effect because it stores a value on a global variable. So it interacts with an external state.

So, why are side effects an important thing in functional programming? Identifying side effects is very important because they are parts of code that are non-deterministic. If they are called several times, they do not do the same actions and/or do not return the same values. Since these functions are not deterministic, they cannot be reused easily and they are more difficult to test. This is the reason why side effects must be identified and isolated. However, this does not mean that side effects must be removed. Any useful work by a program is done through side effects (reading or writing to a file, communicating through a network channel, drawing on a screen, reading input from a keyboard or a mouse, and so on). So, the idea is really to isolate and reduce the footprint of side effects so that most of the code of an application is deterministic and more easy to test. Side effects contain necessary behaviors for a program to execute actions.

This means that a functional code contains two kinds of functions: side effects and functions that are not side effects. Any function that does not contain a side effect is a pure function. A pure function is a function whose output depends only on its input. Here are some examples of pure functions:

```
def addition(a, b):
    return a + b

def hello(who):
    return "Hello {}".format(who)
```

Both of these example return a value that depends only on their input parameters. The benefit of pure functions is that they have deterministic behavior. If they are called multiple times with the same parameters as input, they will always return the same value. This behavior is called **referential transparency**. A referentially transparent function can, in theory, be tested only by calling it multiple times with an exhaustive list of input combinations. Obviously, reality is quite different and exhaustive testing is, most of the time, not possible. Still, pure functions lead to easier testing and fewer bugs.

Higher-order functions

The last concept that is important to know when starting with functional programming is higher-order functions. A higher-order function is a function that accepts a function as an input parameter and/or returns a function as an output parameter. There are different reasons to use higher-order functions:

- By taking functions as input, higher-order functions allow you to implement generic behavior on different types of actions. This allows you to factorize some code.

- Returning a function as an output allows you to capture the values of input arguments, thanks to closures, and return a function that operates on a fixed set of parameters.

Both of these situations are covered in the example of the *Closures* section:

```
def act_on(what):
    def exec(f):
        f(what)
    return exec
```

The `exec` function is a higher-order function that is an example of the first case. It takes a function as an input and calls it. The example is really trivial, but should any code be added in the `exec` function, it would add some behavior available to any function being passed as an input.

The second case is exactly what `act_on` does. The `exec` function that is returned by `act_on` embeds the value of `what` that was provided as an input. This is a very common way to save some context information and use it later.

Functional reactive programming

The time has come to detail how to structure ReactiveX code in a functional way. It is tempting to name code designed this way **functional reactive programming** (**FRP**). Even though this name seems natural, it would be incorrectly named. FRP is something that was described by Conal Elliott in 1997 in a paper named *Functional Reactive Animation*. Functional reactive programming, as described by Conal Elliott, is composed of two types of values:

- Events that correspond to real events, or generated ones
- Behaviors that vary other continuous time

Events are the types of values that are implemented in ReactiveX observables. They can correspond to real events such as mouse location changes, some key presses on a keyboard, or a read operation that completes. Events are used to represent discrete values that change at specific times.

On the other hand, behaviors represent a value that is dependent on the time. So it is basically a formula, or a function, that is applied to the time. Behaviors always have a value, and they are used to represent continuous values depending on the current time. Behaviors are not available in ReactiveX. By the way, behaviors, as defined in the original paper, are available in no framework. This is due to the fact that the notion of a continuous value on a computer system does not exist. Some frameworks approximate behaviors by implementing them via sampling (that is, polling).

Since FRP is definitely not something that can be achieved with ReactiveX, writing functional code on top of a reactive framework should not be named FRP. However, with reactive programming and functional programming being more and more popular, and as they are more and more combined, this is often a source of confusion. The number of questions related to this on development discussion channels confirms this. Another similar name is used by several libraries: **functional and reactive programming (FARP)**. The difference is both subtle and very clear: FARP is not FRP, but reactive code written in a functional way. This is the terminology that will be used in this book.

Observable cycles

From now on, all principles needed to write asynchronous reactive code in a functional way should be clear: reactive programming, asynchronous programming, and functional programming. Before combining all these concepts, there is one last thing to look at—one issue that any real code will face: observable cycles.

The observable cycle issue

What is the observable cycle issue? The observable cycle issue is a natural consequence of flow-based programming. Flow-based programming, as well as ReactiveX programs, consist of defining a directed graph of streams/observables. There are no constraints on the structure of this graph. So, the final code may consist of either a directed acyclic graph or a directed cyclic graph. Some definitions should clarify what the differences between these graphs are:

- A graph is a structure composed of nodes that are connected to each other by edges
- A directed graph is a graph whose edges have a direction

- An acyclic graph is a graph in which it is not possible to start traversing it from a node and looping back to it during traversal
- A cycle graph is a graph in which, when traversing it from a node, it is possible to loop back to this node during traversal

The following diagram shows two simple examples of a directed cycle graph and a directed acyclic graph:

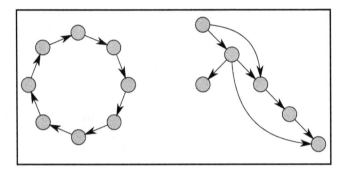

Figure 3.1: A directed cyclic graph on the left, and a directed acyclic graph on the right

All the ReactiveX examples that have been used up to now in this book were directed acyclic graphs of observables. In order to understand what a directed cyclic graph of observables is, let's consider two components, A and B. Both components accept an observable as input and return an observable as output. The output observable of component A is the input of component B, and the output of component B is the input of component A. In other words, these components are inter-dependent. The following figure shows this:

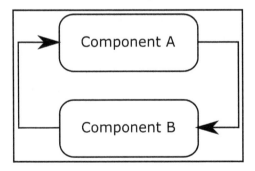

Figure 3.2: A cycle between two components

This is a very common situation, which most of the time occurs with several components forming a cycle. Let's try to implement it:

```
from rx import Observable

def component_a(input):
    return input.map(lambda i: i*2)
def component_b(input):
    input.subscribe(
        on_next=lambda i: print("item: {}".format(i)),
        on_error=lambda e: print("error: {}".format(e)),
        on_completed=lambda: print("completed")
    )
    return Observable.from_([1, 2, 3])

b_out = component_b(???)
a_out = component_a(b_out)
```

The implementation of the two components as two functions is straightforward. Component A is just a wrapper on the map operator and multiplies each item by 2. Component B subscribes to its input to print each item and returns a sequence of integers. The issue occurs when we need to connect both components together. How can we set the input of component B to the input of component A? The good news is that with Python—and this example—it is as simple as this:

```
b_out = component_b(a_out)
a_out = component_a(b_out)
```

However, there are more complex cases in which this kind of construct is not possible. In these cases, something is needed to decouple the output of component A from the input of component B while still being able to connect them together. This can be done by implementing something which acts both as an observable and an observer. This object could be passed as an input of component B, and then the output observable of component A could subscribe to this object. This is exactly the purpose of Subject.

ReactiveX Subject

A Subject is a kind of proxy or bridge that implements both an observable and an observer. Several variants of subjects exist in ReactiveX and in RxPY. The RxPY implementation of the Subject object corresponds to the PublishSubject in ReactiveX terminology. Its behavior is a follows: it emits—to an observer—the items of its source observable that are emitted after the observer subscribes to the Subject. This behavior is shown in the following figure:

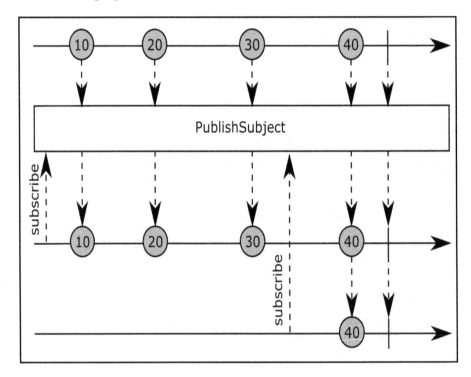

Figure 3.3: The PublishSubject, or Subject, in RxPY

If the source observable of the subject was a cold observable, then it becomes a hot observable. This means that the items sent by the source observable before a subscription are lost. The next chapter will detail hot and cold observables. In the case of an error, then Subject completes immediately with this error.

Here is an example of the usage of `Subject`:

```
from rx.subjects import Subject

proxy = Subject()
proxy.subscribe(
    on_next=lambda i: print("s1 item: {}".format(i)),
    on_error=lambda e: print("s1 error: {}".format(e)),
    on_completed=lambda: print("s1 completed")
)
a = Observable.from_([1,2,3])
a.subscribe(proxy)
print('subscribed to a')

proxy.subscribe(
    on_next=lambda i: print("s2 item: {}".format(i)),
    on_error=lambda e: print("s2 error: {}".format(e)),
    on_completed=lambda: print("s2 completed")
)
```

This code prints the following results:

```
s1 item: 1
s1 item: 2
s1 item: 3
s1 completed
subscribed to a
s2 completed
```

The first subscription to the `proxy` subject is done before the subscription to the a observable; that is, before the subject subscribes to the a observable. So it receives all items of the a observable and prints them until completion. Once the a observable is completed, and by consequence the proxy subject is completed, a second subscription is done on the proxy. Since the `proxy` observable has already completed, this second subscription immediately receives the completion notification.

Solving the cycle issue with Subject

Now let's see how to use `Subject` to implement the directed cyclic graph of the previous example. Instead of referencing the a_out variable directly, `Subject` is used:

```
b_in_proxy = Subject()
b_out = component_b(b_in_proxy)
a_out = component_a(b_out)
a_out.subscribe(b_in_proxy)
```

The complete code of this example is available at: `https://github.com/PacktPublishing/` `Hands-On-Reactive-Programming-with-Python` in the `cycle_subject.py` script.

Structuring functional and reactive code

Finally, all principles have now been covered, as well as the tools needed to implement functional and reactive code. By the way, the previous example is already a functional application: `component_a`, is a pure function, and `component_b` is a side effect. However, the main code that instantiates and connects both components cannot be a pure function because it uses `component_b` which is a side effect. If the instantiation of this side effect is moved to a dedicated side effect initialization part of the code then the rest of the code would be completely composed of pure functions. This is the concept of the Cycle.js framework, a JavaScript framework that allows for writing functional and reactive code. These principles have been used by other frameworks since its creation, and they are applicable to Python and RxPY. With just a few changes to *Figure 3.2*, the architecture of a reactive application with a cycle becomes the following one:

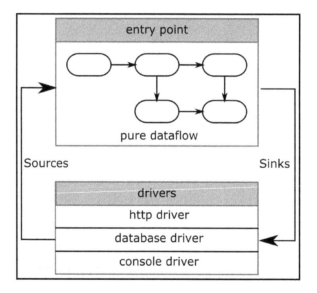

Figure 3.4: The architecture of a functional reactive cycle

There are three parts in this architecture:

- **Application logic**: This part is exclusively composed of pure functions.
- **Drivers**: Drivers are where side effects are implemented. A driver is a function that takes a stream of requests as input and returns a stream of responses.
- **Bootstrapping**: The bootstrapping of the connection between drivers and the entry point.

The entry point of the application is written as a pure function, where inputs and outputs are observables. A nice consequence of this design is that the entry point is not a special case in the application. It is a component that just happens to be the entry point, and it can be reused as a component in other applications. So an application is composed of several components that share this same prototype, and any of them could be used as an entry point.

Drivers can implement any side effects: network clients and servers, access to a database, printing to the console, retrieving a random value, and so on. Drivers can be split into three categories depending on their communication patterns:

- Some drivers use sink and source observables.
- Some drivers are source drivers. They only produce data.
- Some drivers are sink drivers. They only consume data.

The entry point and the drivers communicate with observables. The communication from the entry point to the drivers is done with sink observables. The communication from the drivers to the entry point is done with source observables. A bootstrap function is in charge of doing the instantiation of the drivers and connecting them to the entry point. This bootstrapping allows you to circularly connect the observables together.

The HTTP echo server with an HTTP driver

The time has come to rewrite the HTTP echo server as a functional and reactive application. This application contains an observable cycle. The HTTP server driver returns HTTP requests and takes HTTP responses as input, while the server logic takes HTTP requests as input and returns HTTP responses:

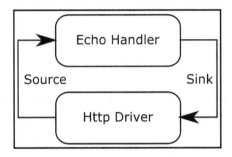

Figure 3.5: The echo server reactivity diagram

ReactiveX operators

This new implementation of the echo server makes use of two new ReactiveX operators: empty and merge. Let's see what they do before going into the new implementation of the server.

The empty operator

The empty operator returns an observable that completes immediately without sending any item:

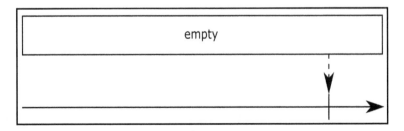

Figure 3.6: The empty operator

The prototype of the `empty` operator is the following one:

```
Observable.empty(scheduler=None)
```

The `empty` operator can be used in the following way:

```
empty = Observable.empty()

empty.subscribe(
    on_next=lambda i: print("item: {}".format(i)),
    on_error=lambda e: print("error: {}".format(e)),
    on_completed=lambda: print("completed")
)
```

The `empty` operator is useful mainly for testing and for stubbing:

- During unit testing, it can be used to test components against `empty` observables as input.
- When implementing a function step by step, for example when following a test-driven development process, an initial implementation can be done with `empty` observables.

The merge operator

The `merge` operator combines several observables into a single observable by merging all items emitted by the source observables in its output observable. The `merge` operator accepts several observables as input and returns one output observable:

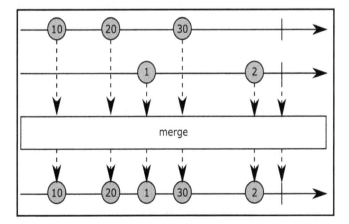

Figure 3.7: The merge operator

The items emitted by each source observable are interleaved on the output observable. As shown in the *Figure 3.7*, the output observable completes once all input observables have completed. However, if a source observable completes on error then the output observable immediately completes on error:

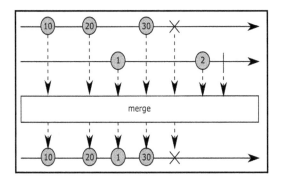

Figure 3.8: The merge operator error behavior

The prototype of the `merge` operator is the following one:

```
Observable.merge(self, *args)
Observable.merge(*args)
```

This method can be used as a method of an `Observable` object, or as a static method of the `Observable` class. The arguments passed as input can be several observables to merge, or a list containing the observables to merge:

```
numbers = Observable.from_([1, 2, 3, 4])
strings = Observable.from_(["one", "two", "three", "four"])

print("Merge from object method:")
numbers.merge(strings) \
    .subscribe(
        on_next=lambda i: print("item: {}".format(i)),
        on_error=lambda e: print("error: {}".format(e)),
        on_completed=lambda: print("completed")
    )
print("Merge from class static method:")
Observable.merge([numbers, strings])    \
    .subscribe(
        on_next=lambda i: print("item: {}".format(i)),
        on_error=lambda e: print("error: {}".format(e)),
        on_completed=lambda: print("completed")
    )
```

Implementation of the HTTP server driver

The HTTP server driver is implemented as a function. It takes an observable of responses as input and returns an observable of requests (referential drivers are upside down, so inputs are outputs and outputs are input). The base implementation is the following one:

```
def http_driver(sink, loop):
    app = None
    runner = None

    def on_subscribe(observer):
        app = web.Application()
        sink.subscribe(
            on_next=on_sink_item,
            on_error=on_sink_error,
            on_completed=on_sink_completed)

    return AnonymousObservable(on_subscribe)
```

When being called, the `http_driver` function returns an observable, whose subscription function is `on_subscribe`. The `http_driver` function declares two variables, `app` and `runner`, which will be used in several nested functions. The subscription function creates the web application and subscribes to the sink stream. So the behavior of the driver is the following: it returns a source stream. When someone subscribes to this source observable then the `on_subscribe` function is called and the driver subscribes to the sink observable. This allows you to chain subscriptions one after each other.

Before looking at the implementation of the `sink.subscribe` callbacks, let's look at three other functions that are needed for the implementation: starting the server, stopping the server, and adding a route and its handler. These functions are nested functions of the `on_subscribe` one. The `http_driver` function contains two levels of nesting, each one allowing you to capture different levels of variables via closures.

The function that starts the server is the following one:

```
def start_server(host, port, app):
    runner = web.AppRunner(app)

    async def _start_server(runner):
        await runner.setup()
        site = web.TCPSite(runner, host, port)
        await site.start()

    loop.create_task(_start_server(runner))
    return runner
```

It creates `runner`, defines a coroutine that starts the server, and schedules the execution of this coroutine on the event loop. Finally, it returns `runner`. The implementation of the `_start_server` coroutine is the same one that was used in Chapter 2, *Asynchronous Programming in Python*. Refer to it if its content is not clear.

The function that stops the server has a similar structure:

```
def stop_server(runner):
    async def _stop_server():
        await runner.cleanup()

    loop.create_task(_stop_server())
```

It declares a coroutine to stop the runner and schedules the execution of this coroutine. The last part of this driver is the creation of new routes and the definition of their handler. Here is its implementation:

```
def add_route(app, methods, path):
    async def on_request_data(request, path):
        data = await request.read()
        response_future = asyncio.Future()
        request_item = {
            'method': request.method,
            'path': path,
            'match_info': request.match_info,
            'data': data,
            'context': response_future,
        }
        observer.on_next(request_item)
        await response_future
        data, status = response_future.result()

        response = web.StreamResponse(status=status, reason=None)
        await response.prepare(request)
        if data is not None:
            await response.write(data)
        return response

    for method in methods:
        app.router.add_route(method, path, lambda r:
            on_request_data(r, path))
```

It takes three parameters as input:

- A reference to the application
- The HTTP methods associated with this route
- The path of the route

At the end of the function, a route is added for each method provided. The handler is common to all routes and is implemented in the on_request_data coroutine. This coroutine is called each time an HTTP client makes a request on one of the configured routes. It works in the following way: for each request, it creates a future and sends an item on the source observable of the drivers, with this future in it. This future will be completed with the content of the answer when an answer is received. Then the value of this future is used to send the HTTP response.

The first line of the coroutine reads the data from the request object. Then, a future is created and a request_item is built with all request information in it, as well as the future in the context field. The item is sent on to the source observable and the coroutine waits for the completion of the future. Once the future has completed (that is, await response_future line), the result of the future is retrieved. The result of the future is a tuple containing two fields: the payload of the answer and the HTTP status of the request.

Then a response object is created, with the status retrieved from the future. This aiohttp response object must be prepared before some data can be written to it. If the future contains some data, then this data is written in the aiohttp response object and the response is returned so that it can be sent as an HTTP response to the client.

Finally, these three functions can be used in the on_next callback of the sink observer:

```python
def on_sink_item(i):
    nonlocal runner
    if i['what'] == 'response':
        response_future = i['context']
        response_future.set_result(((i['data'], i['status'])))
    elif i['what'] == 'add_route':
        add_route(app, i['methods'], i['path'])
    elif i['what'] == 'start_server':
        runner = start_server(i['host'], i['port'], app)
    elif i['what'] == 'stop_server':
        stop_server(runner)

def on_sink_error(e):
    observer.on_error(e)

def on_sink_completed():
```

```
observer.on_completed()
```

`on_sink_item` calls one of the previous functions to start the server, stop the server, or add a route. It also sets the result of the future when a response item is received. This allows you to resume the `on_request_data` coroutine when a response item is received on the sink observable.

Note that the `runner` variable is declared as nonlocal so that the reference of the outermost `runner` variable is updated when the `runner` variable is updated here. Without this statement, the `runner` = `start_server` expression would create a local variable, `on_sink_item`, and it could not be used to stop the server later.

The two other callbacks forward any errors or completion of the sink stream to the source stream. Some additional logic could be added in the error callback; for example, to stop the server. In any case, forwarding these events is important so that they can be caught downstream by other components or drivers.

Bootstrapping the event loop

Now that the driver implementation is done, one has to instantiate it. As explained in the Observable cycles section, this server contains an observable cycle. This cycle is handled with `Subject`. Here is the code for the bootstrapping phase:

```
http_proxy = Subject()
sources = {
    'http': http_driver(http_proxy, loop),
}

sinks = echo_server(sources)
sinks["http"].subscribe(http_proxy)
```

The application logic of the server is implemented as a component in the `echo_server` function. Its implementation is detailed as follows: the source and sinks of this component are Python dictionaries that contain one field named HTTP. This field contains an observable carrying HTTP requests in the `sources` dictionary and HTTP responses in the `sinks` dictionary. It is possible to use an observable directly for the `sources` and `sinks` since they contain only one field, but this is a base structure that will be more complex as features are added to this server.

The first line creates a subject and stores it in the `http_proxy` variable. Then the `sources` object is created with an HTTP field set with the result of the `http_driver` function. As seen before, this returns a stream of HTTP requests. The input parameters are the subject created before and a reference to the `asyncio` events loop.

Then the `echo_server` component is called, with `sources` as an input parameter. This function returns a `sinks` object, whose HTTP field contains an observable with the HTTP responses. Finally, the cycle is completed by making the HTTP `sink` subscribe to the HTTP proxy.

The whole code of this bootstrapping is implemented in the `main` function, which looks like this:

```
def main():
    loop = asyncio.get_event_loop()
    http_proxy = Subject()
    sources = {
        'http': http_driver(http_proxy, loop),
    }

    sinks = echo_server(sources)
    sinks["http"].subscribe(http_proxy)

    loop.run_forever()
    loop.close()
```

The default `asyncio` event loop is retrieved at the beginning so that it can be provided to the HTTP driver, and then the event loop is run forever after the cycle is set up.

Adding the program logic

Now that all the elements needed to implement the asynchronous reactive server are implemented, the application logic can be added. This part is implemented as a function that takes an object of observables as input and returns an object of observables as output. It is a component.

The following figure shows the reactivity diagram of this component:

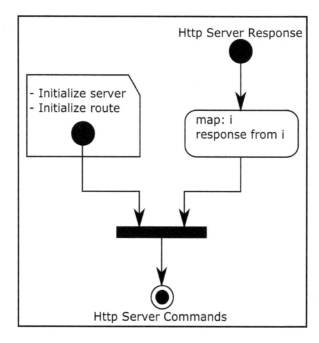

Figure 3.9: The echo_server component reactivity diagram

The empty skeleton of this function is the following one:

```
def echo_server(source):
    return {
        'http': Observable.empty()
    }
```

This component is implemented as a pure function. Its behavior depends only on the value of the input parameter; that is, the content of the http observable contained in the source object. For now, this function returns an empty observable. This will be completed once the body of the function is completed.

The first part of this component is the configuration and initialization of the HTTP server. This is done in a dedicated observable that contains the definition of the HTTP route and the request to start the server:

```
init = Observable.from_([
    {
        'what': 'add_route',
        'methods': ['GET'],
        'path': '/echo/{what}',
    }, {
        'what': 'start_server',
        'host': 'localhost',
        'port': 8080
    }
])
```

The first item will add a new route for the GET method on the /echo/ path. Note the usage of a variable resource, the {what} part of the path, to retrieve the text to echo. The second items effectively start the server on localhost and port 8080.

The second part of the component consists of answering the echo requests. The echo requests come from the observable present in the http field of the source dictionary. The answer is simply built by mapping the source request item to a response item:

```
echo = source['http'] \
    .map(lambda i: {
        'what': 'response',
        'status': 200,
        'context': i['context'],
        'data': i['match_info']['what'].encode('utf-8'),
    })
```

The implementation is straightforward and consists of lambda. The returned item is a response item, with status 200 (the status code for OK in an HTTP response), and the data retrieved from the variable resource that was declared in the route. This value is retrieved from the match_info field of the request item. This text value must be encoded so that aiohttp can put it in the body of the response. The response items are available in the echo observable.

Now that all the logic is implemented, these two observables must be returned so that they can feed the HTTP driver. This is done with the `merge` operator:

```
return {
    'http': Observable.merge(init, echo),
}
```

The full code of the `echo` component is the following one:

```
def echo_server(source):
    init = Observable.from_([
        {
            'what': 'add_route',
            'methods': ['GET'],
            'path': '/echo/{what}',
        }, {
            'what': 'start_server',
            'host': 'localhost',
            'port': 8080
        }
    ])

    echo = source['http'] \
        .map(lambda i: {
            'what': 'response',
            'status': 200,
            'context': i['context'],
            'data': i['match_info']['what'].encode('utf-8'),
        })

    return {
        'http': Observable.merge(init, echo),
    }
```

The full code of the server is available in the `rx_http_echo.py` script. It can be tested the same way as with the previous implementation of `asyncio`. Start the server in a terminal, and then in another Terminal, use `curl` to test it:

```
$ curl http://localhost:8080/echo/hello
hello
$ curl http://localhost:8080/echo/foo
foo
```

This implementation does not stop the server. As an exercise, you can add another route such as `/exit` that will ask the HTTP driver to stop the server.

Summary

This chapter introduced some semantics of functional programming and how they apply these to Python code. This is by no means a complete guide to functional programming, but it covers everything that is needed to start out with functional programming: lambdas, closures, side effects, pure functions, and higher-order functions.

You should now have all the key elements to start writing functional and reactive applications. Hopefully, just like the many JavaScript developers using it today, you will find the architecture proposed in this chapter elegant, easy to use once you have the correct mindset, and scalable (in term of code size).

The application of this architecture on the `echo` server showed you how to solve real-life challenges, such as observable cycles. Moreover, by keeping the application logic pure, it becomes easy to add new features by implementing new components and using them through composition. Another benefit of this architecture that was not detailed here, however, is that testing the application logic is easy since it is pure. Many difficulties in unit testing come from side effects that are not present in this code. A typical benefit of testing a pure function is that you never need mocks, but just provide input arguments and check the return value.

The next chapter will cover in detail how observables and observers work. It will explain the different ways to create observables, how to subscribe to them, and how to unsubscribe from them. It will also explain the different types of observables, which has not been discussed yet.

Questions

- What is a pure function?
- What is a higher-order function?
- Why should side effects be as small as possible?
- What is an observable cycle?
- How can you wait in a coroutine until a item is received on an observable?
- How can you combine two observables into a single one?
- Would you implement some code that writes pixels to a screen as a component or as a driver? Why?

Further reading

The original paper from Conal Elliott describing the principles of FRP is available on its website: `http://conal.net/papers/icfp97/`. A follow-up paper was written some years later, addressing the implementation difficulties of behaviors. The thesis paper for push-pull functional reactive programming is available here: `http://conal.net/papers/push-pull-frp/`.

4
Exploring Observables and Observers

In this chapter, we will go into detail on observables: how to create them, how to subscribe to them, how to handle their errors, and how to use them with AsyncIO. In the first part of this chapter, we will describe all of the possible ways to create observables, from existing objects, iterable objects, or custom code logic. Each time a new observable is needed, one of these methods is best for the situation.

In the second part of this chapter, we will explain another important notion of ReactiveX: hot and cold observables. Knowing whether an observable is hot or cold is the key to using it correctly. The third part of this chapter will cover the different ways to listen to an observable and how to deal with errors. Finally, the last part will illustrate how observables can cohabit with AsyncIO and how to bridge futures and observables. This is a frequent requirement when writing drivers based on AsyncIO packages.

The following topics will be covered in this chapter:

- Creating observables
- Hot and cold observables
- Subscription and disposal
- Error handling
- Observables and AsyncIO

Creating observables

Most of the code of a ReactiveX application is composed of operators that are chained together. However, at some point, the source of these events must be exposed as observables. ReactiveX provides many ways to create an observable from any source of data. Many factory operators are already available to convert virtually any source of data or event to an observable, and, should none of these operators be applicable to a situation, it is possible to create an operator from custom code logic.

All of the factory operators in RxPY are implemented as static methods of the `Observable` class. This means that they are invoked by using `Observable.xxx`, where `xxx` is the factory operator, and they return an observable. Also, almost all of these operators take a scheduler as an optional parameter. A scheduler allows you to control how the items are emitted on the observable. They are only mentioned in this chapter briefly, and they will be covered in detail in `Chapter 5`, *Concurrency and Paralellism in RxPY*.

Creating observables from values

The first category of factory operators allows us to create observables from values, or from iterables. The `from_` operator, which was already documented in `Chapter 1`, *An Introduction to Reactive Programming,* falls into this category. This category contains operators that are used in many cases, so it is important to know them in order to avoid reimplementing a factory that already exists.

The of operator

The `of` operator is a variant of the `from_` operator. This operator creates an observable from a variable number of arguments. The marble diagram of this operator is shown in the following diagram:

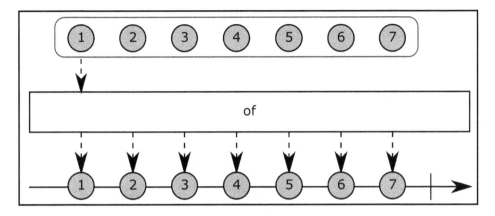

Figure 4.1: The of operator

Its prototype is as follows:

```
Observable.of(*args, **kwargs)
```

The scheduler can be provided as the optional `scheduler` keyword argument. This operator can be used with values directly passed to it, as follows:

```
numbers = Observable.of(1, 2, 3, 4)
numbers.subscribe(
        on_next=lambda i: print("item: {}".format(i)),
        on_error=lambda e: print("error: {}".format(e)),
        on_completed=lambda: print("completed")
    )
```

Upon subscription, the sequence provided as the argument of the `of` operator is emitted on the observable before it completes, as follows:

```
item: 1
item: 2
item: 3
item: 4
completed
```

The `of` operator can also be used to create an observable from the arguments of a function. The following example returns the same values as the previous one:

```
def create_numbers_observable(*args):
    return Observable.of(*args)

create_numbers_observable(1, 2, 3, 4).subscribe(
        on_next=lambda i: print("item: {}".format(i)),
```

Exploring Observables and Observers

```
        on_error=lambda e: print("error: {}".format(e)),
        on_completed=lambda: print("completed")
    )
```

The just operator

The `just` operator returns an observable that emits only one item, and then it completes immediately. The marble diagram of this operator is shown in the following figure:

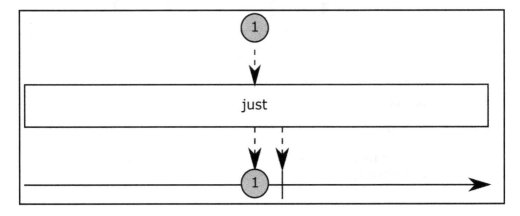

Figure 4.2: The just operator

Its prototype is as follows:

```
Observable.just(value, scheduler=None)
```

The following is an example of how to use it:

```
number = Observable.just(1)
number.subscribe(
        on_next=lambda i: print("item: {}".format(i)),
        on_error=lambda e: print("error: {}".format(e)),
        on_completed=lambda: print("completed")
    )
```

Upon subscription, the number 1, provided in the just operator, is emitted as the only item of the observable before the observable completes:

```
item: 1
completed
```

[98]

The range operator

The `range` operator creates an observable that emits integer items within a range of values. Its marble diagram is shown in the following figure:

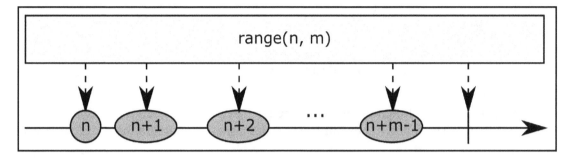

Figure 4.3: The range operator

Its prototype is as follows:

```
Observable.range(start, count, scheduler=None)
```

The `start` parameter is the initial value of the sequence of numbers that is emitted on the observable. The `count` parameter indicates the number of items to send. So, creating a sequence from 1 to 4 can be done as follows:

```
numbers = Observable.range(1, 4)
numbers.subscribe(
        on_next=lambda i: print("item: {}".format(i)),
        on_error=lambda e: print("error: {}".format(e)),
        on_completed=lambda: print("completed")
    )
```

The preceding sample code prints the values from 1 to 4 before completing, as follows:

```
item: 1
item: 2
item: 3
item: 4
completed
```

Like many other operators, this one is available in most, if not all, implementations of ReactiveX. However, in Python, this operator is almost syntactic sugar for the `from_` operator, combined with the built-in Python `range` function. The same result from the preceding code can be obtained as follows:

```
numbers = Observable.from_(range(1, 5))
numbers.subscribe(
        on_next=lambda i: print("item: {}".format(i)),
        on_error=lambda e: print("error: {}".format(e)),
        on_completed=lambda: print("completed")
    )
```

Using the Python `range` function instead of the `range` operator makes it possible to use other steps than 1. The following example generates a sequence of odd numbers, from 1 to 9:

```
numbers = Observable.from_(range(1, 10, 2))
numbers.subscribe(
        on_next=lambda i: print("item: {}".format(i)),
        on_error=lambda e: print("error: {}".format(e)),
        on_completed=lambda: print("completed")
    )
```

The preceding code will provide the following output:

```
item: 1
item: 3
item: 5
item: 7
item: 9
completed
```

The repeat operator

The `repeat` operator allows for repeating the emission of an item or a sequence. The marble diagram of the `repeat` operator is shown in the following figure:

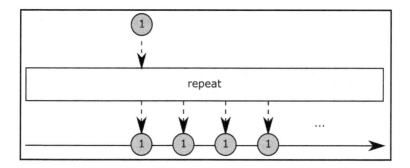

Figure 4.4: The repeat operator

This operator has two prototypes, as follows:

```
Observable.repeat(value=None, repeat_count=None, scheduler=None)
Observable.repeat(self, repeat_count=None)
```

The first implementation is a static class method. It can be used to create an observable that repeats value items for repeat_count times. If the value is not set, items with a None value are emitted. The second implementation is a method that repeats its source observable for repeat_count times. In both methods, the repeat_count argument is optional. When repeat_count is not set, the repetition is infinite. If the repeat_count is less than one, then no items are emitted.

The first variant of the implementation can be used in the following way:

```
ones = Observable.repeat(1, 5)
ones.subscribe(
        on_next=lambda i: print("item: {}".format(i)),
        on_error=lambda e: print("error: {}".format(e)),
        on_completed=lambda: print("completed")
    )
```

The preceding code will provide the following output:

```
item: 1
item: 1
item: 1
item: 1
item: 1
completed
```

The second variant is used in a chain of operators, like in the following simple example:

```
numbers = Observable.from_([1,2,3])
numbers.repeat(3).subscribe(
        on_next=lambda i: print("item: {}".format(i)),
        on_error=lambda e: print("error: {}".format(e)),
        on_completed=lambda: print("completed")
)
```

First, the `numbers` observable is created. Upon subscription, it emits the sequence 1, 2, 3. This sequence is then repeated three times. This provides the following result:

```
item: 1
item: 2
item: 3
item: 1
item: 2
item: 3
item: 1
item: 2
item: 3
completed
```

 In this case, the whole sequence is repeated, and not each item of the source observable. Repeating each item of an observable can be done by combining the static variant of the `repeat` operator with the `flat_map` operator. The `flat_map` operator will be discussed in Chapter 5, *Concurrency and Parallelism in RxPY*.

The never and throw operators

The `empty` operator was discussed in Chapter 3, *Functional Programming with ReactiveX*. This operator is one of a triplet of similar operators: `empty`, `never`, and `throw`. The behavior of each of these operators should be clear from their names, as follows:

- The `empty` operator creates an empty observable that completes immediately
- The `never` operator creates an observable that never completes
- The `throw` operator creates an observable that immediately completes on error

The following figure shows the marble diagram of the never operator:

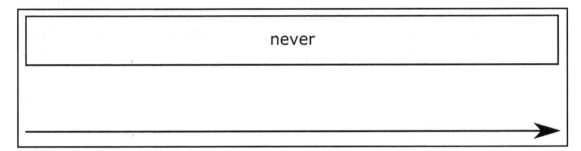

Figure 4.5: The never operator

The following figure shows the marble diagram of the throw operator:

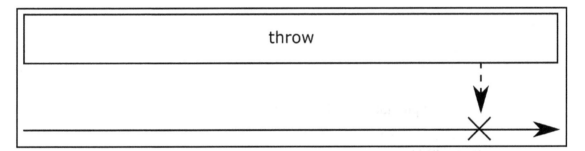

Figure 4.6: The throw operator

Their prototypes are as follows:

```
Observable.never()
Observable.throw(exception, scheduler=None)
```

Note that the `never` operator does not have a scheduler parameter. Since it never emits anything, there is no need for scheduling! The `throw` operator accepts any object in the `exception` parameter. If the provided value is an exception, then it is sent as-is. If the provided value is not an exception, then this value is encapsulated in an `exception` object before being notified. So, the observer of this observable will always receive an exception in its `on_error` handler.

The following code shows two ways to use the `throw` operator:

```
error = Observable.throw("Something wrong happened")
error.subscribe(
        on_next=lambda i: print("item: {}".format(i)),
        on_error=lambda e: print("error: {}".format(e)),
        on_completed=lambda: print("completed")
    )

exception = Observable.throw(NotImplementedError("I do nothing"))
exception.subscribe(
        on_next=lambda i: print("item: {}".format(i)),
        on_error=lambda e: print("error: {}".format(e)),
        on_completed=lambda: print("completed")
    )
```

The preceding code will provide the following results:

```
error: Something wrong happened
error: I do nothing
```

Observables driven by time

The second category of factory operators allows us to create observables from time. They are used less frequently than the previous category of factory operators. One of the main use cases of these operators is to deal with timeouts.

The timer operator

The `timer` operator creates an observable that emits an item after an absolute or relative time has elapsed. After this first emission, the observable emits items periodically if a period value has been provided. The following figure shows the marble diagram of the `timer` operator without a period:

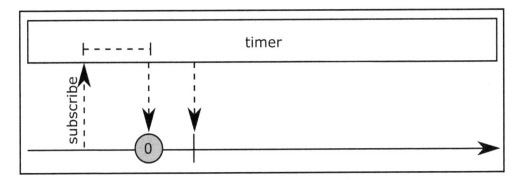

Figure 4.7: The timer operator as a single shot

The following figure shows the marble diagram of the `timer` operator with a period:

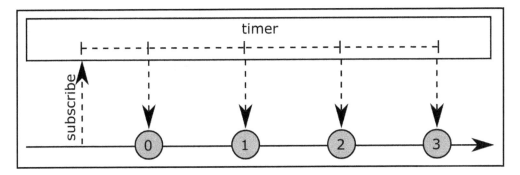

Figure 4.8: The timer operator with a periodic item emission

The prototype of this operator is as follows:

```
Observable.timer(duetime, period=None, scheduler=None)
```

The `duetime` parameter can be an absolute or relative value. Absolute values are provided as `timedate` objects. Relative values are provided as integers in units of milliseconds.

The `period` parameter is optional. When it is omitted, the observable emits a single item, the 0 number, and completes. Otherwise, the observable emits increasing numbers at the period provided. The `period` parameter is an integer that represents milliseconds.

The following is an example of a single shot `timer` observable:

```
import datetime

print("starting at {}".format(datetime.datetime.now()))
one_shot = Observable.timer(1000)
one_shot.subscribe(
        on_next=lambda i: print("tick {} at {}".format(
            i, datetime.datetime.now())),
        on_error=lambda e: print("error: {}".format(e)),
        on_completed=lambda: print("completed")
)
```

The preceding code will provide the following results:

```
starting at 2018-06-21 23:25:08.451966
tick 0 at 2018-06-21 23:25:09.456590
completed
```

As expected, the item was received one second after the program started. The following example (with a period) never ends unless it is interrupted:

```
import datetime

print("starting at {}".format(datetime.datetime.now()))
tick = Observable.timer(1000, period=500)
tick.subscribe(
        on_next=lambda i: print("tick {} at {}".format(
            i, datetime.datetime.now())),
        on_error=lambda e: print("error: {}".format(e)),
        on_completed=lambda: print("completed")
)
```

The output is as follows:

```
starting at 2018-06-21 23:38:26.375393
tick 0 at 2018-06-21 23:38:27.379811
tick 1 at 2018-06-21 23:38:27.878076
tick 2 at 2018-06-21 23:38:28.379091
tick 3 at 2018-06-21 23:38:28.877043
tick 4 at 2018-06-21 23:38:29.381027
...
```

The first item is received after one second, but the other ones are received every 500 milliseconds. Note that the value of the item increases at each emission.

The interval operator

In cases in which some items must be emitted at a fixed interval, the `interval` operator can be used instead of the `timer` operator. Its behavior is the same as the `timer` operator, wherein the same value is provided in `duetime`, a `period` parameter. This is how it is implemented. Its marble diagram is shown in the following figure:

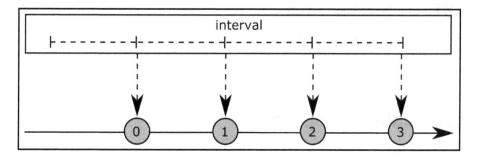

Figure 4.9: The interval operator

Its prototype is as follows:

```
Observable.interval(period, scheduler=None)
```

The `period` parameter is the value, in milliseconds, of the period of item emission. This operator can be used as follows:

```
import datetime

ticks = Observable.interval(1000)
ticks.subscribe(
        on_next=lambda i: print("tick {} at {}".format(
            i, datetime.datetime.now())),
        on_error=lambda e: print("error: {}".format(e)),
        on_completed=lambda: print("completed")
)
```

The preceding example provides the same results as the second example of the `timer` operator, as follows:

```
tick 0 at 2018-06-23 22:07:32.488799
tick 1 at 2018-06-23 22:07:33.491213
tick 2 at 2018-06-23 22:07:34.493068
tick 3 at 2018-06-23 22:07:35.495030
tick 4 at 2018-06-23 22:07:36.500543
...
```

Custom observables

The last category of factory observables allows us to create observables from any source of event, or any code logic. The following operators allow us to create observables from other functions.

The from_callback operator

The `from_callback` operator is a higher order function. It returns a function that returns an observable. This observable emits a single item: the result of a callback function provided as a parameter of the operator. This callback function is called when the observable is being subscribed. The marble diagram of this operator is shown in the following figure:

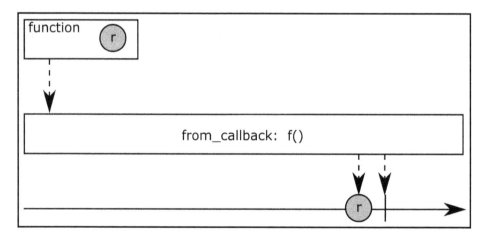

Figure 4.10: The from_callback operator

Its prototype is as follows:

```
Observable.from_callback(func, selector=None)
```

The return value of the `from_callback` operator is a function. This function returns an observable, and must be called with the parameters to pass when `func` is called later on. The `func` callback is called when the `of` observable is being subscribed.

An optional `selector` parameter can be provided. This is a function called with the result of `func` as input parameters. When the `selector` parameter is provided, the item emitted on the observable is the return value of the `selector` parameter.

This operator does not accept a `scheduler` parameter. The whole call flow is always synchronous.

The following code is an example of its usage:

```
def foo(what, handler):
    print("foo: {}".format(what))
    handler("hello " + what)
callback = Observable.from_callback(foo)
cbk_obs = callback("world")
print("subscribing...")
cbk_obs.subscribe(
    on_next=lambda i: print("item: {}".format(i)),
    on_error=lambda e: print("error: {}".format(e)),
    on_completed=lambda: print("completed")
)
```

When `from_callback` is called, a function is returned and stored in the `callback` variable. This `callback` operator is then invoked with the `world` parameter. The result of this call is an observable whose single item is the result of `foo` being called with the `world` parameter. Upon subscription, `foo` is called and a `hello world` item is received:

```
subscribing...
foo: world
item: hello world
completed
```

The create operator

The create operator is the operator most often used to create custom observables. The implementation of almost all other factory operators is done on top of this one. Its marble diagram is shown in the following figure:

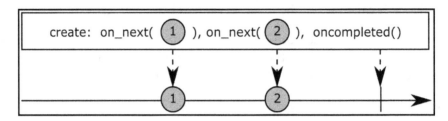

Figure 4.11: The create operator

Its prototype is as follows:

```
Observable.create(subscribe)
```

The subscribe parameter is a function which will be called each time an observer subscribes to the observable. The prototype of the subscribe function is as follows:

```
subscribe(observer)
```

Its only argument is the observer that subscribed to the observable. The following code shows a simple way to use it:

```
def on_subscribe(observer):
    observer.on_next(1)
    observer.on_next(2)
    observer.on_next(3)
    observer.on_completed()

numbers = Observable.create(on_subscribe)
numbers.subscribe(
    on_next=lambda i: print("item: {}".format(i)),
    on_error=lambda e: print("error: {}".format(e)),
    on_completed=lambda: print("completed")
)
```

The `on_subscribe` subscription function emits three items on the observer by calling its `on_next` method. Then it completes the observable by calling the `on_completed` method of the observer. This `subscribe` function is used to create the `numbers` observable. The subscription provides the following result:

```
item: 1
item: 2
item: 3
completed
```

The preceding example was very simple. Let's look at a more realistic example of a very common pattern of the `create` operator—implementing an observable that reacts from the items of another observable (in other words, an operator). The preceding example sums items from the source observable as long as they are even. Every time an odd number is received, the current sum is emitted on the output observable and its value is reset to the value of the odd number.

Let's start with the subscription to this custom operator, shown as follows:

```
numbers = Observable.from_([2,2,4,5,2])
sum_even(numbers).subscribe(
    on_next=lambda i: print("item: {}".format(i)),
    on_error=lambda e: print("error: {}".format(e)),
    on_completed=lambda: print("completed")
)
```

An observable of numbers is created. This observable is provided to the `sum_even` function, and the resulting observable is subscribed. The skeleton of the `sum_even` function is as follows:

```
def sum_even(source):
    def on_subscribe(observer):
        accumulator = 0
        source.subscribe(on_next, on_error, on_completed)
    return Observable.create(on_subscribe)
```

The preceding code just returns an observable, with the nested `on_subscribe` subscription function. The `on_subscribe` function initializes the sum `accumulator` to 0 and subscribes to the source observable. So, when an `observer` subscribes to the observable returned by `sum_even`, `on_subscribe` is called, and the `source` observable is also subscribed. This is a chain of subscriptions. Finally, the callbacks of the `source` observer must be implemented as nested functions of `on_subscribe`, as follows:

```
def on_next(i):
    nonlocal accumulator
```

```
            if i % 2 == 0:
                accumulator += i
            else:
                observer.on_next(accumulator)
                accumulator = i
        def on_error(e):
            observer.on_error()
        def on_completed():
            nonlocal accumulator
            observer.on_next(accumulator)
            observer.on_completed()
```

The `on_next` implementation should be clear. The `accumulator` is updated with the sum of items when they are even and is reset when they are odd. The value of the `accumulator` is emitted every time an odd number is received. The error and completion of the `source` observable are propagated to `observer` of the output observable. The complete code is as follows:

```
def sum_even(source):
    def on_subscribe(observer):
        accumulator = 0
        def on_next(i):
            nonlocal accumulator
            if i % 2 == 0:
                accumulator += i
            else:
                observer.on_next(accumulator)
                accumulator = i
        def on_error(e):
            observer.on_error()
        def on_completed():
            nonlocal accumulator
            observer.on_next(accumulator)
            observer.on_completed()
        source.subscribe(on_next, on_error, on_completed)
    return Observable.create(on_subscribe)

numbers = Observable.from_([2,2,4,5,2])
sum_even(numbers).subscribe(
    on_next=lambda i: print("item: {}".format(i)),
    on_error=lambda e: print("error: {}".format(e)),
    on_completed=lambda: print("completed")
)
```

The preceding code provides the following output:

```
item: 8
item: 7
completed
```

The two items received correspond to the sum of 2, 2, 4, and the sum of 5 and 2. The completion is correctly received after these two items.

Hot and cold observables

The preceding sections covered most of the factory operators available in RxPY. All of these operators start to emit items at subscription time. This is the default behavior in ReactiveX. Nothing happens until an observer subscribes to an observable. It is the subscription that makes the observable start emitting its items. This behavior is very important to understand when coding with ReactiveX, and it has a name: cold observables. Another behavior of observables is possible: hot observables.

So, what is the difference between cold and hot observables?

Cold and hot observables can be described as similar to the different ways of watching TV shows. Sometimes people watch TV shows on demand, and sometimes people watch TV shows live.

When somebody watches a TV show on demand, the content is sent to his TV only when he effectively asks to view the show (that is, when he presses the play button). If another person, or one thousand other people, want to view the same show, each of them will also receive this content; exactly when they request it, they will all receive their own video stream. This allows each person to pause the playback, go forward, or resume the playback without any impact on the other people viewing. This is the behavior of a **cold observable**. A cold observable starts to emit items at subscription time, and each time a new subscription occurs, a new sequence of items is started.

The following figure shows this behavior; each observer receives its own sequence, starting at subscription time:

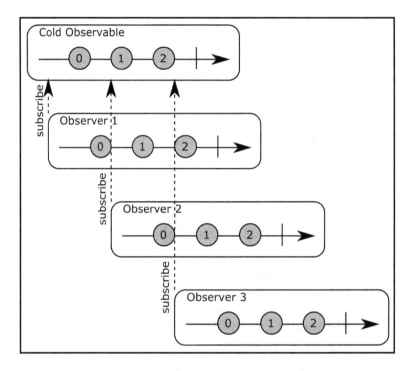

Figure 4.12: A cold observable

On the other hand, when somebody watches a live show on TV then he does not choose when the event will start. The viewer has to be in front of his TV when the show starts; otherwise, he will miss the beginning of it. Also, if thousands of people watch the same live show, they all see the same content. At the very same time, they all receive the same video stream. This is great for events that people want to watch as they happen in real time, such as sports events, music shows, and so on. This is the behavior of a **hot observable**. A hot observable emits items whenever their triggering event happens. These items are emitted whatever the number of subscribers to it.

If an observer does not register before the observable starts to emit items then they will miss some items. The following figure shows this behavior; all observers receive the same items at the same time when they are emitted by the observable:

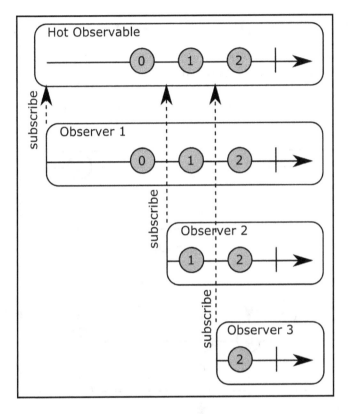

Figure 4.13: A hot observable

Both behaviors are necessary, and the best pattern must be used for each use case. Most of the time, cold observables correspond to the required behavior. That is probably why they are the default type of observable in ReactiveX. If a hot observable is needed, there are two ways to implement it.

The first way is with the `create` operator. Since it can be used to implement any logic, one can expose a hot observable with the `create` operator. For example, with the `create` operator, it is possible to create an observable which emits an item each time lightning hits the ground somewhere on earth. This is a typical hot behavior; observers need to know when lightning occurs, but there is no way for them to force lightning to happen.

The second one is with dedicated operators that can convert a cold observable to a hot observable. Let's look at how to use them in the next section.

Operators – publish and connect

The publish operator converts an observable to a connectable observable. A connectable observable does not start to emit items when an observer subscribes to it, but when its connect method is called. The combination of publish and connect allows us to make an observable hot, but also to ensure that several observers will receive the whole sequence of items. The following figure shows its marble diagram:

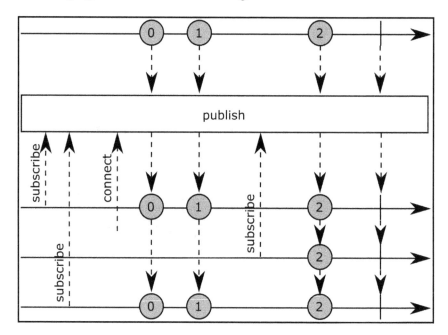

Figure 4.14: The publish operator

The prototypes of the publish and connect operators are as follows:

```
Observable.publish(self)
ConnectableObservable.connect(self)
```

Both of the operators are methods, but `connect` is a method of the `ConnectableObservable` class. The following example shows how the `publish` and `connect` operators modify the behavior of an observable:

```
numbers = Observable.from_([1,2,3])
pub_numbers = numbers.publish()
pub_numbers.connect()

pub_numbers.subscribe(
    on_next=lambda i: print("item: {}".format(i)),
    on_error=lambda e: print("error: {}".format(e)),
    on_completed=lambda: print("completed")
)

pub_numbers.subscribe(
    on_next=lambda i: print("item: {}".format(i)),
    on_error=lambda e: print("error: {}".format(e)),
    on_completed=lambda: print("completed")
)
```

Executing the preceding code provides the following result:

```
completed
completed
```

No items were received by either subscriptions! This is the expected behavior; the `numbers` observable is published and connected before the subscriptions. As explained previously, the subscription to the observable occurs when `connect` is called, not when observers subscribe to the `ConnectableObservable`. In this case, the three numbers are emitted before any observer is subscribed to the `pub_numbers` observable. When they subscribe later, the observable is already completed. If the call to `connect` is moved between the two subscriptions, the code sample provides the following output:

```
item: 1
item: 2
item: 3
completed
completed
```

In this case, the first subscription occurred before connecting to the
`ConnectableObservable` class. So, when the observable started to emit items, the first
subscription received them. The second subscription still missed all of them, because the
observable completed previously. Finally, if the call to `connect` is moved to the end of the
code, the output will be as follows:

```
item: 1
item: 1
item: 2
item: 2
item: 3
item: 3
completed
completed
```

Both of the subscriptions received each item. Their print statements are interleaved because
all of the observers are notified of an item before the next item is emitted.

Operators – ref_count and share

There are cases wherein calling the connect method at the correct time is not easy, or is not
necessary. In many cases, a cold observable can be converted to a hot observable whenever
a first observer subscribes to it, as long as some subscriptions are ongoing. The `ref_count`
operator does just that: it converts a cold observable to a hot observable as soon as a first
subscription occurs. Its prototype is as follows:

```
ConnectableObservable.ref_count(self)
```

It is a method of the `ConnectableObservable` class. So, it must be used after a call to
`publish`, as follows:

```
numbers = Observable.from_([1,2,3])
pub_numbers = numbers.publish().ref_count()

pub_numbers.subscribe(
    on_next=lambda i: print("item: {}".format(i)),
    on_error=lambda e: print("error: {}".format(e)),
    on_completed=lambda: print("completed")
)

pub_numbers.subscribe(
    on_next=lambda i: print("item: {}".format(i)),
    on_error=lambda e: print("error: {}".format(e)),
    on_completed=lambda: print("completed")
)
```

This example is very similar to the previous one, with `ref_count` chained to the `publish` call. The result of this example is as follows:

```
item: 1
item: 2
item: 3
completed
completed
```

Only the first subscription received the items. In this case, the first subscription triggered the emission of the items, and, when the second subscription occurs, the observable has already completed. This difference between the `ref_count` operator and the `connect` operator is important to understand: the `connect` operator allows us to control when the observable starts to emit items, but `ref_count` doesn't.

Using the `ref_count` operator can be a little bit tedious because one has to use two operators. This can be avoided by using the `share` operator, which just chains a `publish` and `ref_count` call, as follows:

```
#pub_numbers = numbers.publish().ref_count()
pub_numbers = numbers.share()
```

Subscription and disposal

So far, only one way to subscribe to an observable has been described: with callbacks. However, it is not the only way. We will now cover the different ways to subscribe to an observable, and will also cover how one can unsubscribe from an observable.

Subscribing to an observable

When an observer subscribes to an observable, it listens to the observable with three handlers, as follows:

- `on_next`, which is called each time an item is emitted on the observable
- `on_error`, which is called when the observable completes on error
- `on_completed`, which is called when the observable completes on success

Handling each of these three kinds of events is optional. However, the `on_error` handler should always be implemented to avoid losing errors silently, which can make a whole program stop working. There are two ways to implement these handlers. The first way is by subclassing the `Observer` class and implementing the three handlers, as follows:

```python
class MyObserver(Observer):
    def on_next(self, item):
        print("on_next {}".format(item))

    def on_completed(self):
        print("on_completed")

    def on_error(self, error):
        print("on_error: {}".format(error))

numbers = Observable.from_([1, 2, 3])
numbers.subscribe(MyObserver())
```

It is also possible to register callbacks with keyword arguments. The following is the same example, but with lambdas as handlers:

```python
numbers = Observable.from_([1, 2, 3])
numbers.subscribe(
    on_next = lambda i: print("on_next {}".format(i)),
    on_error = lambda e: print("on_error: {}".format(e)),
    on_completed = lambda: print("on_completed")
)
```

Disposing a subscription

The `subscribe` method of the `Observable` class returns a disposable object. When a subscription is not used anymore, it must be disposed to free all of the resources that the observable may have allocated:

```python
numbers = Observable.from_([1, 2, 3])
subscription = numbers.subscribe(
    on_next = lambda i: print("on_next {}".format(i)),
    on_error = lambda e: print("on_error: {}".format(e)),
    on_completed = lambda: print("on_completed")
)
subscription.dispose()
```

Custom disposal

When the `create` factory operator is used, it is possible to provide a custom disposal function. This function will be called when the `dispose` method of the disposable object returned by the subscription is called. Consider the following example, similar to the previous one, but with the observable being a custom one:

```
def on_subscribe(observer):
    def dispose():
        print("disposing custom observable")
    observer.on_next(1)
    observer.on_next(2)
    observer.on_next(3)
    observer.on_completed()
    return dispose

numbers = Observable.create(on_subscribe)
subscription = numbers.subscribe(
    on_next = lambda i: print("on_next {}".format(i)),
    on_error = lambda e: print("on_error: {}".format(e)),
    on_completed = lambda: print("on_completed")
)
subscription.dispose()
```

Here, the `subscribe` function returns a `disposal` function. Running the preceding example provides the following result:

```
on_next 1
on_next 2
on_next 3
on_completed
disposing custom observable
```

The `dispose` function of the custom observable was called when the subscription was disposed. This allows us to free resources allocated on the subscription. A typical use case is to unsubscribe from another observable.

Error handling

ReactiveX provides several ways to deal with errors. As explained in Chapter 1, *An Introduction to Reactive Programming,* errors are not special in a ReactiveX code flow. Rather, an error in ReactiveX is one possible way to end an observable. The other way is to complete it (which means that it has succeeded). There are two ways to deal with errors, depending on where the error is caught in the operators chain, as follows:

- An observer handles errors in its on_error callback or method
- A chain of operators can use dedicated operators to deal with errors

The first case is something that must be done in all cases. If a single observer does not handle errors then the errors go to a black hole. This is an easy way to waste hours trying to debug some code and finally see that the error was just silently dropped. If handling the errors is not obvious, then a log is the minimal implementation that allows us to debug them.

The second case allows for some interesting tricks, such as gracefully handling the errors and continuing to emit items, instead of stopping the observable.

The catch_exception operator

The catch_exception operator allows us to catch any error coming from its source observable and to continue to emit items. When the error occurs in the source observable, the catch_exception operator continues the sequence with another sequence of items. Its marble diagram is shown in the following figure:

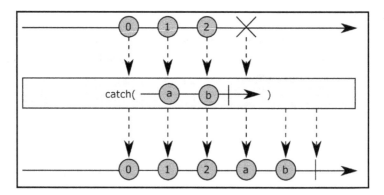

Figure 4.15: The catch_exception operator

Its prototype is as follows:

```
Observable.catch_exception(self, second=None, handler=None):
```

The optional `second` argument is either an observable to chain when an error occurs in the `source` observable or a function that returns an observable. The optional `handler` argument is an exception handler that must return a future. This future will be wrapped in an observable. Only one of the two arguments must be used. The following is an example of this operator:

```
err = Observable.throw("error!")
err.catch_exception(lambda e: Observable.from_([1,2,3])) \
    .subscribe(
        on_next=lambda i: print("item: {}".format(i)),
        on_error=lambda e: print("error: {}".format(e)),
        on_completed=lambda: print("completed")
    )
```

The following is the output of this example:

```
item: 1
item: 2
item: 3
completed
```

The error has been caught correctly and has been replaced with another observable.

The retry operator

The `retry` operator repeats the sequence of the `source` observable for a number of times when an error is raised. Its marble diagram is shown in the following figure:

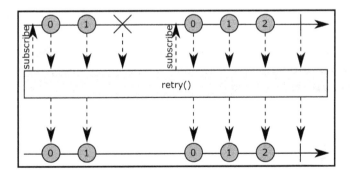

Figure 4.16: The retry operator

Its prototype is as follows:

```
Observable.retry(self, retry_count=None):
```

The `retry_count` argument indicates how many times the operator will subscribe to the observable. So, the number of retry attempts is `retry_count`, minus 1. The following is an example of how to use it:

```
subscribe_count = 0
def on_subscribe(observer):
    global subscribe_count
    subscribe_count += 1
    if subscribe_count == 1:
        observer.on_next(1)
        observer.on_error("error!")
    else:
        observer.on_next(1)
        observer.on_next(2)
        observer.on_next(3)
        observer.on_completed()

err = Observable.create(on_subscribe)
err.retry(2) \
    .subscribe(
        on_next=lambda i: print("item: {}".format(i)),
        on_error=lambda e: print("error: {}".format(e)),
        on_completed=lambda: print("completed")
    )
```

The preceding code provides the following results:

```
item: 1
item: 1
item: 2
item: 3
completed
```

A first, the subscription emits the item 1 and then raises an error. The `retry` operator attempts a second subscription, which succeeds. So the numbers 1, 2, and 3 are emitted before the observable completes.

Observables and AsyncIO

This last section will cover some operators that are specifically designed to deal with asynchronous operations. Some of them allow us to convert synchronous code to asynchronous code and others allow us to convert futures to streams, and vice versa.

The start operator

The start operator schedules the execution of a function asynchronously and emits its result in an observable. The marble diagram of the start operator is shown in the following figure:

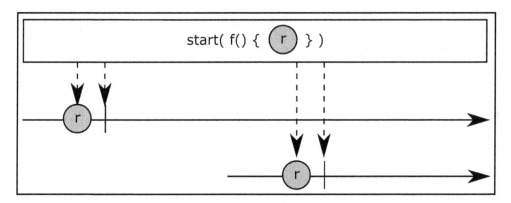

Figure 4.17: The start operator

Its prototype is as follows:

```
Observable.start(func, scheduler=None)
```

The function provided as an argument is scheduled immediately, not during the subscription. If no scheduler is provided, the timeout scheduler is used (see Chapter 5, *Concurrency and Parallelism in RxPY*, for details on schedulers), with a timeout value of 0; that is, no timeout. In this case, the execution of the func function is still done in the context of a timer thread. Let's see this in action, as follows:

```
def foo():
    print("foo from {}".format(threading.get_ident()))
    return 1

number = Observable.start(foo)
print("subscribing...")
```

```
number.subscribe(
        on_next=lambda i: print("on_next: {} from {}".format(
            i, threading.get_ident())),
        on_error=lambda e: print("error: {}".format(e)),
        on_completed=lambda: print("completed")
    )
```

The preceding code sample will provide the following output:

```
foo from 123145595981824
subscribing...
on_next: 1 from 140736035734400
completed
```

When the `start` operator is called, the execution of the `foo` function is scheduled immediately. The log confirms that it is called before the subscription to the observable on the 123145595981824 thread. Once the subscription is done, the result of `foo` is received on the observable, in the context of the main thread of the application; that is, 140736035734400.

This behavior is different when the `asyncio` scheduler is being used. In this case, the `foo` function is executed from the event loop. An example is as follows:

```
from rx.concurrency import AsyncIOScheduler

scheduler = AsyncIOScheduler()

def foo():
    print("foo from {}".format(threading.get_ident()))
    return 2


loop = asyncio.get_event_loop()
done = loop.create_future()

number = Observable.start(foo, scheduler=scheduler)
print("subscribing...")
number.subscribe(
    lambda i: print("on_next: {} from {}".format(
        i, threading.get_ident())),
    lambda e: print("on_error: {}".format(e)),
    lambda: done.set_result(0)
)

print("staring mainloop from {}".format(threading.get_ident()))
loop.run_until_complete(done)
loop.close()
```

In this new example, an `AsyncIOScheduler` is passed to the `start` operator, and this changes the way actions are scheduled, as follows:

```
subscribing...
staring mainloop from 140736035734400
foo from 140736035734400
on_next: 2 from 140736035734400
```

In this case, the subscription happens first; then the event loop is started, the `foo` function is called, and finally, the result of `foo` is emitted on the observable. The `foo` function is called after the event loop starts. When the observable is created, the execution of `foo` is scheduled on the event loop. However, since the event loop has not started yet, its execution is pending. Once the event loop starts, `foo` is executed and its return value is emitted. Also, in this case, both the execution of `foo` and the reception of the item are done in the context of the main thread of the application; that is, `140736035734400`.

The from_future operator

The `from_future` operator converts a `future` object to an observable that emits zero, or one item. The marble diagram of this operator is shown in the following figure:

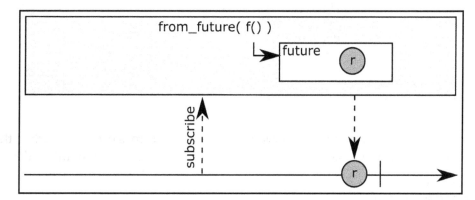

Figure 4.18: The from_future operator

Its prototype is as follows:

```
Observable.from_future(future)
```

This operator converts `future` to an observable that emits the result of `future` if it succeeds, or the error raised by `future` if it does not. The following is an example of its usage:

```
import asyncio
from rx import Observable


async def foo(future):
    await asyncio.sleep(1)
    future.set_result(2)


loop = asyncio.get_event_loop()
done = loop.create_future()
asyncio.ensure_future(foo(done))

number = Observable.from_future(done)
print("subscribing...")
number.subscribe(
    lambda i: print("on_next: {}".format(i)),
    lambda e: print("on_error: {}".format(e)),
    lambda: print("on_completed")
)

print("starting mainloop")
loop.run_until_complete(done)
loop.close()
```

The `done` future is converted to an observable. This `done` future is completed when the `foo` coroutine completes, after a second of delay. The following is the result of this code:

```
subscribing...
starting mainloop
on_next: 2
on_completed
```

The `on_next` trace is printed a second after the `mainloop` has started.

There is a complementary operator to `from_future` and `to_future`. The `to_future` operator converts an observable to a future.

Summary

This chapter detailed the different ways to create observables, from either existing objects or custom code logic. The factory operators that we documented are the ones that allow us to start any operator chain in ReactiveX. Of this list of operators, `from_`, `create`, and `just` are probably used the most frequently.

Understanding the difference between cold and hot observables is very important when developing a ReactiveX application. If this notion is not clear to you, you will not understand why some values are received several times on a cold observable or why some values are never received on a hot observable.

The previous chapters already contained examples of observable subscriptions. Now the different ways to subscribe to an observable, as well as how to handle errors, should be clear.

Finally, the last part of this chapter presented some tools that allow us to bridge observables and futures. These operators are useful in some cases, but it is also possible to make AsyncIO and ReactiveX cohabit via other code logic if they do not match the logic of an application.

The next chapter will be dedicated to concurrency and parallelism. RxPY has provided many ways to handle concurrency. Next, we will study how to use the AsyncIO event loop with RxPY. However, RxPY also allows us to do parallelism since Python has some limitations in this field.

Questions

- How do you create an observable that emits only one value?
- How do you create an observable that emits one item from each line of a text file?
- Does the `just` operator return a cold or a hot observable?
- What operator can you use to convert a cold observable to a hot observable and to start to emit items when a first observer subscribes to it?
- Why is it important that observers handle errors?
- How can you convert an observable error to an observable item?
- Why should subscriptions be disposed?

5
Concurrency and Parallelism in RxPY

The previous chapters covered asynchronous programming principles, the difference between CPU operations and I/O operations, and how to create observables. Chapter 2, *Asynchronous Programming in Python*, detailed the two patterns that allow us to handle concurrency, and which is most adapted to which use case. Unfortunately real life, and so coding, is rarely Boolean; sometimes an asynchronous application also has to deal with CPU-intensive operations, or even worse, blocking code. This chapter details how ReactiveX allows us to handle such situations, with tools that are easy to use and efficient, such as schedulers. The first part of this chapter is a reminder of the concurrency issues that can happen, and how schedulers can solve these issues. The second part details the schedulers available in RxPY, and when and how to use them.

The following topics will be covered in this chapter:

- Concurrency and schedulers
- Available schedulers

Concurrency and schedulers

Chapter 2, *Asynchronous Programming in Python*, explained the principles of concurrency, and its two categories:

- I/O concurrency
- CPU concurrency

An asynchronous framework is designed to deal with I/O concurrency by multiplexing all I/O requests on a single process and thread. The AsyncIO framework and ReactiveX are both tools in this category. As such, they are a perfect fit for applications that are I/O bound, such as network-based applications and tasks involving interactions with databases. However, there are situations where a full asynchronous design cannot be applied. This can occur in two cases:

- When doing CPU-intensive actions
- When using blocking APIs

Both of them break the behavior of an asynchronous system because they block the event loop for a very long time, and prevent other tasks from executing. On some asynchronous frameworks, handling such cases is simply not possible. The code must be fully asynchronous and not use CPU-intensive operations or blocking APIs, which is not always possible; so one has to ignore these behaviors and the application will break sooner or later.

Fortunately, AsyncIO and RxPY acknowledge that such cases exist, and they provide tools to deal with them. More than that, ReactiveX and RxPY allow us to deal with these situations once again in an easy way. So what does it mean to handle CPU concurrency in asynchronous code? Since the issue is that the current core is saturated by an action, there are only two solutions. Both of them have been covered in Chapter 2, *Asynchronous Programming in Python*: multithreading and multiprocessing. These are the two ways to use all the available CPU cycles of all cores. ReactiveX and RxPY allow us to use multithreading in an application and provide a way to schedule where each operator will execute. In practice, this means that it is possible to specify, for each operator in an operator chain, on what execution context they will run. In an AsyncIO application, there are two kinds of execution context:

- The event loop
- A thread (eventually running its own event loop)

The selection of an execution context is possible in three different ways:

- When creating an observable
- By using the subscribe_on operator
- By using the observe_on operator

These three methods allow us to control the execution context of two parts of an observable chain: the source of the chain and each operator in a chain. The source of the chain is the first observable of the chain, usually created with a factory operator. It is possible to control on what execution context the items of this observable are emitted, either by providing a scheduler object to the factory operator or by using the subscribe_on operator. Consider the following code:

```
numbers = Observable.from_([1,2,3,4])

subscription = numbers \
    .map(lambda i: i*2) \
    .map(lambda i: "number is: {}".format(i)) \
    .subscribe(
        on_next = lambda i: print("on_next {}".format(i)),
        on_error = lambda e: print("on_error: {}".format(e)),
        on_completed = lambda: print("on_completed")
)
```

The default behavior of RxPY is to consume all the source observable synchronously, at subscription time. So in this example, all items are emitted and transformed with the two map operators within the execution of the subscribe operator. When the subscribe call returns, the numbers observable is completed. The first way to change this is by providing a scheduler object to the from_ operator. This can be done by changing the first line to something like the following:

```
scheduler = SomeScheduler()
numbers = Observable.from_([1,2,3,4], scheduler=scheduler)
```

With this code, the items of the numbers observable are not emitted anymore when subscribe is called. Rather, they are scheduled for emission when subscribe is called. Depending on the type of the scheduler, this can mean different things: either emitting the items in the context of another thread or emitting items in the context of the AsyncIO event loop. The same behavior can be applied by using the subscribe_on operator:

```
scheduler = SomeScheduler()
numbers = Observable.from_([1,2,3,4])

subscription = numbers \
    .map(lambda i: i*2) \
    .map(lambda i: "number is: {}".format(i)) \
    .subscribe_on(scheduler) \
    .subscribe(
        on_next = lambda i: print("on_next {}".format(i)),
        on_error = lambda e: print("on_error: {}".format(e)),
        on_completed = lambda: print("on_completed")
)
```

Note the addition of the `subscribe_on` call before the subscription. Also note that there is no scheduler provided to the `from_` operator. Calling the `subscribe_on` operator controls on which execution context the source observable of the chain will emit its items. The `subscribe_on` operator can be use anywhere in the chain, but only once. This method is more flexible than providing the scheduler when creating the observable. Sometimes the code that creates the observable is not aware of the scheduler to use, but another piece of code that completes the observable chain has this knowledge.

These two methods allow us to control how the source items are emitted. Another operator allows us to specify the execution context that is used for all operators following its call to `observe_on`:

```
scheduler = SomeScheduler()
another_scheduler = AnotherScheduler()
yet_another_scheduler = AnotherScheduler()
numbers = Observable.from_([1,2,3,4])

subscription = numbers \
    .map(lambda i: i*2) \
    .observe_on(another_scheduler) \
    .map(lambda i: "number is: {}".format(i)) \
    .subscribe_on(scheduler) \
    .observe_on(yet_another_scheduler) \
    .subscribe(
        on_next = lambda i: print("on_next {}".format(i)),
        on_error = lambda e: print("on_error: {}".format(e)),
        on_completed = lambda: print("on_completed")
    )
```

The first `map` operator is executed in the context of `scheduler` (as requested with the call to `subscribe_on`), the second `map` operator is executed in the context of `another_scheduler`, and the subscription callbacks are called in the context of `yet_another_scheduler`. So an observable chain can switch between several execution contexts, simply by calling the `observe_on` operator several times. Once again, compared to the classic way of executing code in another thread and handling synchronization, ReactiveX provides an easy and elegant solution to a complex topic. The following figure shows marble diagram for the `subscribe_on` and `observe_on` operators for this last example:

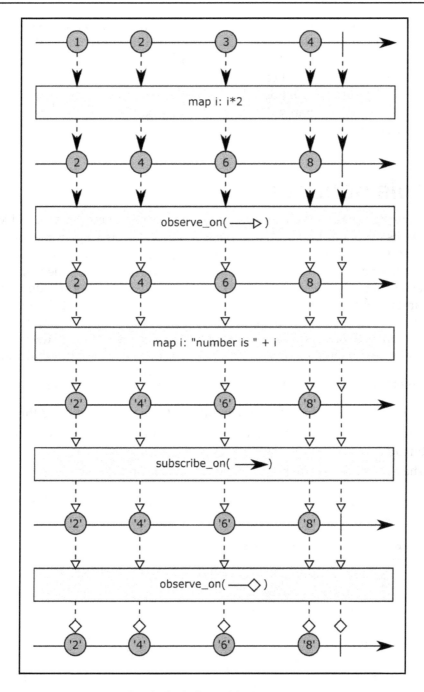

Figure 5.1: The subscribe_on and observe_on operators

In this figure, the shape of the vertical arrows identifies an execution context. The execution context of the source observable corresponds to the scheduler provided in the subscribe_on call, even though it is called later in the chain. The first map operator runs in this execution context. Then, a first call to observe_on changes this execution context (the empty triangles). The second map operator runs in this second execution context. Finally, observe_on again changes the execution context (the empty diamonds) before the final observable is emitted.

Available schedulers

The subscribe_on, observe_on, and factory operators take the scheduler object as a parameter. As its name implies, a scheduler is an object that is responsible for scheduling the emission of the items of an observable. Scheduling the emission means that, instead of calling the observer callbacks directly in the context of the observable, the emission of the items is transferred to another context. RxPY implement two kinds of scheduler: thread schedulers and event loop schedulers. However, the scheduler principle is very generic and it could be possible to implement much more specific schedulers, such as transferring execution to another IP of a chipset or even another device (even though these use cases should rather be implemented as drivers if the code is designed as functional and reactive).

Three schedulers are of interest when developing an AsyncIO application:

- The NewThread scheduler, to schedule execution on a dedicated thread
- The ThreadPool scheduler, to schedule execution on a fixed set of worker threads
- The AsyncIO scheduler, to schedule execution on the event loop

All the schedulers are implemented in the concurency module of RxPY. So, they can be imported this way:

```
from rx.concurrency import NewThreadScheduler
from rx.concurrency import ThreadPoolScheduler
from rx.concurrency import AsyncIOScheduler
```

The NewThread scheduler

The `NewThread` scheduler spawns new threads to emit items. Depending on the operator being used to control scheduling, it spawns a new thread either for each subscription or for each emitted item. Its prototype is the following one:

```
NewThreadScheduler.__init__(self, thread_factory=None)
```

The optional `thread_factory` argument can be provided as an alternative way to spawn threads. If no thread factory is provided, the scheduler uses the `threading.Thread` class to spawn new threads and configures them as daemon threads.

The `NewThreadScheduler` object can be used as a parameter of a factory operator, or as a parameter of the `subscribe_on` operator to control source observable emissions:

```python
from rx import Observable
from rx.concurrency import NewThreadScheduler
import threading

new_thread_scheduler = NewThreadScheduler()
numbers = Observable.from_([1,2,3,4], scheduler=new_thread_scheduler)

subscription = numbers \
    .map(lambda i: i*2) \
    .map(lambda i: "number is: {}".format(i)) \
    .subscribe(
        on_next = lambda i: print("on_next({}) {}"
            .format(threading.get_ident(), i)),
        on_error = lambda e: print("on_error({}): {}"
            .format(threading.get_ident(), e)),
        on_completed = lambda: print("on_completed({})"
            .format(threading.get_ident())))
)
print("main({})".format(threading.get_ident()))
```

This example gives the following result:

```
main(140736035734400)
on_next(123145577897984) number is: 2
on_next(123145577897984) number is: 4
on_next(123145577897984) number is: 6
on_next(123145577897984) number is: 8
on_completed(123145577897984)
```

The items are all emitted on a dedicated thread (123145577897984), which is different from the `main` thread of the interpreter (140736035734400). If several subscriptions are made to the `numbers` observable, then each subscription runs on its own thread.

Another way to use the `NewThreadScheduler` object is to schedule each emission of an item on a dedicated thread. This is done with the `observe_on` operator. The following figure shows this behavior:

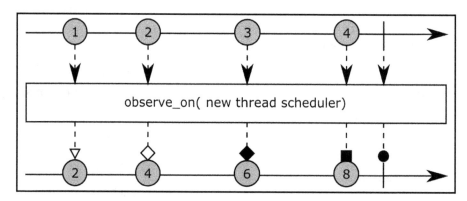

Figure 5.2: The observe_on operator with NewThreadScheduler

With the `observe_on` operator, each item is scheduled on a dedicated ephemeral thread. The following code example shows this behavior:

```
from rx import Observable
from rx.concurrency import NewThreadScheduler
import threading

new_thread_scheduler = NewThreadScheduler()
numbers = Observable.from_([1,2,3,4])

subscription = numbers \
    .map(lambda i: i*2) \
    .observe_on(new_thread_scheduler) \
    .map(lambda i: "number is: {}".format(i)) \
    .subscribe(
        on_next = lambda i: print("on_next({}) {}"
            .format(threading.get_ident(), i));
        on_error = lambda e: print("on_error({}): {}"
            .format(threading.get_ident(), e)),
        on_completed = lambda: print("on_completed({})"
            .format(threading.get_ident())))
)
print("main({})".format(threading.get_ident()))
```

This new example gives the following result:

```
main(140736035734400)
on_next(123145577897984) number is: 2
on_next(123145583153152) number is: 4
on_next(123145577897984) number is: 6
on_next(123145583153152) number is: 8
on_completed(123145577897984)
```

With this code, each item emission after the observe_on call is running on a dedicated thread. In this output example, the thread identifiers of items 4 and 8, as well as 2 and 6, are the same on completion because the interpreter recycles the thread identifiers of closed threads. Nevertheless, they all run a dedicated thread, spawned for each of these items.

The ThreadPool scheduler

Spawning a new thread each time an item is received is an anti-pattern in most cases. Spawning a thread and deleting it is a costly operation. So doing this for each item of an observable implies a performance hit. ThreadPoolScheduler allows us to execute each item operation on a dedicated thread, but instead of spawning a thread for each item, a pool of threads is used and recycled. These threads are created once and recycled without being deleted. This allows us to use a small number of threads without creating and deleting many of them. The prototype for this operator is the following one:

```
ThreadPoolScheduler.__init__(self, max_workers=None)
```

The max_workers parameter allows us to configure how many workers will be spawned in the thread pool. If no value is specified, then the number of workers is set to five times the number of CPU cores. This is a setting that is adapted to blocking I/O operations where most threads will wait for an I/O operation to complete. However, when the need is to deal with CPU bound tasks, then another, smaller, value must be used. Using the most adapted value is always dependent on the application, but a good starting point for a CPU bound application is to use the number of cores plus one. This allows us to maximize the usage of each core, even when they go idle for short periods of time.

ThreadPoolScheduler can be used to schedule subscriptions, just like NewThreadScheduler:

```
import threading

threadpool_scheduler = ThreadPoolScheduler()
numbers = Observable.from_([1,2,3,4], scheduler=threadpool_scheduler)
```

```
subscription = numbers \
    .map(lambda i: i*2) \
    .map(lambda i: "number is: {}".format(i)) \
    .subscribe(
        on_next = lambda i: print("on_next({}) {}"
            .format(threading.get_ident(), i)),
        on_error = lambda e: print("on_error({}): {}"
            .format(threading.get_ident(), e)),
        on_completed = lambda: print("on_completed({})"
            .format(threading.get_ident())))
)
print("main({})".format(threading.get_ident()))
```

This example gives the following result:

```
main(140736035734400)
on_next(123145554874368) number is: 2
on_next(123145554874368) number is: 4
on_next(123145554874368) number is: 6
on_next(123145554874368) number is: 8
on_completed(123145554874368)
```

With this single subscription, the result is the same as with `NewThreadScheduler`. The whole chain is executed on a different thread (`123145554874368`) from the `main` one (`140736035734400`). However, if many subscriptions are done, in this case the same threads will be used instead of spawning a new thread at each subscription.

This scheduler can also be used to execute each item's operations in a different thread of the pool. The following figure shows this behavior:

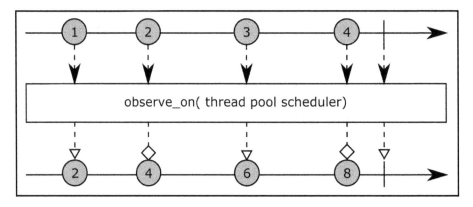

Figure 5.3: The observe_on operator with ThreadPoolScheduler

In this diagram, there are two threads in the pool. Each thread is used alternately to emit the items of the source observable. The following example shows this behavior:

```python
import threading

threadpool_scheduler = ThreadPoolScheduler()
numbers = Observable.from_([1,2,3,4])

subscription = numbers \
    .map(lambda i: i*2) \
    .observe_on(threadpool_scheduler) \
    .map(lambda i: "number is: {}".format(i)) \
    .subscribe(
        on_next = lambda i: print("on_next({}) {}"
            .format(threading.get_ident(), i)),
        on_error = lambda e: print("on_error({}): {}"
            .format(threading.get_ident(), e)),
        on_completed = lambda: print("on_completed({})"
            .format(threading.get_ident()))
)
print("main({})".format(threading.get_ident()))
```

This example gives the following result:

```
main(140736035734400)
on_next(123145565384704) number is: 2
on_next(123145554874368) number is: 4
on_next(123145560129536) number is: 6
on_next(123145565384704) number is: 8
on_completed(123145575895040)
```

In this run, four different threads are used to schedule the emission of the four items and completion. One thread is used twice, to emit items 2 and 8.

The AsyncIO scheduler

Last but not least, `AsyncIOScheduler` allows us to schedule the emissions of an observable on an AsyncIO event loop. Obviously, when writing an application based on AsyncIO and ReactiveX, this is the most used scheduler. The prototype of this scheduler is the following one:

```python
AsyncIOScheduler.__init__(self, loop=None)
```

The optional `loop` parameter allows us to specify the event loop to use with the scheduler. The default value uses the current event loop. Using this scheduler is the same as the other ones:

```python
import asyncio
import threading

loop = asyncio.get_event_loop()
asyncio_scheduler = AsyncIOScheduler()
numbers = Observable.from_([1,2,3,4], scheduler=asyncio_scheduler)

subscription = numbers \
    .map(lambda i: i*2) \
    .map(lambda i: "number is: {}".format(i)) \
    .subscribe(
        on_next = lambda i: print("on_next({}) {}"
            .format(threading.get_ident(), i)),
        on_error = lambda e: print("on_error({}): {}"
            .format(threading.get_ident(), e)),
        on_completed = lambda: print("on_completed({})"
            .format(threading.get_ident()))
)

print("starting event ")
loop.run_forever()
loop.close()
```

This sample code gives the following result:

```
starting event loop
on_next(140736035734400) number is: 2
on_next(140736035734400) number is: 4
on_next(140736035734400) number is: 6
on_next(140736035734400) number is: 8
on_completed(140736035734400)
```

The important point here is the fact that the items are emitted after the event loop starts, although the subscription has been done before. This is the purpose of `AsyncIOScheduler`: it ensures that items are emitted in the context of the event loop, and if the event loop is not started yet, then the emission of items is deferred until the event loop starts. If the same code is used without using `AsyncIOScheduler`, then the output is the following one:

```
on_next(140736035734400) number is: 2
on_next(140736035734400) number is: 4
on_next(140736035734400) number is: 6
on_next(140736035734400) number is: 8
```

```
on_completed(140736035734400)
starting event loop
```

In this case, all items are processed before the event loop runs. This is an expected behavior because, without any scheduler provided, the subscription is synchronous. All items are already emitted when the `subscribe` function returns, so do not forget to use `AsyncIOScheduler` when using an AsyncIO event loop. Otherwise, when the event loop starts, the observables have already completed and nothing happens after that!

Summary

This chapter described how to deal with two issues that can happen when writing an asynchronous application: dealing with CPU-intensive tasks and dealing with blocking tasks. Solutions to both problems can be handled via schedulers and two operators: `subscribe_on` and `observe_on`. Schedulers are objects that allow us to control on which execution context the ReactiveX operators will run. A chain of operators can use as many different execution contexts as needed.

Using schedulers allows us to keep a *synchronous-like* code style. With their API, it is possible to execute each operator of a chain on different threads. ReactiveX and RxPY provide a very developer-friendly syntax that makes multithreading easier to use than with most other libraries and frameworks.

The three schedulers that have been detailed in the second part of this chapter are the only ones that should be needed when writing an AsyncIO application. The AsyncIO scheduler is without any doubt the most used one since it has to be provided to virtually all factory operators of an AsyncIO application. There are however some more schedulers available. Most of them deal with the event loops of other frameworks such as Twisted, Gevent, and Tornado.

The next chapter starts a series covering the implementation of a realistic application: an audio transcoding server. Going step by step in its implementation, you will see how to implement a functional and reactive asynchronous application, but also how to deal with the typical issues of asynchronous programming.

Questions

- Why is using a blocking function a problem in an asynchronous application?
- Why is using a CPU-intensive task a problem in an asynchronous application?
- What is the aim of a scheduler?
- What are the two possible ways to select the scheduler of a source observable?
- How is it possible to change the execution context inside a chain of operator?
- Why is it very important to use `AsyncIOScheduler` in an AsyncIO reactive application?

6
Implementation of an Audio Transcoding Server

This chapter and the next two cover a realistic example of an application. This application uses the features and libraries described in previous chapters. It is based on RxPY, runs on an AsyncIO event loop, and uses the `aiohttp` package. The application is developed in a functional and reactive way. The first part describes how the project is structured. Since this application is more than a code snippet, its code is structured as a Python package. This part also contains some advice to improve the readability of the RxPY code. The second part presents Cyclotron, a framework that implements the code written in Chapter 3, *Functional Programming with ReactiveX*, to deal with observable cycles in a functional way. The third part documents the new operators being used in this chapter. Finally, the fourth part details the implementation of the application.

Functional programming is well adapted to event-based tasks. This is why it is used a lot in communication applications such as message brokers. Using this programming paradigm in combination with reactive programming allows us to structure code very well without sacrificing performance.

The following topics will be covered in this chapter:

- Structuring the project
- Introduction to Cyclotron
- Operators used in this application
- Implementation of the server

Technical requirements

The transcoding server relies on the `sox` audio manipulation library. On top of the Python package (which contains only the Python bindings), the `sox` library must be installed on the host system. On a Debian-based Linux system, type the following command to install it:

```
$ sudo apt-get install sox
```

On macOS, the easiest way to install it is via `brew`:

```
brew install sox
```

Structuring the project

The application that will be developed in this chapter and the following two chapters must be more structured than a simple script with the whole code in it. So, this project will be structured as a Python package, which can be installed with the setup tools. Moreover, since it relies on more dependencies besides the small code examples used in the previous chapters, using the Python setup tools helps us deal with dependencies. But before looking at the structure of the project, let's start by looking into the functional specifications of this application.

The application is a daemon that allows us to transcode audio files from MP3 to the FLAC format. FLAC is a lossless audio codec. The transcoded files are stored in a specified directory. The daemon exposes an HTTP API that allows a client to upload an audio file so that it is transcoded and stored. The application must be configurable via a JSON configuration file. The following settings must be present in it:

- The listening host address and port of the HTTP server
- The location to store transcoded files

The following is a configuration file example:

```
{
  "encode": {
    "storage_path": "/tmp"
  },
  "server": {
    "http": {
      "host": "0.0.0.0",
      "port": 8080
    }
  }
}
```

}

The reactivity of this application is shown in the following figure:

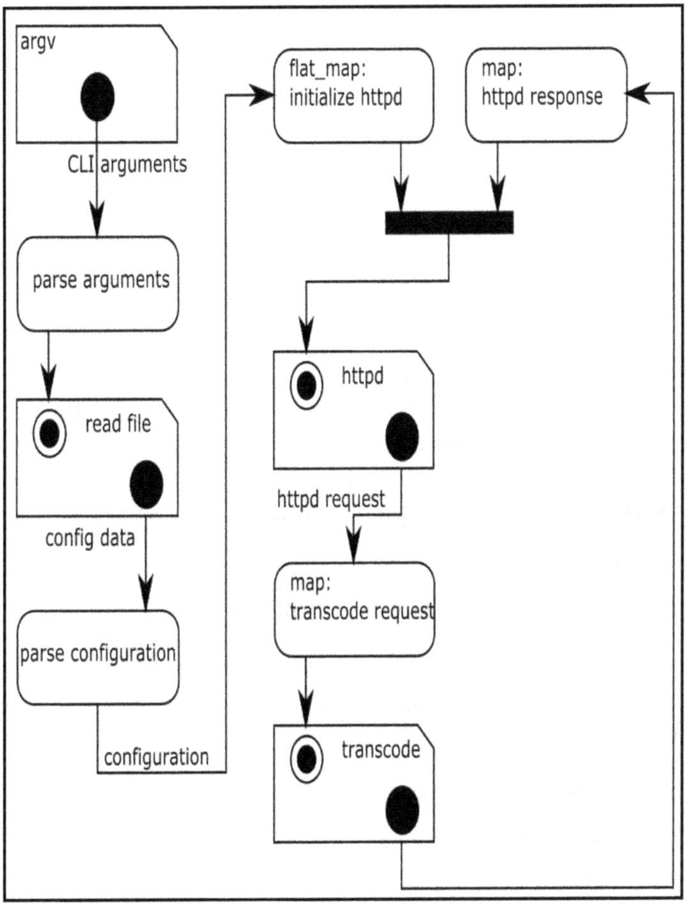

Figure 6.1: The audio encoder server reactivity diagram

There are three main parts in this project:

- Parsing the configuration file
- Encoding the audio files
- Exposing the audio encoding service

Each of these parts relies on one or several drivers. The size of the drivers is kept as small as possible so that, as far as possible, the code consists of pure functions.

The base structure

The structure of the project is the classical structure of a minimal Python package:

```
/audio-encode-server
    /audio_encode_server
        /__init__.py
        /server.py
        /encoder.py
    /script
        /audio-encode-server
    /config.sample.json
    /README.rst
    /setup.py
```

The name of the package is `audio-encode-server`. The name of the package is the name that is used when installing a Python package from `pip`. In this directory, there is the top-level module of the package: `audio_encode_server`. The name is the same as the package but with underscores instead of minus characters, because module names cannot contain minus characters in their names. In this directory, there are several Python files, one for each feature of the server. In this first implementation, only two files are needed:

- One to implement the server itself
- Another one to implement the encoder driver

The `script` directory contains the scripts to install with the package. Here, there is only one shell script that is used to start the daemon. Then, there is a sample configuration file that can be used as-is:

- The server listens on localhost
- The server listens on port `8080`
- The server stores files in `/tmp`

There is also a `README` file in `reStructuredText` format, the format used to write Python documentation (with the sphinx tool). Finally, the `setup.py` file allows us to install this package with the setup tools. It contains information such as the name of the package, the scripts to install, and the dependencies of the package.

Maximizing code readability

One of the main benefits of using AsyncIO and ReactiveX is that it allows us to write code that can be read quite easily. However, there are two things that can make RxPY code less readable than the ReactiveX equivalent in other languages (especially compared to JavaScript):

- The intensive use of dictionaries
- The way to deal with continuation lines

The following code snippet shows a typical way to chain RxPY operators:

```
obs = Observable.from_([{'count': 5, 'what': 'apple'},
                        {'count': 3, 'what': 'orange'}]) \
    .filter(lambda i: i['what'] == 'apple') \
    .map(lambda i: i['count']) \
    .map(lambda i: {'count': i, 'double': i*2} ) \
...
```

When a lot of operators are chained together, in most cases there is a need to return an object that is a composition of several operations on this item. For example, in the last line of this snippet, the `map` operator returns an object that is composed of the item itself and its double value. This new object is defined as a dictionary. Using dictionaries is probably the first solution that most people use because it is very natural in Python. However, the drawback is that the syntax in using dictionaries is more complex than accessing a field of an object like a class instance. This is something that can be improved.

When a lot of operators are chained together, they are usually written as one operator per line. This makes the code easier to read. However, in Python, line continuation must be done with a backslash, except when a parenthesis is open. The presence of many of these backslashes also adds clutter to the code flow. But more than that, it is not possible to insert a comment in a multiline block like this one. When 10 or more operators are chained together, it usually means that several features are implemented. In these cases, being able to insert comments between two operator lines is something nice to have.

Let's see how to improve these two syntactic defects.

Using named tuples

An alternative to dictionaries in Python is `namedtuple`. As the name implies, a named tuple is a tuple where each entry can be accessed via a name instead of being accessed via its index. The benefits of using named tuples instead of dictionaries are the following:

- Named tuples fields can be accessed with their field names and dot notation: `foo.x` allows us to access the x field of the `foo` tuple.
- Named tuples are as efficient as tuples. Accessing a field of a tuple is much faster than a field of a dictionary. With a dictionary, each field is accessed via its hash value, and a lookup is necessary for each access to a dictionary field. This is not the case with tuples and named tuples. Their fields are immediately accessible. So, creating and using them is more efficient.
- Named tuples, as with tuples, are immutable. This is also a good property for functional and reactive code where object lifetimes are very short, and they should not be modified.

Named tuples are implemented in the `collections` module of the standard library. Before being used, a named tuple must be declared. Once it is declared, it can be used like a class constructor. Here is the previous code snippet with dictionaries being replaced with `namedtuple`:

```python
from collections import namedtuple

Basket = namedtuple('Basket', ['count', 'what'])
FruitCount = namedtuple('FruitCount', ['count', 'double'])

obs = Observable.from_([Basket(count=5, what='apple'),
                        Basket(count=3, what='orange')]) \
    .filter(lambda i: i.what == 'apple') \
    .map(lambda i: i.count) \
    .map(lamda i: FruitCount(count=i, double=i*2)) \
...
```

This simple change makes the code simpler. All the quotes, square brackets, colons, and curly braces have disappeared. The constructor style notation to create the objects, and the dot style notation to access the fields, is simpler to follow.

Using dataclasses

Before Python 3.7, namedtuple was the easiest way to use class-like objects without having to implement a class for each object with the associated constructor. Since Python 3.7, dataclasses can also be used for this purpose. dataclass allows a class to easily declare that it contains only data. This is available in the dataclasses module of the standard library. The same snippet can be written as follows with dataclasses:

```
from dataclasses import dataclass

@dataclass
class Basket:
    count
    what

@dataclass
class FruitCount:
    count
    double

obs = Observable.from_([Basket(count=5, what='apple'),
                        Basket(count=3, what='orange')]) \
    .filter(lambda i: i.what == 'apple') \
    .map(lambda i: i.count) \
    .map(lamda i: FruitCount(count=i, double=i*2)) \
    ...
```

Compared to namedtuple, using dataclass is the same, but the definition is done as a class definition. If an application requires Python 3.7 at a minimum, then data classes can be used. However, named tuples still require less code to declare, and their immutability is a nice sanity check in functional code.

Avoiding backslashes

The last small thing that prevents RxPY code from being as readable as synchronous procedural code is the usage of backslashes for continuation lines. When an operator chain is quite small, like in the previous examples, then using backslashes is natural. However, it becomes a visual distraction when longer operator chains are used. The easy way to fix this is to wrap expressions in parentheses. Since line continuation is implicit inside an open parenthesis, there is no need to add backslashes.

Moreover, comments are allowed inside the parentheses. This allows us to finally write the code snippet this way:

```
from collections import namedtuple

Basket = namedtuple('Basket', ['count', 'what'])
FruitCount = namedtuple('FruitCount', ['count', 'double'])

obs = (
    Observable.from_([Basket(count=5, what='apple'),
                      Basket(count=3, what='orange')])
    .filter(lambda i: i.what == 'apple')
    # Now I count apples
    .map(lambda i: i.count)
    .map(lamda i: FruitCount(count=i, double=i*2))
)
...
```

These small changes, when applied in many functions with longer operator chains, really make the difference between easily following the code flow and being distracted by some syntactic overhead.

Introduction to Cyclotron

So far, the code written in this book was done completely from scratch. This is great to learn how to write code, but there is some boilerplate that always has to be written:

- Creating and running the AsyncIO event loop
- Managing observable cycles with subjects

Cyclotron is a set of Python packages that aims at implementing this boilerplate instead of having to rewrite it again and again. It also defines a common prototype for ReactiveX components and drivers so that they can be shared between projects. Cyclotron is composed of several packages:

- cyclotron: This is a very small package that manages the connection of observables, with the support of observable cycles.
- cyclotron-std: This package contains drivers and helpers to use some features of the Python standard library with RxPY.
- cyclotron-aio: This package contains helpers to deal with AsyncIO. It allows us to start the event loop and contains some drivers based on other AsyncIO packages.

The following packages are available on PyPI and can be installed with `pip`:

```
pip3 install cyclotron
pip3 install cyclotron-std
pip3 install cyclotron-aio
```

The main feature of Cyclotron is implementing the base code of the functional and reactive design that was described in `Chapter 3`, *Functional Programming with ReactiveX*. For this, Cyclotron defines the following entities:

- Runners
- Components and drivers
- Sources and sinks

Runners are functions that are used to execute the entry point of the program, with drivers being configured and connected together (eventually with cycles in the connection). The `cyclotron` package contains a basic runner that just connects the observables together and starts the drivers. This runner can be used directly in applications that do not use AsyncIO. Applications that are based on AsyncIO can use the runner provided in the `cyclotron-aio` package. This one is based on the runner of the `cyclotron` package, but it also starts the AsyncIO event loop.

Components are functions that take observables as input and return observables as output. Components are reusable via composition. The entry point of a runner is a component, and components can use other components. This makes the entry point of the application a function like any other component of the application. A nice benefit of this property is the fact that a complete application can be used as a component in another application. The following figure shows an example of an application using several components:

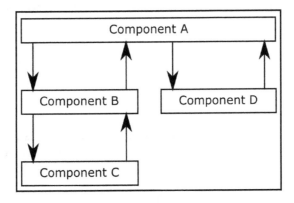

Figure 6.2: Component composition; the topmost component is the entry point of the application

Drivers are specialized components; they are components that implement side-effects. However, a driver has a similar prototype to a component. It takes observables as input and returns observables. The important difference between a component and a driver lies in their behavior. A component is a pure function while a driver is a side-effect.

Sources and sinks are the inputs and outputs used by components and drivers. As already shown in *Figure 3.4*, components take a source object as input and return a sink object. On the other hand, drivers take a sink object as input and return a source object. These inputs and outputs are not directly observables, but named tuples with each field being either an observable (for drivers), or another named tuple (for components). As explained in the previous section, using named tuples has several benefits. The syntax to use them is easier than dictionaries, they are very efficient, and they are immutable. The following figure shows a reminder of the inputs and outputs used by components and drivers:

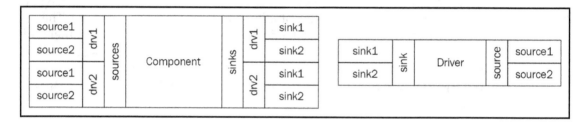

Figure 6.3: Inputs and outputs of components and drivers

Each driver defines a source named tuple that it returns and a sink named tuple that it accepts. The fields of these named tuples are observables. Each component also defines a source-named tuple that it accepts and a sink-named tuple that it returns. However, since a component can interact with several drivers, the fields of these named tuples are not directly observables, but the source and sink named tuples defined by the drivers.

Let's clarify how to use all these entities with another implementation of the CLI echo example studied in Chapter 1, *An Introduction to Reactive Programming*.

The command-line echo example

The command-line echo application simply outputs the arguments passed on the command-line to the console. This subpart details its functional and reactive implementation with Cyclotron.

First, more imports than previously are needed:

```
from collections import namedtuple
```

```
from rx import Observable
from cyclotron import Component
from cyclotron.rx import run

import cyclotron_std.sys.stdout as stdout
import cyclotron_std.sys.argv as argv
```

In addition to `Observable` of the `rx` module, `namedtuple` as well as several `cyclotron` modules are used. The `Component` constructor and the `run` function are the minimal requirements to start an application. Then two drivers of `cyclotron-std` are used. The `stdout` driver is a sink-only driver that outputs received items on the standard output, and the `argv` driver is a source-only driver that exposes the arguments provided in the command-line.

After these imports, three named tuples are declared. There is one for `Drivers` used by the application, one for the entry point `Source` object, and one for the entry point `Sink` object:

```
Drivers = namedtuple('Drivers', ['stdout', 'argv'])
Source = namedtuple('Source', ['argv'])
Sink = namedtuple('Sink', ['stdout'])
```

The `stdout` and `argv` drivers are used. The objects in the `Drivers` tuple fields are the `Component` objects that implement the corresponding driver. They are initialized later. The source of the entry point is just the source of the `argv` driver. The `Sink` of the entry point contains only the `Sink` of the `stdout` driver. Once these definitions are available, `Source` and `Sink` can be used in the entry point of the application:

```
def echo(sources):
    console = sources.argv.argv.skip(1).map(lambda i: i + '\n')
    return Sink(
        stdout=stdout.Sink(data=console)
    )
```

The `echo` function is a component. The `sources` input argument is a named tuple of type source. This component returns a `Sink` named tuple. The `console` observable takes all arguments except the first one, and appends a new line after each of them. The `sources.argv` object is a named tuple of type `argv.Source`. This named tuple has only one field named `argv`. It is an observable emitting one item per command-line argument. The `skip` operator used here allows us to skip some items from an observable. In this case one item is removed. This first item corresponds to the name of the binary being used. This first item is skipped so that only the arguments are printed.

The `echo` component returns a `Sink` object, and sets the `stdout` field with an object of type `stdout.Sink`. This named tuple has one field named `data`. This field must contain an observable emitting the items to write on the standard output.

Finally, the application can be initialized and started:

```
if __name__ == '__main__':
    dispose = run(
        entry_point=Component(call=echo, input=Source),
        drivers=Drivers(
            stdout=stdout.make_driver(),
            argv=argv.make_driver(),
        )
    )
    dispose()
```

The `run` function is called with two parameters as input: the component that is the entry point of the application, and the drivers that are being used. A `Component` object is created by using the `Component` constructor with two parameters: the entry point function of the component and the type being used as an input parameter. Each field of the `Drivers` object is a driver `Component` object. Both drivers used here provide a factory method to create them; this factory method is called `make_driver`. This is a very common way to expose drivers factories.

These four snippets put together are a complete implementation of the command-line echo example. The whole code is available at the GitHub repository (`https://github.com/PacktPublishing/Hands-On-Reactive-Programming-with-Python`) for this book, in the `cyclotron_echo_argv.py` script. In a very simple application, like this one, this design adds some overhead, but it becomes negligible very quickly.

Operators used in this application

Now, the structure of the application is ready. Before going into its implementation, some more operators will be described here, four new operators that will be used in the application:

- The `skip` operator
- The `filter` operator
- The `flat_map` operator
- The `let` operator

The skip operator

The `skip` operator omits the first *n* items emitted by the input observable and emits all other items of the input observable on the output observable. The following figure shows the workings of this operator:

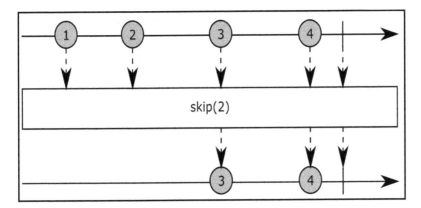

Figure 6.4: The skip operator

The prototype of this operator is the following one:

```
Observable.skip(self, count)
```

The `count` parameter is the number of items to skip before emitting some items.

Here is an example of the `skip` operator in use:

```
numbers = Observable.from_([1, 2, 3, 4, 5])
numbers.skip(2).subscribe(
    on_next = lambda i: print("on_next {}".format(i)),
    on_error = lambda e: print("on_error: {}".format(e)),
    on_completed = lambda: print("on_completed")
)
```

This example gives the following result:

```
on_next 3
on_next 4
on_next 5
on_completed
```

In this example, the first two items have been skipped, and the remaining three items have been forwarded.

The filter operator

The `filter` operator emits only the items of the input observable that match a predicate function. The following figure shows how this operator works:

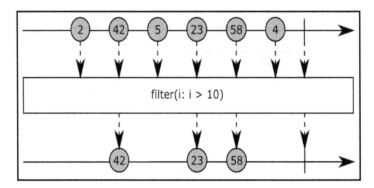

Figure 6.5: The filter operator

The prototype of this operator is the following one:

```
Observable.filter(self, predicate)
```

The `predicate` argument is a function called for each item emitted on the input observable. If this `predicate` evaluates to true, then the item is emitted on the output observable. Otherwise, the item is dropped. The prototype of the `predicate` function is the following one:

```
predicate(item, index)
```

Here, `item` is the item to evaluate and `index` is the index of the item in the sequence, starting from 0. Here is an example of how to use the `filter` operator:

```
numbers = Observable.from_([1, 2, 3, 4, 5])
numbers.filter(lambda i: i > 1 and i < 4) \
    .subscribe(
    on_next = lambda i: print("on_next {}".format(i)),
    on_error = lambda e: print("on_error: {}".format(e)),
    on_completed = lambda: print("on_completed")
)
```

This example gives the following results:

```
on_next 2
on_next 3
on_completed
```

The flat_map operator

The `flat_map` operator allows us to create an observable from each item emitted on the input observable. Then, each item of the resulting observables is merged in the output observable. The following figure shows how this operator works:

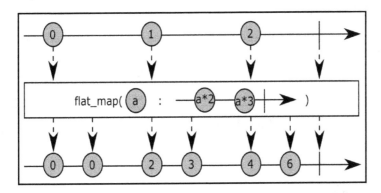

Figure 6.6: The flat_map operator

The prototype of this operator is the following one:

```
Observable.flat_map(self, selector)
```

The `selector` argument is a function called for each input. It takes the item as an input parameter and returns an observable. Here is an example of how to use this operator:

```
numbers = Observable.from_([1, 2, 3, 4])
numbers.flat_map(lambda i: Observable.from_(range(i, i+2))) \
    .subscribe(
        on_next = lambda i: print("on_next {}".format(i)),
        on_error = lambda e: print("on_error: {}".format(e)),
        on_completed = lambda: print("on_completed")
)
```

This example gives the following result:

```
on_next 1
on_next 2
on_next 2
on_next 3
on_next 3
on_next 4
on_next 4
on_next 5
on_completed
```

For each item of the `numbers` observable, `lambda` is called, and it returns two items (the item and another item with its value plus 1). These four dual-item observables are then flattened into a single observable, emitting all their items.

The let operator

The `let` operator allows us to use a function like an operator. It allows us to use a function that takes an observable as input and returns an observable into a chain of operators, in a seamless way. The following figure shows the workings of this `let` operator:

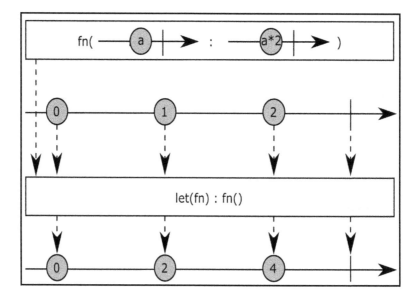

Figure 6.7: The let operator

The prototype of this operator is the following one:

```
Observable.let(self, func, **kwargs)
```

The implementation of the `let` operator is simply a call to the `func` function with the `self` and `kwargs` arguments:

```
func(self, **kwargs)
```

So, the `let` operator basically makes `func` an operator that takes the input stream of the `let` operator as the input parameter, as well as the eventual keyword arguments provided to the `let` call. The `let` operator allows us to factorize some code and implement operators like functions. Here is an example of how to use it:

```
def add_and_multiply(numbers, add_value, multiply_by_value):
    return numbers \
        .map(lambda i: i + add_value) \
        .map(lambda i: i * multiply_by_value)

numbers = Observable.from_([1, 2, 3])
numbers.let(add_and_multiply, add_value=1, multiply_by_value=2) \
    .subscribe(
    on_next = lambda i: print("on_next {}".format(i)),
    on_error = lambda e: print("on_error: {}".format(e)),
    on_completed = lambda: print("on_completed")
)
```

The `add_and_multiply` function performs two operations on each item of the input observable, an addition followed by a multiplication. The use of the `let` operator allows us to insert these two operations into the chain of operators. In this example, the resulting operations are similar to moving the two `map` operators in place of the `let` operator. The result of this code is the following:

```
on_next  4
on_next  6
on_next  8
on_completed
```

This corresponds to the 1, 2, and 3 numbers added to 1 and then multiplied by 2.

Implementation of the encoding server

It is now time to implement the encoding server by using all the new notions and operators that have just been covered. The following sections go into the detail of each element of the server: parsing the configuration file, encoding an MP3 file to FLAC, and serving the encoding service from an HTTP server.

Parsing the configuration file

Parsing the configuration file requires three distinct parts, as shown previously in the reactivity diagram for the application:

- Parsing the command-line arguments
- Reading the configuration file
- Parsing the configuration file and converting it to a Python object

Command-line arguments are retrieved with the `argv` driver of the `cyclotron-std` package, as already seen with the cyclotron echo example. The application accepts only one argument, named `config`. The Python standard library contains a module dedicated to the parsing of arguments: `argparse`. Moreover, the `cyclotron-std` package contains a helper to use the `argparse` module with an observable of arguments as an input. So, all these elements can be used as follows:

```
read_config_file = (
    sources.argv.argv.skip(1)
    .let(argparse.argparse,
        parser=Observable.just(
            argparse.Parser(description="audio encode server")),
        arguments=Observable.from_([
            argparse.ArgumentDef(
                name='--config',
                help="Path of the server configuration file")
        ]))
    .filter(lambda i: i.key == 'config')
    .map(lambda i: file.Read(id='config', path=i.value))
)
```

Let's decompose this code line by line. The whole result of this chain is saved in the `read_config_file` observable variable. This observable is used as a sink for the file driver. It contains requests to read the content of the configuration file. The first step consists of retrieving the `argv` observable from the `argv` driver. The first item is skipped because it contains the name of the Python script being launched. The arguments start from the second item of this observable.

After that are the parsing arguments. The Cyclotron `argparse` function is used to provide the `arguments` observable to the parser. The `argparse` function takes an observable as input and returns an observable. Any function with such a prototype can be used like a custom operator thanks to the `let` operator. The `argparse` function takes two additional arguments as parameters: an observable containing one `Parser` item, and an observable containing some `ArgumentDef` items. There must be one `ArgumentDef` item per argument to support. Here, only the `config` argument is allowed, so there is only one item in the arguments parameter. The observable returned by the `argparse` function contains `Argument` items composed of two fields: `key` and `value`. The `key` field contains the name of the parsed argument (without the leading `--`), and `value` contains the value of this argument.

After this is a sanity check, with only the `config` argument being used. Finally, the value provided in the `config` argument is wrapped in a `Read` request so that its content can be read by the file driver. When the content of the file has been read, it is available in the source of the file driver. It is now ready to be parsed. This is done in a dedicated function:

```
def parse_config(file_data):
    config = (
        file_data
        .filter(lambda i: i.id == "config")
        .flat_map(lambda i: i.data)
        .map(lambda i: json.loads(
            i,
            object_hook=lambda d: namedtuple('x', d.keys())
            (*d.values()))))
    )

    return config.share()
```

The `parse_config` function takes an observable of `ReadResponse` items as input. In practice, this observable contains only one item, with the content of the JSON configuration file. The `ReadResponse` object contains a data field that is itself an observable of bytes. This is why the `flat_map` operator is used here: it allows us to extract the content of the file in the same operator chain. The `data` observable emits a single item that contains the whole content of the file. From that point, the JSON data is available and can be parsed with the `json` module of the standard library. The `lambda` provided in the `object_hook` parameter converts the JSON object to a named tuple instead of a dictionary. Once again, this will make the syntax easier to read when using this object. An important point here is that the `parse_config` function is a pure function. Had the `json.load` function been used instead of `json.loads`, then `parse_config` would be a side-effect since it would read the content of the file. Moreover, by splitting the reading and parsing steps, the parsing step can be reused in other projects, eventually with JSON data coming from sources other than a file.

Finally, the resulting configuration observable is converted to a hot observable with the `share` operator. This configuration observable will be subscribed by several observers. If the `config` observable is not converted to a hot observable, then there will be as many subscriptions at the top of the chain (that is, the `argv` observable) as there are observers. This means that the arguments would be parsed several times and the configuration file would be read several times. Making the `config` observable hot after these steps allows us to read and parse the file only once for all observers.

This function can now be used, fed with the source of the file driver:

```
config = sources.file.response.let(parse_config)
```

Implementation of the encoder driver

The encoder driver is implemented on top of the `sox` library. The API of this library is simple, which makes it well suited for this study. However, it works only on files and not buffers, which would be an issue for a production-grade asynchronous application. This issue is ignored in this chapter to focus on the overall structure of the application. However, the next chapter will explain how to deal with this. Ensure that the `sox` package is installed on your system before running the server. The installation instructions are available in the *Technical requirements* section of this chapter. Before going into the driver implementation, let's start by writing the function that will actually perform the audio conversion. Here is its code:

```
import sox

def mp3_to_flac(data, dest_path, name):
    tmp_filename = '/tmp/transcode-tmp.mp3'
    dest_filename = os.path.join(dest_path, name + '.flac')
    with open(tmp_filename, 'wb') as content_file:
        size = content_file.write(data)
        status = 0 if size == len(data) else -1
    transformer = sox.Transformer()
    transformer.convert(samplerate=16000, n_channels=2, bitdepth=16)
    transformer.build(tmp_filename, dest_filename)
    return dest_filename
```

The sox library is available in the sox module. To use the sox library, one has to create a transformer object, associate audio manipulations to it, and finally apply these manipulations to an input file. The result is written to an output file. The mp3_to_flac function takes three parameters as input:

- The data of the MP3 file to convert
- The path where the result must be saved
- The name of the converted file

The first two lines of the conversion function build a temporary file path and the destination file path. The temporary file path is used to store MP3 data so that sox can convert it. Then, the data is written to the temporary file. After that comes the encoding part. A transformer object is created and a conversion is done. In this case, the audio is converted to 16 KHz, stereo, with 16 bits per sample. Finally, calling the build method on the transformer does the audio conversion. The converted audio is available in the dest_filename file. This name is returned by mp3_to_flac. The sox library determines the format of the input and output files from their extension. This is why the filenames are constructed with the .mp3 and .flac extensions.

The next step is to define the APIs of the drivers. This means defining the Source and Sink objects that they deal with. Here is what is needed in this driver:

```
Source = namedtuple('Source', ['response'])
Sink = namedtuple('Sink', ['request'])

# Sink events
Initialize = namedtuple('Initialize', ['storage_path'])
EncodeMp3 = namedtuple('Encode', ['id', 'data', 'key'])

# Source events
EncodeResult = namedtuple('EncodeResult', ['id', 'file'])
```

The Source and Sink objects are only composed of one observable each:

- A response observable for Source
- A request observable for Sink

There are two possible `Sink` request items:

- The initialization of the driver
- A request to encode some data

The initialization item contains the path in which to store the encoded files. The encoding request contains the `id` of the request, the `data` of the audio file, and a `key`. The `id` of the request will be provided back on the response. This allows the user of the encoding driver to match responses with previous requests. The `key` is the name to use when encoding the file. There is only one source item, which is sent each time a file has been converted. This item contains two fields: the `id` of the request and the name of the converted file, including its absolute storage path.

Now the skeleton of the driver can be written:

```
def make_driver():
    def encoder(sink):
        return Source(
            response=Observable.create(on_subscribe)
        )

    return Component(call=encoder, input=Sink)
```

The `make_driver` function is a factory to create the driver object. This function returns a `Component` object whose entry point is the `encoder` function, with input parameters of type `Sink`. The encoder function is the actual implementation of the driver. It takes a `Sink` object as input and returns a `Source` object. The `response` observable is created with a subscription callback whose implementation is nested in the `encoder` function:

```
def on_subscribe(observer):
    storage_path = None

    def on_next(item):
        if type(item) is Initialize:
            nonlocal storage_path
            storage_path = item.storage_path
        elif type(item) is EncodeMp3:
            encoded_file = mp3_to_flac(
                item.data, storage_path, name=item.key)
            observer.on_next(
                EncodeResult(id=item.id, file=encoded_file))
        else:
            observer.on_error("unknown item: {}".format(type(item)))

    sink.request.subscribe(
        on_next=on_next,
```

```
        on_error=lambda e: observer.on_error(e),
        on_completed=lambda: observer.on_completed(),
    )
```

Let's start by studying the end of this function. When an observer subscribes to the `response` observable, the driver subscribes to the `request` observable. This allows us to chain subscriptions in an upstream way. When the final observer subscribes, this starts a subscription chain up to the source observable. The `request` subscription forwards errors and completion to the `response` observable. This allows us to propagate errors and completion. Since there is no special action to take in these cases, the driver just forwards these events.

At the beginning of the function, a variable is declared to store the storage path of the encoded files. Finally, the handling of the request items is done in the `on_next` function. The two types of item are handled, and any other object raises an error. On receipt of the `Initialize` item, the storage path is updated. On reception of an `EncodeMp3` item, the `mp3_to_flac` function is called, and an `EncodeResult` object is sent to the observer. The driver is now ready to be used by the application!

Using the encoder driver

There are two blocks needed to use the encoder driver:

- Doing the initialization
- Sending the transcoding requests

The initialization must provide the storage path present in the configuration file. This is straightforward:

```
encode_init = (
    config
    .map(lambda i: encoder.Initialize(storage_path=i.encode.storage_path))
)
```

Then, the encoding requests must be created each time an HTTP request comes in. Here is the code for doing this:

```
encode_request = (
    sources.httpd.route
    .filter(lambda i: i.id='flac_transcode')
    .flat_map(lambda i: i.request)
    .map(lambda i: encoder.EncodeMp3(
        id=i.context,
        data=i.data,
```

```
        key=i.match_info['key']))
  )
```

The HTTP requests are emitted on the route observable of the source of the `httpd` driver. Only requests that correspond to the FLAC encoding route are used here. This may have been omitted since there is only one route in this application. For each route, the `httpd` driver sends one item with a `request` field that contains a `request` observable. This `request` observable emits one item per request. These requests are merged with the `flat_map` operator. The `i.request` object is already an observable, so it is possible to use it in the rest of the chain by directly returning it in the `flat_map` call. Finally, each request is mapped to an `EncodeMp3` object. The `id` of the request is filled with the context of the `http` request. This allows us to retrieve it when the file is encoded. Also, the key of the encoded file is retrieved from the URL of the request available in the key match information, defined when declaring the HTTP route. The final `encode_request` observable emits one `EncodeMp3` item per HTTP request coming from remote clients.

The two encode observables can then be merged together so that they are provided to the sink of the encoder driver:

```
encoder_request = Observable.merge(encode_init, encode_request)
```

Exposing the REST APIs

Now that the code logic is in place, the remaining part is configuring and starting the HTTP server. In this application, the `httpd` driver from the `cyclotron-aio` package will be used. Its implementation is similar to the one that we performed in Chapter 3, *Functional Programming with ReactiveX*. This is also done with two code blocks:

- One for the initialization of the server
- One to return the responses when the audio encoding completes

Here is the initialization part:

```
http_init = (
    config
    .flat_map(lambda i: Observable.from_([
        httpd.Initialize(request_max_size=0),
        httpd.AddRoute(
            methods=['POST'],
            path='/api/transcode/v1/flac/{key:[a-zA-Z0-9-\._]*}',
            id='flac_transcode',
        ),
        httpd.StartServer(
```

```
                host=i.server.http.host,
                port=i.server.http.port),
        ]))
    )
```

The `httpd` driver needs at least three items on its control sink observable to complete the initialization:

- One with initialization parameters
- One or several to configure the routes
- A final one to start the server

The initialization message disables the maximum size accepted in the request payloads. This is necessary to accept requests with MP3 file content because the default limit is 2 MB, which is smaller than most existing audio files. Then, the unique route is declared. It accepts the HTTP POST method on a path that ends with a matching value named `key`. This value is the name to use when encoding the file. The `id` of the route is not really used in this case since there is only one route. Finally, the server is started with the host and port values provided in the configuration file.

The second code block is simpler:

```
http_response = (
    sources.encoder.response
    .map(lambda i: httpd.Response(
        data='ok'.encode('utf-8'),
        context=i.id,
    ))
)
```

The `http_response` observable is a map of the encoding response to an HTTP response. An `'ok'` text payload is put in the response, and the HTTP request context is retrieved from the encoding response `id` field. `http_reponse` and `http_init` can then be merged to create the observable provided to the `httpd` driver sink:

```
http = Observable.merge(http_init, http_response)
```

Putting it all together

Now, all the drivers and base blocks are available. These elements must be combined together, via a component that is the entry point of the application. Let's define the APIs of this component:

```
Drivers = namedtuple('Drivers', ['encoder', 'httpd', 'file', 'argv'])
Source = namedtuple('Source', ['encoder', 'httpd', 'file', 'argv'])
Sink = namedtuple('Sink', ['encoder', 'httpd', 'file'])
```

Four drivers are used in total:

- The encoder especially implemented for this application
- The `httpd` driver from the `cyclotron-aio` package
- The `file` and `argv` drivers from the `cyclotron-std` package

Each of these drivers emits source items that are used by the application. So, the `Source` object also contains the same four fields. However, the `argv` driver has no sink. So, the `Sink` object is only composed of three driver sinks.

These objects can now be used to start the application:

```
def audio_encoder(sources):
    ...
    return Sink(
        encoder=encoder.Sink(request=encoder_request),
        file=file.Sink(request=file_requests),
        httpd=httpd.Sink(control=http),
    )


def main():
    dispose = run(
        entry_point=Component(call=audio_encoder, input=Source),
        drivers=Drivers(
            encoder=encoder.make_driver(),
            httpd=httpd.make_driver(),
            file=file.make_driver(),
            argv=argv.make_driver(),
        )
    )
    dispose()
```

The `main` function uses the `run` function of the `cyclotron-aio` package. This call connects the drivers with the entry point function and starts the AsyncIO event loop. The entry point of the application is the `audio_encoder` function. It returns three sink objects, one for each driver sink. The content of the `audio_encoder` function is not fully reproduced here, it is the code previously written. The whole code is available in the in the GitHub repository (`https://github.com/PacktPublishing/Hands-On-Reactive-Programming-with-Python`) of this book.

In order to easily start the server, a wrapper is needed to call the `main` function. This is done with a shell script, inserted in the script folder of the package:

```
#!/usr/bin/env PYTHONUNBUFFERED="1" python

from audio_encode_server.server import main

main()
```

This script is declared in the `scripts` section of the `setup.py` file. This allows us to copy it into the binary path of the `virtualenv` system, and so to execute it from any location in a shell Terminal.

Using the encoding server

Finally, the time has come to test this audio encoder! In order to test it easily, some audio recordings are available in the `audio-dataset` folder of the code files. It is obviously possible to use any other MP3 file. This application is structured as a Python package, so it can be installed with the Python setup tools. From a `virtualenv` environment, type the following shell command to install the server:

```
(venv-rx)$ python3 setup.py install
```

This installs the application package, as well as all its dependencies. When developing an application, it can be annoying to install it many times to test some code changes. In such cases, the setup tool's `develop` command is useful:

```
(venv-rx)$ python3 setup.py develop
```

The `develop` command creates a symbolic link in the Python packages directory to the current package. This allows us to always use the current code, without having to install the application after each change. The server can now be started:

```
(venv-rx)$ audio-encode-server --config ./config.sample.json
```

Curl can be used again to test the application. An encoding request can be done with this command-line, from another shell:

```
curl -X POST --data-binary @../audio-dataset/banjo1.mp3
http://localhost:8080/api/transcode/v1/flac/banjo1
```

This should print an `ok` log when the request completed. The MP3 file encoded in FLAC should be available in the `/tmp/banjo1.flac` file. Changing the `banjo1` name at the end of the URL will encode the audio in another filename.

Summary

This chapter is an application of all the notions learned in the previous chapters. While relatively small, starting its development by using the layout of a Python package allows us to easily extend it later (which will be done in the next chapters). Also, readability tips, such as using named tuples for items types and using parentheses in operator chains, make this code even easier to follow.

Cyclotron packages are very useful when it comes to structuring code in a functional and reactive way. They avoid writing observable connection boilerplate, and provide directions to write functional code. Cyclotron allows us to write the code logic of the application as pure functions, while keeping side-effects in dedicated locations called drivers.

The audio transcoding application is quite small. It consists of only 200 lines of Python code. However, it already implements a lot of things:

- Using a JSON file to configure it
- Exposing HTTP APIs with an embedded server
- Transcoding an audio file

Implementing the same application in an asynchronous way would be very challenging in many other programming languages.

The current implementation of this application should allow you to grasp how to use ReactiveX operators and combine them in practice. There are still some issues in this code, and some of them will be fixed in the following chapters. However, you should now be ready to write your own applications with RxPY.

The next chapter is dedicated to an example of dealing with non-asynchronous libraries. It explains how to use the Amazon Web Services S3 storage SDK in an asynchronous application. This will also be an opportunity to introduce Docker, a tool that will be used in `Chapter 11`, *Deploying and Scaling Your Application*, to deploy this application.

Questions

- What are the benefits of using named tuples instead of dictionaries to define operator item types?
- What is the difference between a component and a driver in Cyclotron?
- How is it possible to use a function almost like a custom operator?
- What is the type of the object returned by the function provided to the `flat_map` operator?
- Why is it better to parse the JSON configuration file with the loads function rather than the load function?
- Why is the fact that `sox` works directly on files an issue?
- Find another problem in the current implementation of the audio transcoding.

Further reading

The `argparse` module of the standard library supports many features to parse command-line arguments. Its documentation contains many examples of how to use them: `https://docs.python.org/3.6/library/argparse.html`.

More information on Cyclotron packages is available from their GitHub repository: `https://github.com/MainRo/cyclotron-py`.

Cyclotron is heavily inspired by Cycle.js, a functional and reactive framework for JavaScript. Many of the principles of Cycle.js are also applicable to Cyclotron. So, the home page of the Cycle.js project makes for very interesting reading: `https://cycle.js.org`.

7
Using Third-Party Services

This chapter describes some enhancements to the audio transcoding server. The first part describes how to use S3, a database dedicated to object management, to store encoded audio files instead of writing them directly to the filesystem. The second part introduces the Docker engine, and how to use it to install an S3 server on your own machine. The next part is dedicated to the usage of this new storage backend in the transcoding server, in place of directly writing files onto the local disk. The last part shows possible ways to deal with blocking APIs in asynchronous applications, as well as how to benefit from multiple cores for CPU-bound operations.

The following topics will be covered in this chapter:

- An introduction to S3 storage
- Installing Docker and Minio
- Using S3 as storage
- Dealing with blocking API and CPU-bound operations

Technical requirements

The Docker part of this chapter has been tested on a Debian system. It is possible to use Docker on macOS and Windows, but this is not documented here. Some links to the Docker documentation are provided in the relevant paragraphs.

An introduction to S3 storage

The **Simple Storage Service** (usually named **S3**) is a storage service provided by Amazon in its **Amazon Web Services** (**AWS**) cloud offering. S3 was one of the first services provided by AWS. It was made publicly available in March 2006, and presented as the Amazon in-house storage solution accessible to everybody. S3 is not only very different from a relational database, but also different from a NoSQL database (which also grew in popularity at the same time). S3 is based on the very simple principle of storing a value with an associated key, and retrieving that value via this key. In its simplest definition, it is just a key/value store. There is no notion of searches, transactions, or joins in S3. It looks more like a filesystem than a database. However, it benefits from the usual cloud promises: scalability, availability, redundancy, and easy access via APIs.

S3 relies on only a few concepts:

- Buckets
- Objects
- Keys

A bucket is a flat container that can hold an infinite number of objects. Several buckets can be created per AWS account. An object is a binary blob. So it can be a file of any type, text-based or binary-based. The key is a UTF-8 string that is used to identify an object. Even though, in principle, any UTF-8 character can be used in the key name, only characters that are valid in URLs should be used. This is because access to the objects is done via REST APIs, where the object key is part of the URL. Being a flat container, an S3 bucket has no notion of hierarchy: all objects are stored at a single root level in the bucket. However, it is possible to simulate a hierarchical structure by using the slash / character in the keys. In this case, the AWS S3 console displays such keys as a folder-like layout. The following figure shows how S3 is organized:

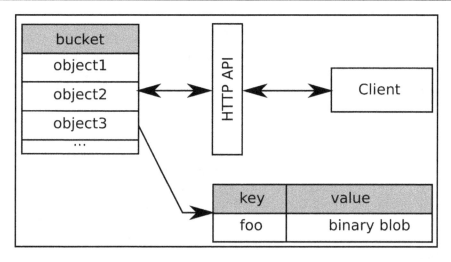

Figure 7.1: The Simple Storage Service, S3

Buckets can be created either on the AWS console, or via HTTP APIs. Each object is a binary blob, identified by a unique key in the bucket. An object also has some metadata associated with it, such as the creation date. Custom metadata can be added when an object is created. Once the object is created, it is immutable: its content and its metadata cannot be changed. If any part has to be changed, then another object with the same key must be put in the bucket, which replaces the existing object and the associated metadata.

Amazon provides command-line tools to use S3 and also an SDK that is available for many programming languages. S3 is one of the most popular AWS services. There are two main reasons for this: it is easy to use and it is quite cost-efficient. However, the simplicity of this service comes with restrictions. The two main ones are the fact that objects are immutable, and also the fact that there is no search. So, S3 is adapted to use cases where a key/value store is needed, with values being large objects. But, in order to retrieve the objects, one has to know the key in advance. There is no way to search for an object based on its content or metadata.

Installing Docker and Minio

Using AWS to host an S3 bucket is the most obvious way to use S3. However, there are compatible alternatives that allow us to host an S3 service on-premises. This is the solution used in this chapter, so that the evolutions presented here can be tested without access to an AWS account. Also, this is an opportunity to get familiar with Docker, which will also be used in Chapter 10, *Testing and Debugging*.

An introduction to Docker

Docker is an application execution environment that simplifies the packaging and deployment of applications. Originally it started as a simpler way to use Linux containers. Today it is a huge ecosystem with many tools, and a repository of publicly available application images.

Before looking at a quick overview on how to use it, it is important to understand what Docker is, and how it compares to other—more or less—similar solutions. First of all, why is something like Docker really useful? There are many solutions to packaging applications, and all operating systems provide their own packaging system (even several, sometimes). Docker does not aim to be a replacement for the Windows application installer, macOS packages, or Debian packages. Docker aims to simplify the setup and isolation of an application (or, most of the time, a service). It is first and foremost an isolation tool for a Linux distribution.

Historically, there have been three main categories of solution to isolate the execution of some software:

- Emulators
- Virtual machines
- Containers

Emulators are the oldest isolation solutions available. They are also probably the solution that offers the strongest guarantee of isolation from the host system. An emulator is software that implements the instruction set of a CPU, as well as the interfaces of some other hardware devices (such as serial ports and disk interfaces). The instruction set that is implemented is not necessarily that of the host system. This allows us to execute ARM code on an x86 system, for example. QEMU is a famous open source emulator that supports many kinds of hardware architecture such as ARM and MIPS. Nowadays, emulators are mainly used for two cases: testing software on specialized hardware more easily, and retrogaming. Many people use an emulator without knowing it when they play old Atari or Amiga games on a PC or a Raspberry Pi! So, emulators are a great solution for running software for another hardware architecture other than the one on the host system. However, they have a big drawback: they are very slow. Since they have to execute each instruction of the target architecture in software, the performance hit is huge.

Emulators are great for testing software for other hardware architectures. However, there are many cases where the need is just to execute software for the same hardware, but in another operating system. This is what virtual machines allow us to do. A typical example is somebody who uses Windows on a PC, but wants to also execute some Linux applications. By executing a Linux distribution inside a virtual machine, it is possible to have Linux and Windows running at the same time. Virtual machines are much more efficient than emulators because they can directly use the CPU, and execute instructions natively. However, this comes at the cost of being less isolated: it is easier for the software running inside the virtual machine to escape from it and execute some code on the host operating system. At some point, CPUs implemented dedicated instructions to improve both the efficiency and security of virtual machines. Virtual machines are now heavily used in cloud environments.

Still, virtual machines have an important overhead: each virtual machine runs a full operating system, including the kernel. Sometimes, the requirement is even simpler and only some applications need to be isolated from the host, by using the same operating system, on the same hardware architecture. This is where containers come into action. A container is not a feature in itself, but an accumulation of many different isolation mechanisms provided by an operating system. All recent operating systems provide some form of isolation, but it so happens that one of them is heavily used in cloud environments, running on 1-CPU architecture: Linux on an x86-64 CPU. As cloud technologies grew, the need to isolate services on big servers, while having a minimal impact on performance, became more and more important. In the early days of cloud computing, virtual machines where used to isolate services. But it so happens that very good isolation can be achieved on Linux with far fewer overheads. When features such as capabilities, cgroups, namespaces, and iptables are combined together, it is possible to execute other Linux distributions that share the same kernel environment as the host. This is the basis of a Linux container.

The following figure shows the principles used in each of these isolation technologies:

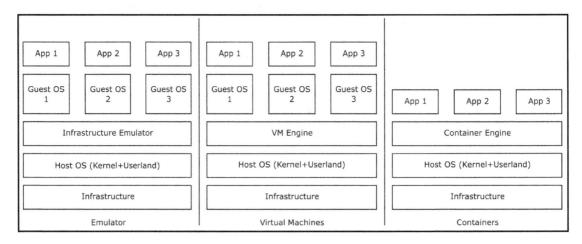

Figure 7.2: Emulator, virtual machine, and container isolation architectures

Emulators provide the best isolation, but at a higher performance cost, because each code instruction is executed as instructions on another instruction set. Virtual machines are much more efficient, at the cost of less isolation than on an emulator. Finally, containers provide even less isolation guarantees, but are the most efficient solution. The fact that containers are less isolated by design does not mean that they are not secured: they are deployed in many services where isolation between applications is required.

There are many container management solutions for Linux, and Docker is one of them. One promise from Docker is to package your application once, and then execute it anywhere. But, as usual with such promises, there is a catch: a Docker image is universal only if you consider that running Linux on an x86-64 processor is universal! The fact is that running Docker from another operating system (namely Windows or macOS) relies on the execution of a virtual machine running a Linux distribution that hosts the Docker containers. So, in the end, Docker is just a way to execute an isolated Linux system hosted by another Linux system on an x86-64 processor. This solution is very efficient because many resources are shared with the Linux host system, and the container is usually a very specialized system which contains only what is needed to execute the service.

The original Docker solution evolved quickly to propose many features on top of container management:

- Docker itself allows us to create and manage containers.
- Docker Compose allows us to create systems that are based on several containers. It also simplifies the definition of resources accessible to the container.
- Swarm allows us to create clusters of physical machines so that the deployment of many instances of containers is easier.
- Docker Stack leverages Swarm to scale Docker instances easily.

For several of these features, other companies propose alternative solutions, such as Kubernetes from Google, which allows us to do orchestration instead of Swarm.

Docker installation on Linux

Let's now see how to install and play with Docker on Linux. Only the Linux installation is described here. (See the Docker documentation for installation on other systems.) The following describes the installation on an Ubuntu system. The procedure is very similar on other Linux distributions, and also detailed in the Docker documentation.

The first step is to add the Docker gpg key to the apt registry, as can be seen in the following example:

```
$ curl -fsSL https://download.docker.com/linux/ubuntu/gpg | sudo apt-key
add -
```

Then the Docker repository can be added, as can be seen in the following code:

```
sudo add-apt-repository \
    "deb [arch=amd64] https://download.docker.com/linux/debian \
    $(lsb_release -cs) \
    stable"
```

Finally, update the apt registry and install Docker, as shown in the following example:

```
$ sudo apt-get update
$ sudo apt-get install docker-ce
```

Now the Docker daemon is running, ready to be used. Before using it, there is one last thing to configure. Since Docker uses privileged features of Linux, it requires administration rights to use it. In practice, this means that all Docker commands have to be executed as `root` or via `sudo`. Both solutions can be dangerous and are annoying to use. A simple way to use Docker without `sudo` is to add users allowed to use Docker in the Docker group. For example, user `alice` can use Docker without `sudo` after running the following command:

```
$ sudo usermod -aG sudo alicedocker
```

Getting started with Docker

Now that Docker is properly installed and configured, let's see how to use it. First, Docker manages all Linux distribution images that can be run. They are stored locally on the computer that runs these images. Retrieving a new image is done with the `pull` command, as can be seen in the following example:

```
$ docker pull hello-world
```

This will retrieve the `hello-world` image from the public Docker image registry (https://hub.docker.com/). The list of images available locally now contains the `hello-world` image, as can be seen in the following code:

```
$ docker images
REPOSITORY        TAG        IMAGE ID        CREATED       SIZE
hello-world       latest     2cb0d9787c4d    2 weeks ago   1.85kB
```

This image can now be executed. A running image is called an instance. A Docker image can be instantiated several times, making several instances of the application able to run at the same time. As can be seen in the following example, an image is started with the run command:

```
$ docker run hello-world

Hello from Docker!
This message shows that your installation appears to be working correctly.

To generate this message, Docker took the following steps:
 1. The Docker client contacted the Docker daemon.
 2. The Docker daemon pulled the "hello-world" image from the Docker Hub.
 (amd64)
 3. The Docker daemon created a new container from that image which runs
the
 executable that produces the output you are currently reading.
 4. The Docker daemon streamed that output to the Docker client, which sent
```

```
it
 to your terminal.

To try something more ambitious, you can run an Ubuntu container with:
 $ docker run -it ubuntu bash

Share images, automate workflows, and more with a free Docker ID:
 https://hub.docker.com/

For more examples and ideas, visit:
 https://docs.docker.com/engine/userguide/
```

The `hello-world` image was executed, and completed. The following list of running instances can be seen with the `ps` command:

```
$ docker ps -a
CONTAINER ID IMAGE COMMAND CREATED STATUS PORTS NAMES
e955b00349ff hello-world "/hello" About a minute ago
Exited (0) About a minute ago stoic_leavitt
```

The `-a` option displays the instances that are running, and also those that are not running anymore. This allows it to display the `hello-world` instance that is now completed. When instances are started without providing an explicit name, Docker generates one for us. This is why the instance was named `stoic_leavitt`. This stopped instance can be restarted with the `start` command. Should this instance run a daemon, it could be stopped with the `stop` command.

As can be seen in the following example, removing a stopped instance from the `ps` list is done with the `rm` command:

```
$ docker rm stoic_leavitt
stoic_leavitt
```

Now the `ps` command does not list `stoic_leavitt` anymore. However, the `images` command still contains the `hello-world` image: an instance has been removed, but not its image. Images can be removed with the `rmi` command (remove image), as demonstrated by the following code:

```
$ docker rmi 2cb0d9787c4d
```

The `rmi` command takes the image ID as a parameter, not the image name. From that point, executing another `images` command does not list the `hello-world` image anymore.

These few commands (`pull`, `run`, `start`, `stop`, `rm`, `rmi`) are enough to enable us to use Docker for many situations. Let's now start an S3 service running on Docker.

Using Minio as S3 storage

Using the S3 service from AWS can be really convenient, but there are also some drawbacks to it: it implies a recurrent cost, and you have to put your data on a datacenter (the cloud). In some cases it would be very convenient to use an S3 storage, but the cost and/or the fact of storing the data off-premises is a problem. For example, in a data science team working with relatively small datasets (some 100th of a GB), using Spark is very convenient and easy to set up. One of the sources of data supported by Spark is S3. In this case, it can be easier and less costly to host a small Spark cluster in premises, as well as an S3 database, rather than using cloud services.

Since S3 is the de facto standard, there are many tools that support it. Moreover, there are some alternatives to AWS for hosting such a database: other cloud providers have offers compatible with S3, and there are some server implementations that can be hosted on any machine. Minio is one of these tools, and it is available as an open-source project. The installation instructions and the documentation are available in the homepage (`https://minio.io/`) of the project, and the source code is available on GitHub (`https://github.com/minio`). The current chapter was tested with Minio as an S3 backend. However, you can use AWS S3 if you prefer, or if you already use it. This does not change anything within the code of the application.

Minio can be installed in many different ways, all of them leveraging popular cloud tools and infrastructures. Here, the simplest installation method is used, with Docker, without any duplication or security features enabled. This is only for test purposes, but it is possible to use Minio in production with features such as encryption and replication. To install Minio, first create some directories where data and configuration will be stored, as shown in the following example:

```
mkdir minio
cd minio
mkdir data
mkdir config
```

The data directory will be the location in which to store S3 objects and manage the database. The `config` directory will contain the configuration file of the instance. Then, installing Minio is very easy with Docker, as can be seen in the following example:

```
docker run -d -p 9000:9000 --name minio \
  -v /home/alice/minio/data:/data \
  -v /home/alice/minio/config:/root/.minio minio/minio \
  server /data
```

Note that even though Minio is not in the local registry, it is automatically retrieved from the Docker hub before being started. The `pull` command is done automatically by the `run` command when the image is not found. The Minio instance is started in the background with the `-d` option. Port `9000` is the default HTTP port used by Minio to expose the web interface and the S3 APIs. This port is exposed publicly with the `-p` option. Then, two volume bindings are configured: one to store the S3 database on the data folder of the host, and one to store the configuration files on the host. A volume binding is a link between a file or directory on the filesystems of the host and the container. In this case, the `data` and `config` directories of the host (located at `/home/alice/minio`) are accessible to the container. Minio automatically creates a default configuration file when it is started for the first time.

Once the server is started, it prints the access key and secret key that are needed to connect it to the database. One principle of Minio is that each account runs a dedicated instance. This clearly targets private hosting where each team or project has its own instance running. The credentials are available in the logs, as can be seen in the following code:

```
$ docker logs minio
Endpoint:  http://172.17.0.2:9000  http://127.0.0.1:9000
AccessKey: IU0645L6OOSV96GSEG72
SecretKey: udTdXiaUh1equB7BE9Kn691a/DNGnMguIVEh0iyu

Browser Access:
   http://172.17.0.2:9000  http://127.0.0.1:9000

Command-line Access:
https://docs.minio.io/docs/minio-client-quickstart-guide
   $ mc config host add myminio http://172.17.0.2:9000 IU0645L6OOSV96GSEG72
udTdXiaUh1equB7BE9Kn691a/DNGnMguIVEh0iyu

Object API (Amazon S3 compatible):
   Go:         https://docs.minio.io/docs/golang-client-quickstart-guide
   Java:       https://docs.minio.io/docs/java-client-quickstart-guide
   Python:     https://docs.minio.io/docs/python-client-quickstart-guide
   JavaScript:
https://docs.minio.io/docs/javascript-client-quickstart-guide
   .NET:       https://docs.minio.io/docs/dotnet-client-quickstart-guide
```

In this case, the access key is `IU0645L6OOSV96GSEG72` and the secret key is `udTdXiaUh1equB7BE9Kn691a/DNGnMguIVEh0iyu`. The web interface is accessible from a browser on localhost: `http://localhost:9000`.

It is also accessible from other clients on the LAN. Once logged in from a web browser, the following screen should be displayed:

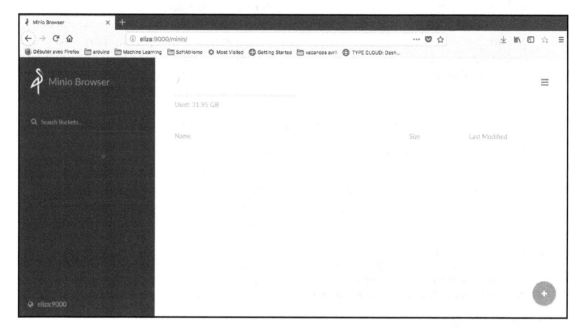

Figure 7.3: The Minio web interface

The instance is ready, but there is no bucket in it yet. Click on the + icon on the lower right, and select **Create bucket**. Name the bucket `audio` and press *Enter* to create the bucket. The new bucket is visible on the left pane, but it is still empty. The following screenshot shows what the menu should look like:

Figure 7.4: Creating a new bucket in Minio

Now the server is configured, and ready to store audio objects.

Using S3 as storage

With an S3 service ready to use (either as a private Minio installation, or directly on AWS), it can now be used to store transcoded audio files instead of storing them directly on a filesystem. Amazon provides an SDK to use many AWS services from Python (S3, EC2, Elasticsearch, and so on). This SDK is open-source (`https://github.com/boto/boto3`), and available on PyPI in the `boto3` package. This is the package that will be used to store the encoded files in the S3 database.

Several evolutions are needed to use S3 storage instead of the local filesystem:

- Implementing an S3 driver
- Returning FLAC data in the encode driver
- Adding S3 information in the configuration file
- Using the new driver in the application

These evolutions mainly consist of using a new driver in the application. So, the reactivity diagram of the application evolves to the following example:

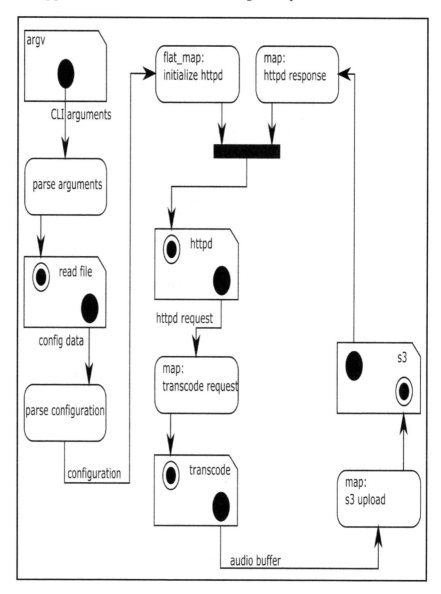

Figure 7.5: The audio transcoding server with S3 storage

The main change is the addition of the S3 driver after the transcode driver. Also, the output of the transcode driver is now a buffer.

Implementation of the S3 driver

Storing files on a database is a side-effect: the action of storing an object on a database is not deterministic, and the result of this action does not only depend on the input arguments (it can fail for many reasons, such as the quota being exceeded or a network error). So, this feature must be implemented as a driver. For this driver, new imports are needed, as can be seen in the following example:

```
from collections import namedtuple
from io import BytesIO
from rx import Observable
import boto3
from boto3.session import Session

from cyclotron import Component
```

The `boto3` package contains the AWS SDK, and the `Session` object will be used to configure the connection with the S3 database. The `BytesIO` class is needed to use the S3 upload function with a buffer as input. The other imports are the usual ones and use RxPY and Cyclotron. The next step consists of defining the API of this driver, that is, its `Source` and `Sink` definitions. This can be seen in the following example:

```
Source = namedtuple('Source', ['response'])
Sink = namedtuple('Sink', ['request'])

# Sink objects
Configure = namedtuple('Configure', [
    'access_key', 'secret_key',
    'bucket', 'endpoint_url', 'region_name'])

UploadObject = namedtuple('UploadObject', ['key', 'data', 'id'])

# Source objects
UploadReponse = namedtuple('UploadReponse', ['key', 'id'])
```

This driver uses only one observable as input and returns a single observable. So, the `Source` object contains only one field, named `response`, and the `Sink` object contains only one field, named `request`. The S3 driver takes a `Sink` object as input and returns a `Source` object.

There are two possible types of item in the `Sink` observable:

- The `Configure` item contains all the information needed to connect to the S3 database. The access and secret keys are used to authenticate it to the S3 server. The `bucket` name is fixed and provided during configuration. The `endpoint_url` parameter contains the URL of the S3 server, and the region name must match the region operating the server.
- The second type of item is `UploadObject`. It corresponds to a request to upload a new file on the database. The item's fields are `key`, used to identify the object, a buffer containing `data` from the audio file, and a request `id`.

There is one possible type of item in the `Source` response observable: `UploadResponse`. This item is emitted to notify when an upload request has been completed. It contains the `key` of the object that has been uploaded, and the request `id` provided in the `UploadObject` item.

Now the structure of the driver can be written, similarly to the one of the drivers implemented previously. This can be seen in the following example:

```
def make_driver():
    def driver(sink):

        def on_subscribe(observer):
            sink.request.subscribe(
                on_next=on_next,
                on_error=lambda e: observer.on_error(e),
                on_completed=lambda : observer.on_completed())

        return Source(
            response=Observable.create(on_subscribe)
        )

    return Component(call=driver, input=Sink)
```

The `make_driver` function is a factory that returns a `Component` object. The entry point of the `Component` is the `driver` function, and it takes a `sink` object as its input. The `driver` function is the actual driver implementation. It returns a `Source` object, with the `response` field being a custom observable. The `on_subscribe` function is the `subscription` function of this observable. When an observer subscribes to the `response` observable, the `driver` subscribes to the `sink` request observable. Once again, this pattern allows it to chain subscriptions. Note that error and completion coming from the `request` observable are forwarded to the `response` observable.

This means that, if the `request` observable completes for any reason, then the `response` observable will also complete, for the same reason. Finally, the content of the `on_subscribe` function can be implemented as a nested `on_next` function. This can be seen in the following example:

```
def on_subscribe(observer):
    client = None
    bucket = None

    def on_next(item):
        nonlocal client
        nonlocal bucket

        if type(item) is Configure:
            ...
        elif type(item) is UploadObject:
            ...
        else:
            observer.on_error(
                "unknown item: {}".format(type(item)))

    sink.request.subscribe(
        on_next=on_next,
        on_error=lambda e: observer.on_error(e),
        on_completed=lambda : observer.on_completed())
```

Two variables are defined in the scope of the `on_subscribe` function: `client` and `bucket`. These variables are set when the `Configure` item is received, and they are used when an `UploadObject` item is received. Any other received object raises an error. When a `Configure` object is received, a `boto3` client is created, as can be seen in the following example:

```
if type(item) is Configure:
    session = Session(aws_access_key_id=item.access_key,
                    aws_secret_access_key=item.secret_key)
    client = session.client('s3',
                    endpoint_url=item.endpoint_url,
                    region_name=item.region_name)
    bucket = item.bucket
```

First, a `session` object is created from the credentials being received. Then a client for the S3 service is created. Since custom (non-AWS) endpoints must be supported, the endpoint URL is provided here. The region is also provided here. The last line just saves the bucket name for future reference.

When an `UploadObject` item is received, the corresponding audio file is uploaded on the database, as can be seen in the following example:

```
elif type(item) is UploadObject:
    data = BytesIO(item.data)
    client.upload_fileobj(data, bucket, item.key)
    observer.on_next(UploadReponse(key=item.key, id=item.id))
```

The `upload_fileobj` method of the `client` object allows it to upload a file on the database. This function takes a file-like object as input, the name of the bucket, and the key used to identify the object. The data received in the `UploadObject` item contains bytes data. So, this data buffer must be converted to a file-like object. This is done with the `BytesIO` class which takes a bytes-like object as input and returns a file-like object as output. The `BytesIO` class is very interesting in this case because it allows us to create a file-like object without having to create a real file. Once the file is uploaded, an `UploadResponse` item is emitted on the observer of the response observable.

The full code for the S3 driver is available in the GitHub repository (`https://github.com/PacktPublishing/Hands-On-Reactive-Programming-with-Python`) of this book, in the file `audio-encode-server-2/audio_encode_server/s3.py`.

Returning data in the encoding driver

The current implementation of the encoding driver returns the full path of the file that has been encoded. This made sense in the previous implementation because the encoding driver also wrote the transcoded file at its destination location. Now that the transcoded file is saved on a database, this must change. Instead, the encoding driver should return the data from the transcoded file, so that it can be written anywhere. For this, some evolutions are needed in the audio encoding function of the driver, as demonstrated in the following example:

```
def mp3_to_flac(data):
    tmp_filename = os.path.join('/tmp/transcode-tmp.mp3')
    tmp2_filename = os.path.join('/tmp/transcode-tmp.flac')
    with open(tmp_filename, 'wb') as content_file:
        size = content_file.write(data)
        status = 0 if size == len(data) else -1
    transformer = sox.Transformer()
    transformer.convert(samplerate=16000, n_channels=2, bitdepth=16)
    transformer.build(tmp_filename, tmp2_filename)

    # retrieve data in a buffer
    with open(tmp2_filename, mode='rb') as file:
```

```
        flac_data = file.read()

    os.remove(tmp_filename)
    os.remove(tmp2_filename)
    return flac_data
```

Now, this function only takes MP3 data as input, and it returns FLAC data as output. Also, the `sox` APIs only work with filename parameters. So, the destination filename of `sox` is also set to a file in `/tmp`. When the encoding is completed, then the content of the encoded file (located in `tmp2_filename`) is read to the `flac_data` variable. At the end of the function, the two temporary files are deleted, and the FLAC data is returned. A benefit of this change is that the transcoding function now only operates on files located in `/tmp`. This means that it operates on files located in a RAM filesystem, a filesystem with no access to I/O devices. In other words, the `sox` APIs can no longer block on read or write operations. So, this change fixed the issue where the encode driver blocked on I/O calls.

The `EncodeResult` item must also evolve so that the data is returned instead of the filename, as in the following example:

```
EncodeResult = namedtuple('EncodeResult', ['id', 'data', 'key'])
```

The `file` field is replaced with the `data` field, and the `key` provided in the request is also sent back in the response. These changes can be used in the `driver` function to return FLAC data in the response observable. The new code for the encode driver is available in the file present at `audio-encode-server-2/audio_encode_server/encoder.py` on the GitHub repository.

Using the S3 driver

These evolutions can now be used in the server itself. This implies some evolutions in the drivers used by the `audio_encoder` component, as demonstrated in the following example:

```
import audio_encode_server.s3 as s3

Drivers = namedtuple('Drivers', ['encoder', 'httpd', 's3', 'file', 'argv'])
Source = namedtuple('Source', ['encoder', 'httpd', 's3', 'file', 'argv'])
Sink = namedtuple('Sink', ['encoder', 'httpd', 's3', 'file'])
```

The S3 driver has been added, and it is used both in `Source` and `Sink` of the component. Inside the component, a new step has been added between the encoding result and the sending of the HTTP response: the file is uploaded on the S3 database. This is done in the following way:

```
store_requests = (
    sources.encoder.response
    .map(lambda i: s3.UploadObject(
        key=i.key + '.flac',
        data=i.data,
        id=i.id,
    ))
)
```

Instead of directly being used to send the HTTP response, the response from the encoder is mapped to an S3 upload request. The result of the upload request is used to send the HTTP answer, as can be seen in the following example:

```
http_response = (
    sources.s3.response
    .map(lambda i: httpd.Response(
        data='ok'.encode('utf-8'),
        context=i.id,
    ))
)
```

The S3 driver must also be initialized from information stored in the configuration file. A new section is added in the configuration file to store the S3 database parameters. They typically look like the following example:

```
"s3": {
    "access_key": "P0B76GIFPB6T0OD5I67U",
    "secret_key": "3+kGshnhQ7i41UabvMz8buqUKgtGsikmdL1Q+oDR",
    "bucket": "audio",
    "endpoint_url": "http://localhost:9000",
    "region_name": "eu-west-1"
}
```

Thanks to the generic configuration parser that was implemented, this new section can be used directly to initialize the driver, as can be seen in the following example:

```
s3_init = (
    config
    .map(lambda i: s3.Configure(
        access_key=i.s3.access_key,
        secret_key=i.s3.secret_key,
        bucket=i.s3.bucket,
```

```
        endpoint_url=i.s3.endpoint_url,
        region_name=i.s3.region_name,
    ))
)
```

The last step is to merge the S3 observables and return them in the Source object. This is demonstrated in the following code:

```
s3_requests = Observable.merge(s3_init, store_requests)

return Sink(
    encoder=encoder.Sink(request=encoder_request),
    s3=s3.Sink(request=s3_requests),
    file=file.Sink(request=file_requests),
    httpd=httpd.Sink(control=http),
)
```

The whole code is available in the audio-encode-server-2 file in this chapter's repository (https://github.com/PacktPublishing/Hands-On-Reactive-Programming-with-Python). This new implementation can be used in the same way as the first one, as detailed here:

(venv-rx)$ python3 setup.py install

This installs the application package, as well as all its dependencies. The server can then be started in the following way:

(venv-rx)$ audio-encode-server --config ./config.sample.json

And Curl can be used to transcode a file and store it on the S3 database, as shown in this example:

```
curl -X POST --data-binary @../audio-dataset/banjo1.mp3
http://localhost:8080/api/transcode/v1/flac/banjo1
```

After this call, a new banjo1.flac file should exist in the S3 audio bucket. You can download it via the web interface of Minio or AWS and check that it corresponds to the original MP3 file.

Dealing with blocking API and CPU-bound operations

The audio transcoding server implementation is now feature complete: it exposes an HTTP API to encode MP3 files to FLAC, and the resulting file is uploaded on an S3 database. However, there are still several things which are needed to improve it. This part focuses on improvements to the performance of the server. Let's start with a quick analysis of the current performances of the server. The following shell script executes ten instances of `curl` to transcode ten files in parallel. In other words, it simulates ten simultaneous encoding requests:

```
#! /bin/sh

transcode_url="http://localhost:8080/api/transcode/v1/flac"
date
echo "encoding file 0"
curl -X POST --data-binary @banjo0.mp3 $transcode_url/banjo0 &
echo "encoding file 1"
curl -X POST --data-binary @banjo1.mp3 $transcode_url/banjo1 &
echo "encoding file 2"
curl -X POST --data-binary @banjo2.mp3 $transcode_url/banjo2 &
echo "encoding file 3"
curl -X POST --data-binary @banjo3.mp3 $transcode_url/banjo3 &
echo "encoding file 4"
curl -X POST --data-binary @banjo4.mp3 $transcode_url/banjo4 &
echo "encoding file 5"
curl -X POST --data-binary @banjo5.mp3 $transcode_url/banjo5 &
echo "encoding file 6"
curl -X POST --data-binary @banjo6.mp3 $transcode_url/banjo6 &
echo "encoding file 7"
curl -X POST --data-binary @banjo7.mp3 $transcode_url/banjo7 &
echo "encoding file 8"
curl -X POST --data-binary @banjo8.mp3 $transcode_url/banjo8 &
echo "encoding file 9"
curl -X POST --data-binary @banjo9.mp3 $transcode_url/banjo9 &

wait
date
echo "completed"
```

After the ten transcoding requests have started, the script waits for the completion of all of them to print the time. Since the time is also printed at the beginning of the script, this allows us to see how much time was required to do the transcoding. Save this script as encode-all.sh and execute it. It should provide the following result:

```
Lun 23 jul 2018 22:00:48 CEST
encoding file 0
encoding file 1
encoding file 2
encoding file 3
encoding file 4
encoding file 5
encoding file 6
encoding file 7
encoding file 8
encoding file 9
okokokokokokokokokokLun 23 jul 2018 22:01:19 CEST
completed
```

This is the result on a relatively old laptop with a dual core i5 processor (that is: with four execution engines, as the cores are hyperthreaded). The encoding lasted 31 seconds. This timing will be faster on more recent processors. However, a look at the CPU utilization via a monitor shows that something is wrong: only one core has been used, and not even at 100%.

The processor is clearly under-used. The server is composed of three main operations: the HTTP server, the audio encoder, and the S3 uploader. The HTTP server and the S3 uploader are I/O bound operations. So, if they are both implemented in an asynchronous way, they are very efficient. The audio encoder is a CPU-bound operation. But there is bad news here:

- The S3 implementation is synchronous, so it can block the whole event loop
- The audio encoder is CPU-bound, which must be handled with multiprocessing or multithreading

So let's make some changes to improve the performance of the encoding server.

Using thread pools for CPU-bound operations

There are two possible ways to deal with CPU-bound operations:

- Split them into multiple processes
- Split them into multiple threads (provided that several execution engines are available on the CPU)

For now, the multithreading solution will be investigated. More details on how to solve it with multiprocessing will be provided in Chapter 10, *Testing and Debugging*.

As explained in Chapter 5, *Concurrency and Parallelism in RxPY*, two operators allow us to deal with schedulers and execution contexts: observe_on and subscribe_on. In the case of this application, ThreadPoolScheduler can be used. Since the encoding requests use a lot of CPU, and they can run in parallel, a thread pool can be used to execute them concurrently. But, before this can be done, another change is needed in the encode driver. The encoding function uses temporary files to work with the sox package. This is detailed in the following example:

```
def mp3_to_flac(data, dest_path, name):
    tmp_filename = os.path.join('/tmp/transcode-tmp.mp3')
    dest_filename = os.path.join(dest_path, name + '.flac')
    ...
```

The two filename variables are set to the same values for all files being encoded. So, if several files are encoded at the same time, then there will be simultaneous access to these temporary file. This can be fixed in several ways. One way is to use the Python tempfile.mkstemp function to create unique files each time. Another one is to add the thread identifier in the name of the file. This is shown in the following example:

```
import threading

def mp3_to_flac(data, dest_path, name):
    tid = threading.get_ident()
    tmp_filename = os.path.join('/tmp/transcode-{}.mp3'.format(tid))
    tmp2_filename = os.path.join('/tmp/transcode-{}.flac'.format(tid))
```

With this simple change, the encode driver can now be used in a multithreaded context. Then the encode requests must be scheduled on ThreadPoolScheduler to execute them in parallel. First a dedicated scheduler must be created, as can be seen in the following example:

```
from rx.concurrency import ThreadPoolScheduler

encode_scheduler = ThreadPoolScheduler(max_workers=4)
```

Here the thread pool is set to 4 workers. So, four encodings can be done in parallel. Then, the following scheduler can be used:

```
encode_request = (
    sources.httpd.route
    .filter(lambda i: i.id == 'flac_transcode')
    .flat_map(lambda i: i.request)
    .flat_map(lambda i: Observable.just(i, encode_scheduler))
    .map(lambda i: encoder.EncodeMp3(
        id=i.context,
        data=i.data,
        key=i.match_info['key']))
)
```

There is a trick here: directly using the `observe_on` operator does not work. The following items are only scheduled when the previous items are encoded. So that the scheduler can process items in parallel, a new subscription must occur for each item. This is why the `flat_map` operator is used, combined with the `just` operator associated to the scheduler. From that point, each `map` operation occurs in parallel on one of the four threads of the thread pool.

Moving the blocking I/O to a dedicated thread

The second evolution consists of making the S3 upload operation run in a dedicated thread. This upload operation is based on a blocking API, so it should be executed in a dedicated thread to avoid blocking the event loop. In RxPY there is no scheduler to execute some operators on a dedicated thread. However, this is not really needed because the same result is possible by creating a thread pool containing only one thread. So another scheduler is created for the S3 upload operations, as detailed in the following example:

```
s3_scheduler = ThreadPoolScheduler(max_workers=1)
```

For this scheduling, the `observe_on` operator can be used directly to move the execution context from the encoder thread pool to the s3 dedicated thread, as can be seen in the following example:

```
store_requests = (
    sources.encoder.response
    .observe_on(s3_scheduler)
    .map(lambda i: s3.UploadObject(
        key=i.key + '.flac',
        data=i.data,
        id=i.id,
    ))
```

```
)
```

Once the upload is complete, the HTTP response item must be scheduled on the AsyncIO scheduler so that it can be processed on the event loop. Due to a limitation present in RxPY 1.6, this requires some evolutions on the S3 driver: the implementation of the AsyncIO scheduler does not allow us to schedule an item from a thread scheduler to the AsyncIO scheduler. This limitation may be fixed in future versions of RxPY. Should this work, it would be implemented in the following way. First, an AsyncIO scheduler is needed:

```
from rx.concurrency import AsyncIOScheduler

aio_scheduler = AsyncIOScheduler()
```

Then, this scheduler can be used before sending the HTTP response, as detailed in the following example:

```
http_response = (
    sources.s3.response
    .observe_on(aio_scheduler)
    .map(lambda i: httpd.Response(
        data='ok'.encode('utf-8'),
        context=i.id,
    ))
)
```

Unfortunately, this does not work with RxPY 1.6, and the items are lost at this point because they cannot be scheduled. So, instead, the S3 driver has to schedule the emission of its items directly on the AsyncIO event loop. For this, it first needs a reference to the event loop, as can be seen in the following example:

```
def make_driver(loop=None):
    if loop is None:
        loop = asyncio.get_event_loop()
```

The event loop can be provided as a parameter, otherwise the default event loop is used. Then, each emission of items must be done from this event loop. There is a dedicated method for the event loop to do this: `call_soon_threadsafe`. This method schedules the execution of a function on the event loop, even when being called from a thread other than the event loop. So, the `on_next` callback of the S3 driver can now wrap the emission with the following method:

```
elif type(item) is UploadObject:
    data = BytesIO(item.data)
    client.upload_fileobj(data, bucket, item.key)
    loop.call_soon_threadsafe(observer.on_next, UploadReponse(
        key=item.key,
```

```
        id=item.id))

else:
    loop.call_soon_threadsafe(observer.on_error, "unknown item:
{}".format(type(item)))
```

As well as the subscription forwarding callbacks:

```
sink.request.subscribe(
    on_next=on_next,
    on_error=lambda e: loop.call_soon_threadsafe(observer.on_error, e),
    on_completed=lambda: loop.call_soon_threadsafe(observer.on_completed)
```

With these evolutions, the application code runs on three different execution contexts: the event loop, the encoding thread pool, and the S3 upload thread. This is shown in the following figure:

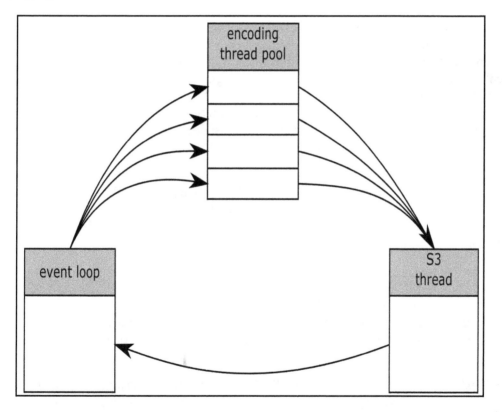

Figure 7.6: Multithreaded execution contexts

Now, encoding the 10 files in parallel completes in 15 seconds instead of 30 seconds. This is a 100% improvement in performance. This is mainly due to the encoding, which now uses four cores. This can be confirmed by looking at a CPU monitor: four cores are now being used, with peaks of 100% usage.

Some other improvements are possible to leverage the asynchronous design of the application more extensively. It is possible to directly use S3's HTTPS APIs instead of using the `boto3` package: this would allow us to upload the files concurrently on the AsyncIO event loop instead of serializing them. However, there is too much to describe here, and it will not introduce new ReactiveX or AsyncIO features. This could be an interesting exercise if you want to implement an existing protocol based on HTTP.

Summary

This chapter is a first step away from an initial application implementation to a software that may be deployed as a service. Docker, and its associated ecosystem, make the deployment of services on the cloud much easier than installing everything manually on virtual machines. It also makes it possible to package the application being developed, and deploy it on a testing infrastructure. For example, testing for software against different versions of Python is possible with `virtualenv`, provided that all these versions are available on the host system. With Docker, it is possible to do the same without even having Python installed on the host system. This saves a lot of time in the long run.

The S3 service is one of the most popular services provided by AWS. This chapter covered one usage of S3: uploading files on a bucket. The simplicity of S3 makes it very adaptable in all applications where files have to be stored and shared among several instances of the application. The most important limitation of S3 compared to a more classical database is its lack of a search capability.

Real situations are always more complex than theory. This chapter provided practical solutions for cases that can come up sometimes: handling CPU-bound tasks and blocking APIs. Thanks to AsyncIO and RxPY, it is possible to make use of multiple cores in an asynchronous application very easily. Very little code had to be changed to add multithreading support in the transcoder server. This would have been much more difficult with many other frameworks.

In the next chapter, we will cover some other improvements to the application, once again leveraging a reactive design: a dynamic reconfiguration of some settings, and better error handling.

Questions

- What are the existing software isolation technologies?
- What is Docker?
- On what kind of system does Docker software run?
- What is the difference between a Docker image and a Docker instance?
- What kind of service is provided by S3?
- How do you search for an object on an S3 bucket?
- How can CPU-bound operations be managed with RxPY?

Further reading

The `boto3` documentation is available here: `https://boto3.readthedocs.io/en/latest/`.

Installing Docker is also possible on macOS and Windows. Interestingly, the installation procedure is even easier than for Linux. The installation instructions for macOS are available here: `https://docs.docker.com/docker-for-mac/install/#install-and-run-docker-for-mac`. The installation instructions for Windows are available here: `https://docs.docker.com/docker-for-windows/install/`.

The complete Docker documentation is available here: `https://docs.docker.com`.

Dynamic Reconfiguration and Error Management

8

This is the last chapter describing the evolution of the audio transcoding server. In this last chapter, two more areas will be detailed—how to handle dynamic configuration and how to manage errors correctly. This chapter is composed of four parts. The first one explains how one can monitor changes in a file. The second part details the new operators that are needed to implement such a feature. The third part covers the implementation of this feature in the encode server. Finally, the last part shows you a smarter way to handle errors than the current one.

The following topics will be covered in this chapter:

- Monitoring file changes
- Operators used for dynamic configuration
- Encode driver reconfiguration
- Error management

Monitoring file changes

Monitoring files is a process often needed in applications. The most demanding applications for such a feature are media indexers. They need to know when some multimedia files have changed, appeared, or disappeared so that they re-index them and update their associated metadata. Another usual use case is simply monitoring a configuration file so that changes can be applied dynamically instead of requiring a restart of the application.

There are two ways to monitor files changes: either by directly polling for modifications in the file, or via the operating system providing some APIs to be notified when files are updated. The first solution has the advantage of being more portable. A solution that works on any system simply consists of reading the contents of the file regularly, and checking for any changes in it. Clearly this is a waste of resources because, to be practical, such a polling mechanism must occur quite often (every 10 seconds for example) while configuration file changes occur rarely. Another solution to avoid reading the whole file is checking for its modification time. This is easier than reading the whole contents, but more of a workaround for the lack of a dedicated solution.

The Linux kernel contains a feature dedicated to file monitoring—inotify. The principles of inotify are very simple—inotify allows you to register for modifications to a file or directory. Whenever a change occurs, the kernel notifies the application of these changes. This event-based mechanism is a perfect fit for a reactive application.

Understanding inotify

The name inotify is a contraction of **inode notify**. Inodes are the names of the filesystem on a Unix system. So files and directories are implemented as inodes in Linux (as well as on macOS since it implements a lot of Unix features). The inotify API is very simple, and is composed of just three functions. These APIs are system calls, accessible via C APIs in the GNU C standard library:

- inotify_init
- inotify_add_watch
- inotify_rm_watch

When an application needs to monitor a directory or a file, it must first create a monitoring context. This is done with the inotify_init function. This function returns a file descriptor. Then, to actually monitor a file, the inotify_add_watch function must be called. This function takes three parameters:

- The file descriptor returned by inotify_init
- The path of the file or directory to monitor
- The list of events to register

The `inotify` API supports many events, triggered when different conditions occur:

- `IN_ACCESS`: It is emitted when the file has been read.
- `IN_ATTRIB`: It is emitted when metadata has changed.
- `IN_CLOSE_WRITE`: It is emitted when the file has closed and was previously open in write mode.
- `IN_CLOSE_NOWRITE`: It is emitted when the file has closed and was previously not open in write mode.
- `IN_CREATE`: It is emitted when a file or a directory has been created. This is only valid when watching directories.
- `IN_DELETE`: It is emitted when a file or a directory has been deleted. This is only valid when watching directories.
- `IN_DELETE_SELF`: It is emitted when the file or directory has been deleted.
- `IN_MODIFY`: It is emitted when the file has changed.
- `IN_MOVE_SELF`: It is emitted when the file or directory has been moved.
- `IN_MOVED_FROM` or `IN_MOVED_TO`: These are emitted when a file has been moved. The first event contains the old name of the file, and the second event contains the new name of the file. This is only valid when watching directories.
- `IN_OPEN`: It is emitted when the file has been open.

The notification of these events is done with the classical reactor pattern explained in Chapter 1, *An Introduction to Reactive Programming*. Once the application does not need to monitor the file anymore, it uses the `inotify_rm_watch` function. The `inotify_add_watch` function can be called many times with the same `inotify` file descriptor. This enables the monitoring of several files, with their events being notified via a single file descriptor. When the application does not need the `inotify` context anymore, it must close the `inotify` file descriptor to free all the associated resources on the kernel.

The following diagram shows how the `inotify` API can be used:

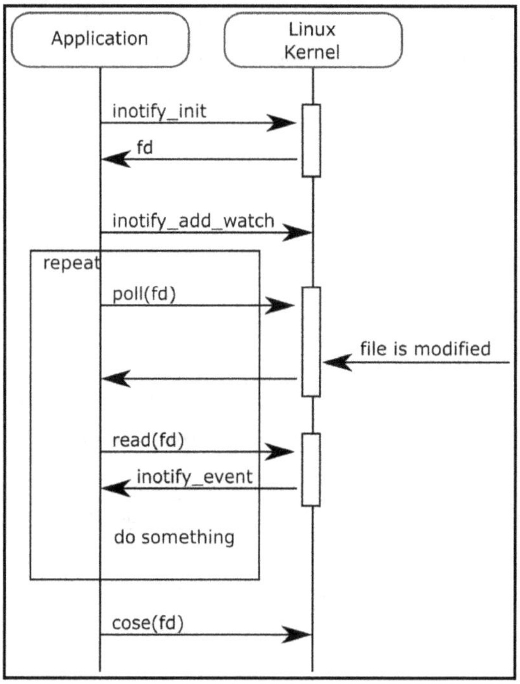

Figure 8.1: Using the Linux inotify API

The `inotify` API fits in well in asynchronous and reactive applications for two reasons. First, it is inherently event-based, so chances are that it can be used naturally in existing event-based code. Then, since it is a kernel API working with file descriptors, it is easy to integrate in existing frameworks based on an event loop. And this means that it can integrate nicely in AsyncIO.

Monitoring file changes with inotify

Fortunately, there is already a Python package that exposes the `inotify` features with Asyncio—`aionotify`. This package is available on `pypi` and can be installed with `pip` (as usual from your `virtualenv`):

```
pip3 install aionotify
```

The `aionotify` API is simple to use (by the way, the original `inotify` API is already simple for a C API), and access to the events leverages coroutines and the `await` notation. See the following example:

```
import asyncio
import aionotify

# Setup the watcher
watcher = aionotify.Watcher()
watcher.watch(alias='test', path='/tmp/foo.txt', flags=
    aionotify.Flags.OPEN
    | aionotify.Flags.CLOSE_WRITE
    | aionotify.Flags.ACCESS
    | aionotify.Flags.MODIFY)

# Prepare the loop
loop = asyncio.get_event_loop()

async def work():
    await watcher.setup(loop)
    for _ in range(10):
        event = await watcher.get_event()
        print(event)
    watcher.close()

loop.run_until_complete(work())
loop.stop()
loop.close()
watcher.unwatch('/tmp/foo.txt')
```

Here, a `watcher` object is created. This class wraps the `inotify_init` function call. Then a `watcher` is added with the `watch` method of the `Watcher` class. The alias argument will be provided when events are emitted. This can be useful when several files are being watched with the same `watcher` object. The path of the file to watch is also provided, as well as the events that must be monitored. Here, four events will be notified when the file is opened, closed, read, and written respectively.

To test this application, an initial `foo` file must be present in the filesystem:

```
echo "bar" > /tmp/foo.txt
```

Then the application can be started:

```
(venv-rx) $ python3 ch8/inotify.py
```

To test it, open the file in a text editor and make some changes in it. The console of the application should display something similar to the following:

```
Event(flags=32, cookie=0, name='', alias='test')
Event(flags=1, cookie=0, name='', alias='test')
Event(flags=32, cookie=0, name='', alias='test')
Event(flags=2, cookie=0, name='', alias='test')
Event(flags=8, cookie=0, name='', alias='test')
Event(flags=32, cookie=0, name='', alias='test')
Event(flags=2, cookie=0, name='', alias='test')
Event(flags=8, cookie=0, name='', alias='test')
```

The flags correspond to the values of the `aionotify.Flags` enumeration. The value `32` is when the file is open. `1` is for access, `2` is for modification, and `8` is when the file is closed. Depending on the editor being used, different values will be printed, depending on what you type in the file and how the editor manages changes in the files. Here, my editor does the following actions each time I save the file: opens the file, makes some modifications, and then closes the file. Other editors keep the file open and write to it either on request from the user or automatically. There are also cases where there is literally a flood of access or modify events. This is something that can be easily handled with RxPY.

Operators used for dynamic configuration

Some more operators are needed to add support for dynamic configuration in the server. Among those, the `debounce` operator is very powerful in the sense that using this operator avoids writing a consequent quantity of code to implement its feature. This is another example of how ReactiveX simplifies a lot of use cases.

The debounce operator

The `debounce` operator allows you to wait for a defined delay until an item is emitted. Each time an item is received, a timer is started with this delay as an expiration time. Items are emitted only when the timer triggers. This has the effect of dropping any item that is received before the delay has completed.

The following figure shows the marble diagram of the debounce operator:

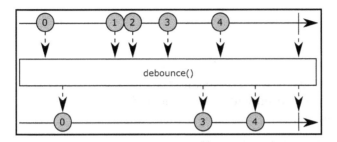

Figure 8.2: The debounce operator

The prototype of this operator is the following:

```
Observable.debounce(self, duetime, scheduler=None)
```

The duetime parameter is the delay in milliseconds that must elapse between two item emissions on the source observable so that an item is emitted on the output observable. The scheduler parameter allows you to provide an alternative scheduler than the default one. If no scheduler is provided, then the timeout scheduler is used. The timeout scheduler is implemented on top of the Python Timer class of the threading module. So, by default, the debounce operator is scheduled on a dedicated thread.

Here is an example of how to use it:

```
import time
from datetime import datetime

def slow_sequence(observer):
    print("sending 1 at {}".format(datetime.now()))
    observer.on_next(1)
    time.sleep(0.8)
    print("sending 2 at {}".format(datetime.now()))
    observer.on_next(2)
    time.sleep(0.8)
    print("sending 3 at {}".format(datetime.now()))
    observer.on_next(3)
    print("sending 4 at {}".format(datetime.now()))
    observer.on_next(4)

numbers = Observable.create(slow_sequence)

numbers.debounce(700).subscribe(
    on_next = lambda i: print("on_next {} at {}".format(i,
datetime.now()))),
```

```
    on_error = lambda e: print("on_error: {}".format(e)),
    on_completed = lambda: print("on_completed")
)

time.sleep(3)
```

Here, a custom `Observable` is created. This custom observable sends two items with a delay of 800 milliseconds between them, and then two items without a delay between them. The `debounce` operator is used with a due time of 700 milliseconds. The result of this example is the following:

```
sending 1 at 2018-08-01 22:14:12.236241
on_next 1 at 2018-08-01 22:14:12.940047
sending 2 at 2018-08-01 22:14:13.038211
on_next 2 at 2018-08-01 22:14:13.741002
sending 3 at 2018-08-01 22:14:13.840345
sending 4 at 2018-08-01 22:14:13.841314
on_next 4 at 2018-08-01 22:14:14.544288
```

The timestamps of the sending logs show that the delay between each item emission is correct: 2 is sent 800 milliseconds after 1, 3 is emitted 800 milliseconds after 2, and 4 is emitted right after 3. Also, the timestamps of the `on_next` logs correspond to the expected behavior—item 1 is received about 700 milliseconds after it has been sent. The small imprecision is due to the implementation of the `Timer` class, which is not designed to be very precise. Item 2 is received 700 milliseconds after is has been sent. Item 3 is not emitted at all because item 4 was received before the due time. Finally, 4 is also received 700 milliseconds after it has been sent.

The take operator

The `take` operator emits only the first items of the source observable. This operator is the complementary operator of the `skip` operator that behaves the opposite way. The following is its marble diagram:

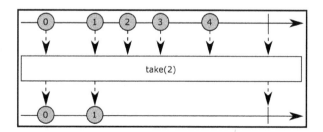

Figure 8.3: The take operator

The prototype of the `take` operator is the following:

```
Observable.take(self, count, scheduler=None)
```

The `count` parameter indicates how many items must be emitted before the output observable completes.

The following is an example of the `take` operator:

```
numbers = Observable.from_([1, 2, 3, 4])

numbers.take(2).subscribe(
    on_next = lambda i: print("on_next {}".format(i)),
    on_error = lambda e: print("on_error: {}".format(e)),
    on_completed = lambda: print("on_completed")
)
```

The example gives the following result:

```
on_next 1
on_next 2
on_completed
```

The first two items of the `numbers` observable are emitted by the `take` operator, and then the `Observable` object completes, skipping the last two items.

The distinct_until_changed operator

The `distinct_until_changed` operator filters continuous identical items. It emits only source items that are distinct from the previous item emitted on the source observable. The following is the marble diagram of this operator:

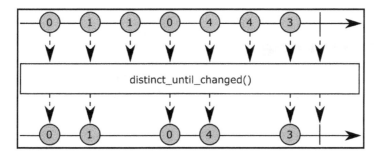

Figure 8.4: The distinct_until_changed operator

Its prototype is the following code:

```
distinct_until_changed(self, key_selector=None, comparer=None)
```

This operator accepts two optional parameters:

- The `key_selector` parameter is a function used to return the value that must be compared. When no `key_selector` is provided, then the item itself is used for comparison.
- The `comparer` parameter allows you to specify another comparison function than the equality operator.

Here is an example of this operator:

```
numbers = Observable.from_([1, 2, 2, 2, 3, 2, 1, 1])

numbers.distinct_until_changed().subscribe(
    on_next = lambda i: print("on_next {}".format(i)),
    on_error = lambda e: print("on_error: {}".format(e)),
    on_completed = lambda: print("on_completed")
)
```

This gives the following results:

```
on_next 1
on_next 2
on_next 3
on_next 2
on_next 1
on_completed
```

Any sequence of the same number in the `Observable` source is translated into a single item being received.

The start_with operator

The `start_with` operator emits items on the output observable before any other item of the source observable. The marble diagram of this operator follows:

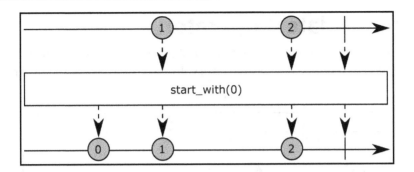

Figure 8.5: The start_with operator

The prototype of this operator is the following:

```
Observable.start_with(self, *args, **kw)
```

The `args` parameter contains the items to emit prior to any other one. Optionally, the first argument can be a scheduler. A scheduler can also be provided with the `scheduler` keyword argument.

The `start_with` operator can be used this way:

```
numbers = Observable.from_([1, 2, 3, 4])

numbers.start_with(0).subscribe(
    on_next = lambda i: print("on_next {}".format(i)),
    on_error = lambda e: print("on_error: {}".format(e)),
    on_completed = lambda: print("on_completed")
)
```

This gives the following result:

```
on_next 0
on_next 1
on_next 2
on_next 3
on_next 4
on_completed
```

The combine_latest operator

The `combine_latest` operator allows you to emit items that are composed from the latest value of the items emitted by each source observable. Here is the marble diagram of this operator:

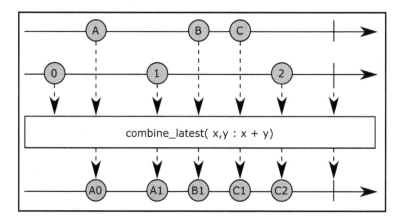

Figure 8.6: The combine_latest operator

This operator can be used as a class method or as a member method:

```
Observable.combine_latest(self, *args)
Observable.combine_latest(cls, *args)
```

The `args` argument contains all the source observables that must be combined. A list can also be provided instead of several arguments. The last argument must be a function that implements the combination logic. This function takes as many input arguments as the source observable provided before.

Here is an example of how to use this operator:

```
numbers = Observable.from_([1, 2, 3, 4])
characters = Observable.from_(["a", "b", "c"])

characters.combine_latest(numbers, lambda c, n: c + str(n)).subscribe(
    on_next = lambda i: print("on_next {}".format(i)),
    on_error = lambda e: print("on_error: {}".format(e)),
    on_completed = lambda: print("on_completed")
)
```

This gives the following result:

```
on_next a1
on_next b1
on_next b2
on_next c2
on_next c3
on_next c4
on_completed
```

For each combination of numbers and characters items, they are concatenated together to form a new sequence of all these combinations.

Encode driver reconfiguration

As an evolution of the audio transcoder server, it would be nice to be able to change the encoding parameters from the configuration file, dynamically, without restarting the server. So the encode section of the configuration must evolve to contain the following information:

```
"encode": {
  "samplerate": 16000,
  "bitdepth": 16
},
```

The two `samplerate` and `bitdepth` parameters for now are hardcoded in the encoder driver. Two steps are necessary to take these settings into account dynamically:

1. Add these settings in the configuration file and use them in the encode driver
2. Monitor the configuration file, reparse it, and use the new settings

With these changes, the reactivity diagram of the application becomes as follows:

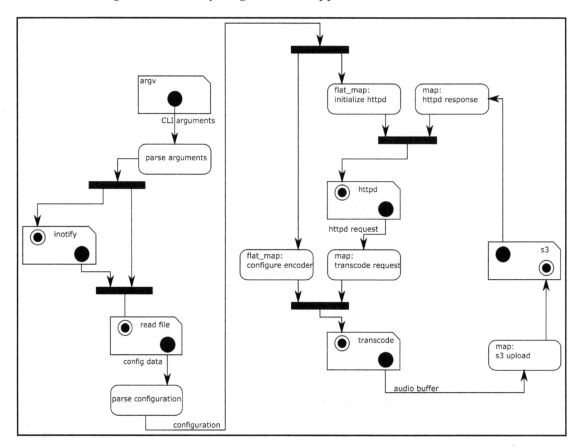

Figure 8.7: Reactivity diagram of the transcode server with dynamic configuration

Configuring the audio encoding

Several changes are necessary to make these settings configurable. The first one is declaring a new sink item:

```
Configure = namedtuple('Configure', ['samplerate', 'bitdepth'])
```

This item contains the values of the two settings that can be configured. Then the mp3_to_flac function must take these values as parameters instead of hardcoding them. The following are the changes in it:

```
def mp3_to_flac(data, samplerate, bitdepth):
    ...
    transformer.convert(samplerate=samplerate, n_channels=2,
bitdepth=bitdepth)
    ...
```

The two samplerate and bitdepth parameters are forwarded to the convert function of the transformer. One last modification is needed to configure the encoding. It consists of saving the information of the Configure item, and using it when an audio file is transcoded:

```
def on_subscribe(observer):
    samplerate = None
    bitdepth = None

    def on_next(item):
        nonlocal samplerate
        nonlocal bitdepth
        if type(item) is Configure:
            samplerate = item.samplerate
            bitdepth = item.bitdepth
        elif type(item) is EncodeMp3:
            encoded_data = mp3_to_flac(
                item.data, samplerate, bitdepth)
            observer.on_next(
                EncodeResult(id=item.id, key=item.key,
                    data=encoded_data))
        else:
            observer.on_error("unknown item: {}".format(type(item)))
```

The samplerate and bitdepth variables are defined in the scope of the on_subscribe function. They are declared as non-local in the on_next function so that they can be modified and used. When the Configure item is received, their value is updated, and when an EncodeMp3 item is received, these values are provided to the mp3_to_flac function.

Finally, the initialization of the encode driver must be updated to send a `Configure` item when the configuration file has been parsed:

```
encode_init = (
    config
    .map(lambda i: encoder.Configure(
        samplerate=i.encode.samplerate,
        bitdepth=i.encode.bitdepth))
)
```

Monitoring the configuration file

Now that the encoding parameters are configurable, let's see how to update this configuration dynamically. For this, the support of `inotify` is needed. This must be implemented in a new driver. Then this driver can be used to monitor the configuration file and trigger the reconfiguration of the encoder driver.

Implementing an inotify driver

The structure of this driver is the same as the previous ones. The first step is to declare the types used in it:

```
Source = namedtuple('Source', ['response'])
Sink = namedtuple('Sink', ['request'])

# Sink objects
AddWatch = namedtuple('AddWatch', ['id', 'path', 'flags'])
Start = namedtuple('Start', [])

# Source objects
Event = namedtuple('Event', ['id', 'path'])
```

This driver has one source observable and one sink observable. However, the API of this driver is not based on request/response. The inputs are requests, but the output is a continuous observable of `inotify` events. So a single request triggers many item emissions on the sink observable.

There are two possible sink items:

- The `AddWatch` item adds a new file to watch on the watcher associated with the driver
- The `Start` item starts the watcher

There is a single `Event` sink item that is emitted each time an `inotify` event is received.

The driver factory accepts a loop argument because the reference to the `asyncio` event loop is needed in this driver. When no loop is provided, then the current event loop is being used:

```
def make_driver(loop = None):
    loop = asyncio.get_event_loop() if loop is None else loop
```

Then the subscription function of the driver follows the same pattern as was previously used:

```
def on_subscribe(observer):
    watcher = aionotify.Watcher()

    def on_next(item):
        if type(item) is AddWatch:
            watcher.watch(alias=item.id, path=item.path,
                flags=item.flags)
        elif type(item) is Start:
            asyncio.ensure_future(read_events())
        else:
            observer.on_error("unknown item: {}".format(type(item)))

    sink.request.subscribe(
        on_next=on_next,
        on_error=lambda e: observer.on_error(e)
```

The `watcher` object is created on subscription to the source observable. This object is configured each time an `AddWatch` item is received, and the driver starts waiting for events when the `Start` item is received. Note that there is no `on_completed` handler on the sink observer. This driver should continue to send events even if the sink observable completes. Stopping the emission should be done when the source observable is disposed of (this is not implemented here to simplify the code). Waiting for the `watcher` events occurs in the `read_events` coroutine. Here is its implementation:

```
async def read_events():
    nonlocal observer
    await watcher.setup(loop)
    while True:
        event = await watcher.get_event()
        loop.call_soon(observer.on_next, Event(id=event.alias,
path=event.name))
    watcher.close()
```

This coroutine is also nested in `on_subscribe`. It first starts by enabling the `watcher` object by calling the `setup` method. This method requires the event loop as a parameter. Then an infinite loop waits for events and forwards events to the source observer. In this example, the coroutine contains an infinite loop. This loop should stop when the source observable is disposed of so that the coroutine can complete.

Monitoring changes in the configuration file

The final step is to use the `inotify` driver in the application. It must first be added in the driver, source, and sink of the application entry point:

```
Drivers = namedtuple('Drivers',
    ['encoder', 'httpd', 's3', 'file', 'inotify', 'argv'])
Source = namedtuple('Source',
    ['encoder', 'httpd', 's3', 'file', 'inotify', 'argv'])
Sink = namedtuple('Sink',
    ['encoder', 'httpd', 's3', 'file', 'inotify'])
```

The `inotify` driver must be created in the constructor of the `Drivers` object when the run function is called. Then it can be configured:

```
monitor_init = (
    parsed_argv
    .flat_map(lambda i : Observable.from_([
        inotify.AddWatch(id='config', path=i.value,
        flags=aionotify.Flags.MODIFY),
        inotify.Start(),
    ]))
)
```

An observable containing configuration and startup items is created from the `parsed_argv` observable. Since the `parsed_argv` observable contains only one item, the `monitor_init` observable will emit two items. This new observable is the sink of the `inotify` driver. The items coming from the `inotify` driver are then used to re-read the configuration file:

```
config_update = (
    sources.inotify.response
    .debounce(5000)
    .map(lambda i: True)
    .start_with(True)
)

read_config_file = (
    Observable.combine_latest(parsed_argv, config_update,
```

```
        lambda config, _: file.Read(id='config',
        path=config.value))
    )
```

The `config_update` observable emits a Boolean item each time the configuration file is changed. The `debounce` operator avoids events flooding. In this case, an event is emitted only when no change occurs within 5 seconds. Finally, the `config_update` observable starts by emitting an item immediately to trigger the initial read of the configuration file.

The `read_config_file` observable is no longer built directly from the `argv` source. Instead, it is a composition of the `argv` value (that is, the path of the configuration file) and the `inotify` events. The usage of the `combine_latest` operator allows you to emit a `Read` item with the path of the configuration file each time.

With all these changes, the configuration file is read and parsed each time it is modified. Moreover, the encode driver take into account these changes. However, there is now an issue—the `config` observable emits an item each time the configuration file is changed instead of only one single item. This means that the configuration of the HTTP and S3 drivers is done each time the configuration file is modified. Since these drivers do not support reconfiguration, it raises errors. This can be fixed by using only the first item emitted by the `config` observable when initializing these drivers:

```
http_init = (
    config.take(1)
    ...

s3_init = (
    config.take(1)
    ...
```

This is done trivially with the `take` operator that emits only the first *n* items of an observable. Here, only the first item is used. Note how this issue is the opposite of what happens with other programming paradigms. In a reactive application, handling change is the default behavior, while doing things only once requires special care. In a typical object-oriented application, adding a dynamic configuration afterwards almost always requires rewriting a significant part of the application. In a reactive application, this is a much more simple evolution.

A last sanity check can be added to avoid reconfiguring the encode driver when it is not needed. If for any reason the configuration file changed but not the encode part of it, then it is useless to reconfigure the encoder driver. This can be done with the following modifications in the `encode_init` observable chain:

```
encode_init = (
    config
    .map(lambda i: i.encode)
    .distinct_until_changed()
    .map(lambda i: encoder.Configure(
        samplerate=i.samplerate,
        bitdepth=i.bitdepth))
)
```

First, the whole configuration is mapped to just contain the `encode` part. Then these items are filtered to be emitted only when they change, thanks to the `distinct_until_changed` operator.

The new code of the transcode server is available in the GitHub repository (`https://github.com/PacktPublishing/Hands-On-Reactive-Programming-with-Python`) of this book, in the `audio-encode-server-4` sub-folder. It creates logs when the encode driver configuration changes. So you can test it and see that the configuration is updated 5 seconds after the the configuration file is modified.

Error management

The audio transcode server is now feature-complete. But unfortunately, it is not very robust for a server that should be able to run for months without issues. This can be seen easily if, instead of an MP3 file, a WAV or FLAC file is provided, or if the S3 server is not started when a transcode request occurs. In these cases, an error is raised, and the server stops.

`Chapter 4`, *Exploring Observables and Observers*, explained several ways to handle errors. The time has come to see how to apply them in a real application. There are two main ways to handle errors in RxPY—with the `on_error` handler, or with dedicated operators. The error handler is already used in all custom observables and this allows you to propagate the errors. However, there are several kinds of error that should be handled gracefully. Typically, if an audio-encoding error occurs, then an HTTP error should be returned to the client. The server should not stop working.

So the behavior of the application should be updated as shown in the following diagram. This diagram does not contains the initialization, since it does not change here:

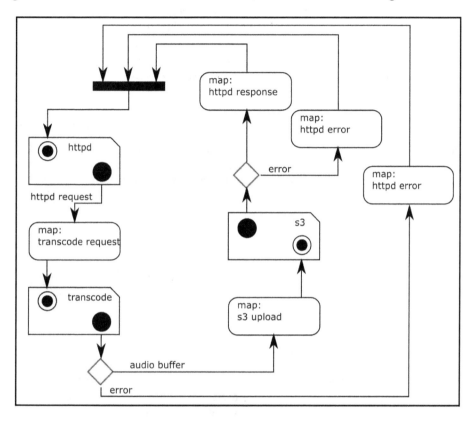

Figure 8.8: Handling errors

In the event of an error, the error must be caught, and an HTTP error must be returned to the client, by passing any other action that is done in the normal way. For example, if a transcode error occurs, then the HTTP error response must be sent immediately, without trying to upload something. In imperative programming, this is usually done with decision statements such as `if` and `else`. In ReactiveX, the situation is different: the whole behavior relies on a chain of observables. If any error occurs in one observable, it is propagated and the whole data flow stops.

So, with the current implementation of the drivers, raising an error does not permit you to handle the error only for the request that failed. An additional layer of abstraction is needed to do this. *Figure 1.8* in `Chapter 1`, *An Introduction to Reactive Programming*, shows how higher-order observables carry other observables. This is the way errors can be managed per request. The transcode and S3 drivers must return higher-order observables instead of observables. Instead of sending items with the result of the response, each response is an observable that either emits one item (with the response value) or completes on error.

Let's do these changes in the encode server. First, an error item must be defined:

```
EncodeError = namedtuple('UploadReponse', ['id', 'key'])
```

And then the result of the encoding must be changed to emit observables instead of items:

```
elif type(item) is EncodeMp3:
    try:
        encoded_data = mp3_to_flac(
            item.data, samplerate, bitdepth)
        observer.on_next(Observable.just(
            EncodeResult(id=item.id, key=item.key, data=encoded_data)))
    except:
        observer.on_next(Observable.throw(
            Exception(EncodeError(
                key=item.key,
                id=item.id))))
```

The whole encoding action is enclosed in a `try` block. If no exception is raised, then an observable containing only `EncodeResult` is sent. However, if an exception is raised, then an observable without an item, but throwing an `EncodeError`, is returned. Now the response observable is a higher-order observable, it returns observables as items.

Correctly handling the errors is more complex than directly using the `catch_exception` operator. The `catch_exception` operator forwards items directly, and when an error is received, it emits items of another observable, provided as a parameter. Here, the items of the encode response source observable must always be forwarded, and any error must be replaced by an item emitted on the response sink of the HTTP driver.

This behavior must be implemented in several steps. First, a higher-order function is needed. This function allows you to route an item on one of two observables, depending on whether an error occurred or not:

```
def make_error_router():
    sink_observer = None

    def on_subscribe(observer):
        nonlocal sink_observer
        sink_observer = observer

    def route_error(item, convert):
        def catch_item(i):
            sink_observer.on_next(convert(i))
            return Observable.empty()

        return item.catch_exception(catch_item)

    return Observable.create(on_subscribe), route_error
```

Let's start with the description of the `route_error` function. This function either returns the item provided as input or sends an item to another observable. Note that the item parameter here is in fact an observable. The items sent on `sink_observer` are converted before being emitted. This allows you to map the errors to other types of objects. Then the `make_error_function` wraps the `route_error` function to return two parameters: an observable that emits error items, and the `route_error` function that must be used in an operator chain to handle errors. This function can be used in the following way, at the beginning of the audio encoder component:

```
def audio_encoder(sources):
    http_encode_error, route_encode_error = make_error_router()
```

The `http_encode_error` observable must be added to the list of streams returned to the HTTP response sink:

```
http = Observable.merge(http_init, http_response, http_encode_error)
```

However, the `route_encode_error` function is not usable directly. Since the results of the encode driver are higher-order observables, these items should be flattened at some point to continue the chain with `EncodeResult` items. So the `flat_map` operator must be used, in combination with the `route_encode_error` function. Wrapping these in another higher-order function will make its usage easier:

```
def catch_or_flat_map(source, error_map, error_router):
    return source.flat_map(lambda i: error_router(i, error_map))
```

The `catch_or_flat_map` function takes three parameters. `source`: a higher-order observable, the mapping function to apply to errors, and the error-routing function returned by `make_error_router`. The result of this function is a **flattened observable** of the items received as input. Any error will be routed to another observable, via the `error_router` function. Using this function is now easy, thanks to the `let` operator:

```
store_requests = (
    sources.encoder.response
    .let(catch_or_flat_map,
        error_router=route_encode_error,
        error_map=lambda i: httpd.Response(
            data='encode error'.encode('utf-8'),
            context=i.args[0].id,
            status=500))
    .observe_on(s3_scheduler)
    .map(lambda i: s3.UploadObject(
        key=i.key + '.flac',
        data=i.data,
        id=i.id,
    ))
)
```

In this case, any encode error is mapped to an HTTP response, with status 500 (internal error), and help text. Non-error items are forwarded in the chain, and provided to the S3 driver so that they can be uploaded.

This whole code is non-trivial to comprehend, because it is composed of several higher-order functions and higher-order observables. Take some time to read it several times and add some logs to see what happens on each step to get it. This code, with the error handling of the S3 driver, is available in the GitHub repository of this book, in the `ch8/audio-encode-server-5` sub-folder.

With these last evolutions, the audio transcoding server is now fully reactive, and asynchronous, and handles errors correctly.

Summary

This chapter concludes the implementation of the audio-transcoding server. This application is now robust enough to be used in production. The two parts studied in this chapter provide other examples of how to use RxPY in non-trivial cases.

The usage of `aionotify` is another example of how to integrate an AsyncIO package with RxPY, and in a functional way. `inotify` is different from the other drivers that have been written before because it does not implement a request/response communication pattern, but an observer one (which is more similar to ReactiveX observables). With this example, you should now be able to use any AsyncIO package in an RxPY application.

The second part covers a very important aspect of any serious application—error management. More specifically, the snippets used to describe how to manage errors in `Chapter 4`, *Exploring Observables and Observers*, are not enough to handle errors in an application like this one. The correct handling of errors in this cases requires more abstractions. This translates to the usage of higher-order functions and higher-order observables. Splitting the behavior into several helper functions makes the code using these functions more readable.

A last word on readability—the `audio_encoder` function is now quite big, too big. As an exercise, try to split it into several functions or even components to make it smaller.

Questions

- What is the purpose of the `inotify` feature ?
- What is the feature provided by the `debounce` operator ?
- What operator can be used to remove duplicate items in an observable ?
- What is the difference between the `take` and `skip` operators ?
- What is a higher-order observable?
- Why, in this application, is throwing an error on the observable chain not a good way to handle errors?

Operators in RxPY

9

The previous chapters covered more than 30 operators. These operators allow us to implement a realistic application, but many others are often needed. This chapter describes more than 40 other operators that are also commonly used, grouped by functional category. As usual, each operator is described with its marble diagram, a comprehensive description, and an example of how to use it to help you decide when to use what operator.

The following topics will be covered in this chapter:

- Transforming observables
- Filtering observables
- Combining observables
- Utility operators
- Conditional operators
- Mathematical operators

Transforming observables

The following operators allow us to make some transformations on the items emitted on source observables. Some of them have already been covered in the previous chapters. They are the following:

Operator	Description	Chapter
map	Maps each item to another value	1
flat_map	Maps each item to an observable and flattens all emitted items in a single observable	6

The buffer operator

The `buffer` operator groups items emitted on the source observable based on different types of window selectors. These selectors can be defined via another observable, an item count, or time information. The following figure shows the marble diagram of the buffer operator:

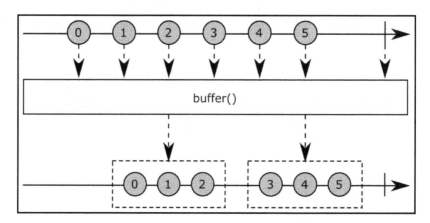

Figure 9.1: The buffer operator

This operator has several prototypes:

```
Observable.buffer(self, buffer_openings=None,
    buffer_closing_selector=None)
Observable.buffer_with_count(self, count, skip=None)
Observable.buffer_with_time(self, timespan,
    timeshift=None, scheduler=None)
Observable.buffer_with_time_or_count(self,
    timespan, count, scheduler=None)
```

The first version allows us to use another observable to control when a new buffer begins. Each time the `buffer_openings` observable emits an item, then the current buffer is emitted, and a new buffer is created. The `buffer_closing_selector` parameter is an optional parameter. When provided, it must be a function that returns an observable whose completion ends the current buffer. On completion, this function will be called again to start a new buffer. The `buffer_closing_selector` parameter can also be provided as the first parameter of this operator. If the first parameter is an observable, then it is used as the `buffer_openings` parameters, and if it is a function, then it is used as the `buffer_closing_selector` parameter.

The following is the first way to use the `buffer` operator:

```
numbers = Subject()
windows = Subject()
numbers.buffer(windows).subscribe(
    on_next = lambda i: print("on_next {}".format(i)),
    on_error = lambda e: print("on_error: {}".format(e)),
    on_completed = lambda: print("on_completed")
)

numbers.on_next(1)
numbers.on_next(2)
windows.on_next(True)
numbers.on_next(3)
numbers.on_next(4)
numbers.on_next(5)
windows.on_next(True)
```

The `numbers` observable is the observable that must be buffered. The `windows` observable emits items each time a new buffering window must start. The following example gives the following result:

on_next [1, 2]
on_next [3, 4, 5]

The first two items are emitted as a single list item. Then, the next three items are emitted as a second item.

The `closing_selector` parameter can be used in the following way:

```
window_selector = None
def closing_selector():
    print("closing_selector")
    global window_selector
    window_selector = Subject()
    return window_selector

numbers = Subject()
numbers.buffer(closing_selector).subscribe(
    on_next = lambda i: print("on_next {}".format(i)),
    on_error = lambda e: print("on_error: {}".format(e)),
    on_completed = lambda: print("on_completed")
)

numbers.on_next(1)
numbers.on_next(2)
numbers.on_next(3)
window_selector.on_completed()
```

```
numbers.on_next(4)
numbers.on_next(5)
window_selector.on_completed()
```

The `numbers` observable is the observable that must be buffered. The `closing_selector` function returns an observable that emits no items. This observable is completed after emitting three items, and then two items. This example gives the following result:

```
closing_selector
on_next [1, 2, 3]
closing_selector
on_next [4, 5]
closing_selector
```

First, the `closing_selector` function is called. This allows the `buffer` operator to subscribe to its completion. When the `window_selector` observable completes, then the first item is emitted (the 1, 2, 3 list). After that, the `closing_selector` function is called again. When the associated observable completes, then a second item is emitted (the 4, 5 list). The `closing_selector` function is called one last time by the operator to start a new buffer.

The second prototype of the `buffer` operator creates buffers based on the item, `count`. The `count` parameter indicates how many items must be grouped together. The optional `skip` parameter indicates how many items must be skipped between each buffer creation. The default value is the one provided in `count`. The `skip` parameter allows us to use overlapping windows for buffering.

This second variant can be used this way:

```
numbers = Observable.from_([1, 2, 3, 4, 5, 6])
numbers.buffer_with_count(3).subscribe(
    on_next = lambda i: print("on_next {}".format(i)),
    on_error = lambda e: print("on_error: {}".format(e)),
    on_completed = lambda: print("on_completed")
)
```

This snippet gives the following result:

```
on_next [1, 2, 3]
on_next [4, 5, 6]
on_completed
```

The six items are grouped by three, and so the resulting observable emits two items.

The third variant of this operator allows us to buffer source items based on time information. The `timespan` parameter is an integer that indicates, in milliseconds, how many time items must be grouped together. The optional `timeshift` parameter indicates how many times in milliseconds must elapse before creating a new buffer. By default, its value is one of the `timespan` parameters. The `timespan` parameter allows us to use overlapping windows for the buffering.

The following is an example using this operator:

```
numbers = Subject()
dispoable = numbers.buffer_with_time(200).subscribe(
    on_next = lambda i: print("on_next {}".format(i)),
    on_error = lambda e: print("on_error: {}".format(e)),
    on_completed = lambda: print("on_completed")
)

numbers.on_next(1)
numbers.on_next(2)
t1 = threading.Timer(0.250, lambda: numbers.on_next(3))
t1.start()
t2 = threading.Timer(0.450, lambda: numbers.on_next(4))
t2.start()
t3 = threading.Timer(0.750, lambda: dispoable.dispose())
t3.start()
```

In this example, items of the `numbers` observable are grouped in a window of 200 ms. Items 1 and 2 are emitted immediately, then item 3 is emitted after 250 milliseconds, item 4 is emitted after 200 more milliseconds, and finally the subscription is disposed of after 300 milliseconds. This gives the following result:

```
on_next [1, 2]
on_next [3]
on_next [4]
```

Numbers 1 and 2 are emitted in the same item because they are received within the same 200 milliseconds. Then, 3 and 4 are emitted as two other items because each one is in a separate 200-millisecond window.

The window operator

The `window` operator is similar to the `buffer` operator, except that it emits a higher-order observable instead of emitting list items. Its marble diagram is shown in the following figure:

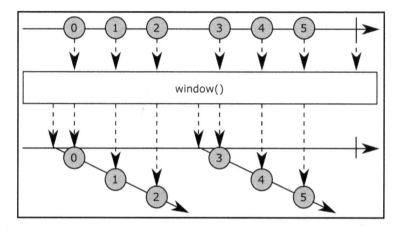

Figure 9.2: The window operator

The prototype of the `window` operator is the following:

```
Observable.window(self, window_openings=None,
    window_closing_selector=None)
```

The two parameters are similar to the ones of the `buffer` operator. The `window_opening` parameter is an observable that emits items each time a new window must be created. The `window_closing_selector` is a function that returns an observable that completes when the current window must end.

This operator can be used in the following way:

```
def wrap_items(i):
    return i.map(lambda j: 'obs {}: {}'.format(i, j))

numbers = Subject()
windows = Subject()
numbers.window(windows).flat_map(wrap_items).subscribe(
    on_next = lambda i: print("on_next {}".format(i)),
    on_error = lambda e: print("on_error: {}".format(e)),
    on_completed = lambda: print("on_completed")
)
```

```
numbers.on_next(1)
numbers.on_next(2)
windows.on_next(True)
numbers.on_next(3)
numbers.on_next(4)
numbers.on_next(5)
windows.on_next(True)
```

This example is very similar to the first example of the `buffer` operator. The main difference is that the result of the `window` operator goes through the `flat_map` operator to serialize each item. Each item is mapped to a string containing the reference of the observable window. This gives the following result:

```
on_next obs <0x105ee6a58>: 1
on_next obs <0x105ee6a58>: 2
on_next obs <0x105ee6da0>: 3
on_next obs <0x105ee6da0>: 4
on_next obs <0x105ee6da0>: 5
```

The first two items are emitted on the same observable, and the last three items are emitted on another observable.

The group_by operator

The `group_by` operator groups items of the source observable, where the groups are determined by a selector function. This operator returns a higher-order observable. The following figure shows the marble diagram of this operator:

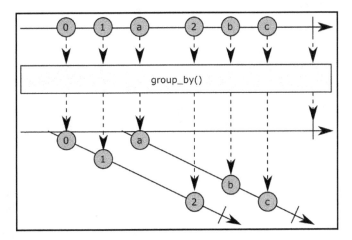

Figure 9.3: The group_by operator

The prototype of this operator is the following:

```
group_by(self, key_selector, element_selector=None,
         key_serializer=None)
```

Here, `key_selector` is a function that returns a key from an item. This key is used to group items per key. The optional `element_selector` parameter is a function used to map each source item in the observable of the group. Its default value is the identity function (that is, the item is mapped to itself). Finally, the `key_serializer` optional parameter is a function used to compare whether two keys are equal or not. Its default value is the equality operator.

Here is an example of this operator:

```
def wrap_items(i):
    return i.map(lambda j: 'obs {}: {}'.format(i, j))

numbers = Observable.from_([1, 2, 3, 4, 5, 6])
numbers.group_by(lambda i: i % 2 == 0).flat_map(wrap_items).subscribe(
    on_next = lambda i: print("on_next {}".format(i)),
    on_error = lambda e: print("on_error: {}".format(e)),
    on_completed = lambda: print("on_completed")
)
```

The `key_selector` is a function returning `True` or `False` depending on whether the item is an even number or an odd one. The items are then flattened before being printed with the name of the observable that carried them. This example gives the following result:

```
on_next obs <0x105f70048>: 1
on_next obs <0x105ee6b70>: 2
on_next obs <0x105f70048>: 3
on_next obs <0x105ee6b70>: 4
on_next obs <0x105f70048>: 5
on_next obs <0x105ee6b70>: 6
on_completed
```

Even and odd items are received interleaved, on two different observables. One observable contains all the even numbers, and the other all the odd numbers.

Filtering observables

The operators listed here emit only some of the items emitted on the source observables, based on their criteria. Some of them have already been covered in the previous chapters. They are the following:

Operator	Description	Chapter
debounce	Maps each item to another value	8
distinct_until_changed	Emits an item only when it is different from the previously emitted item	8
filter	Emits only items that meet a certain criterion	6
skip	Skips items some amount of items	6
take	Emits only some amount of items	8

The first operator

The first operator returns the first item emitted on the source observable. Its marble diagram is shown in the following figure:

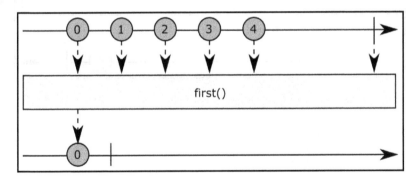

Figure 9.4: The first operator

Its prototype is the following:

```
Observable.first(self, predicate=None)
```

Here, predicate is an optional function used to filter items in the source observable. If no predicate is provided, the first item of the observable is emitted.

Here is an example of this operator:

```
numbers = Observable.from_([1, 2, 3, 4, 5, 6])
numbers.first().subscribe(
    on_next = lambda i: print("on_next {}".format(i)),
    on_error = lambda e: print("on_error: {}".format(e)),
    on_completed = lambda: print("on_completed")
)
```

This example gives the following result:

```
on_next 1
on_completed
```

The last operator

The `last` operator returns the last item emitted on the source observable. The following figure shows its marble diagram:

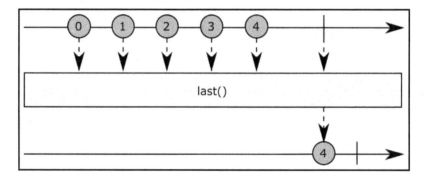

Figure 9.5: The last operator

Its prototype is the following:

```
last(self, predicate=None)
```

Here, `predicate` is an optional function used to filter items in the source observable. If no `predicate` is provided, the last item of the observable is emitted.

Here is an example of this operator:

```
numbers = Observable.from_([1, 2, 3, 4, 5, 6])
numbers.last().subscribe(
    on_next = lambda i: print("on_next {}".format(i)),
    on_error = lambda e: print("on_error: {}".format(e)),
```

```
        on_completed = lambda: print("on_completed")
    )
```

This gives the following result:

```
on_next  6
on_completed
```

The skip_last operator

The `skip_last` operator returns all items emitted by the source observable, but not the last *n* ones. The following figure shows the marble diagram of this operator:

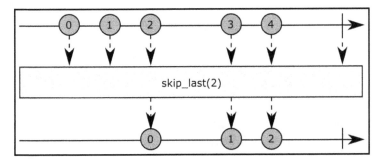

Figure 9.6: The skip_last operator

The prototype of this operator is the following:

```
Observable.skip_last(self, count)
```

Here, `count` is the number of items to skip from the source observable.

Here is an example of this operator:

```
numbers = Observable.from_([1, 2, 3, 4, 5, 6])
numbers.skip_last(2).subscribe(
    on_next = lambda i: print("on_next {}".format(i)),
    on_error = lambda e: print("on_error: {}".format(e)),
    on_completed = lambda: print("on_completed")
)
```

This gives the following result:

```
on_next  1
on_next  2
on_next  3
```

```
on_next 4
on_completed
```

The take_last operator

The `take_last` operator returns only the *n* last items emitted by the source observable. The following figure shows the marble diagram of this operator:

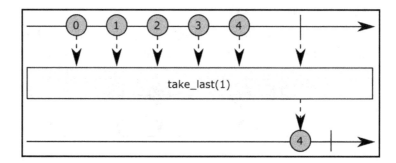

Figure 9.7: The take_last operator

The prototype of this operator is the following:

```
take_last(self, count)
```

Here, `count` is the number of items to keep from the source observable.

Here is an example of this operator:

```
numbers = Observable.from_([1, 2, 3, 4, 5, 6])
numbers.take_last(2).subscribe(
    on_next = lambda i: print("on_next {}".format(i)),
    on_error = lambda e: print("on_error: {}".format(e)),
    on_completed = lambda: print("on_completed")
)
```

This gives the following result:

```
on_next 5
on_next 6
on_completed
```

The ignore_elements operator

The `ignore_elements` operator emits no items. This operator completes when its source observable completes. The following figure shows the marble diagram of this operator:

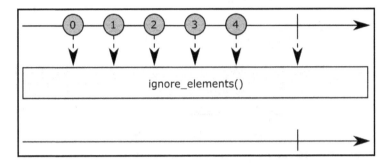

Figure 9.8: The ignore_elements operator

The prototype of this operator is the following:

```
Observable.ignore_elements(self)
```

Here is an example of this operator:

```
numbers = Observable.from_([1, 2, 3, 4, 5, 6])
numbers.ignore_elements().subscribe(
    on_next = lambda i: print("on_next {}".format(i)),
    on_error = lambda e: print("on_error: {}".format(e)),
    on_completed = lambda: print("on_completed")
)
```

This gives the following result:

```
on_completed
```

It is not visible in this example, but the observable returned by the `ignore_elements` operator completes when the `numbers` observable completes. This operator is useful in cases where the completion is the only meaningful information. For example, one can wait for completion of the observable before subscribing to another observable (typically with the `concat` operator). In such a case, the resulting observable emits the items of the second observable but only once the first observable has completed.

The sample operator

The `sample` operator emits the last item received on its source observable, either at fixed intervals or on receipt of items from another observable. The following figure shows the marble diagram of this operator when sampling is done by time:

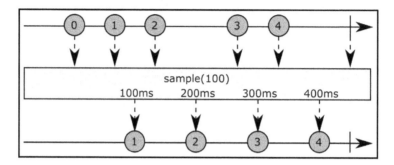

Figure 9.9: The sample operator with time-based sampling

The following figure shows the marble diagram of the `sample` operator when sampling is done via another observable:

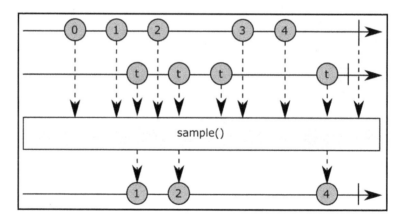

Figure 9.10: The sample operator with sampling being based on an observable

The prototype of this operator is the following:

```
Observable.sample(self, interval=None, sampler=None, scheduler=None)
```

Here, the `interval` and `sampler` parameters are exclusive. The `interval` parameter specifies the sampling period in milliseconds. The `sampler` parameter is an observable that controls the sampling. Each time it emits an item, sampling of the source observable is performed. The `scheduler` parameter can be used to specify the scheduler to use. The default value uses the timeout scheduler.

Here is an example of this operator, with sampling controlled via a `sampler` observable:

```python
numbers = Subject()
sampler = Subject()
numbers.sample(sampler=sampler).subscribe(
    on_next = lambda i: print("on_next {}".format(i)),
    on_error = lambda e: print("on_error: {}".format(e)),
    on_completed = lambda: print("on_completed")
)

numbers.on_next(1)
numbers.on_next(2)
sampler.on_next(True)
numbers.on_next(3)
numbers.on_next(4)
numbers.on_next(5)
sampler.on_next(True)
```

This example gives the following result:

```
on_next 2
on_next 5
```

Here, two items are received, corresponding to the last value emitted by the `numbers` observable each time the `sampler` observable emitted an item.

The distinct operator

The distinct operator returns only unique items from its source observable. The following figure shows its marble diagram:

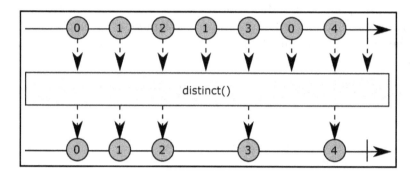

Figure 9.11: The distinct operator

Its prototype is the following:

```
Observable.distinct(self, key_selector=None, comparer=None)
```

Here, key_selector is a function that returns a key from each item. The default value uses the item as a key. The comparer parameter is a function used to compare two keys. Its default value uses the equality operator. Both parameters are optional.

Here is an example of the distinct operator:

```
numbers = Observable.from_([1, 2, 1, 3, 3, 2, 4, 5])
numbers.distinct().subscribe(
    on_next = lambda i: print("on_next {}".format(i)),
    on_error = lambda e: print("on_error: {}".format(e)),
    on_completed = lambda: print("on_completed")
)
```

This example gives the following result:

```
on_next 1
on_next 2
on_next 3
on_next 4
on_next 5
on_completed
```

All duplicate items have been removed from the `numbers` observable.

The element_at operator

The `element_at` operator returns the nth item of the source observable. The following figure shows its marble diagram:

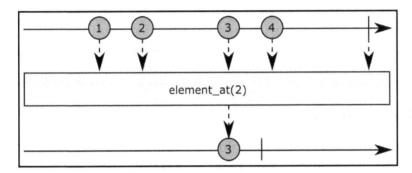

Figure 9.12: The element_at operator

The prototype of this operator is the following:

```
Observable.element_at(self, index)
```

Here, `index` is the index of the item to return, starting from index 0.

Here is an example of the `element_at` operator:

```
numbers = Observable.from_([1, 2, 3, 4, 5, 6])
numbers.element_at(3).subscribe(
    on_next = lambda i: print("on_next {}".format(i)),
    on_error = lambda e: print("on_error: {}".format(e)),
    on_completed = lambda: print("on_completed")
)
```

This gives the following result:

```
on_next 4
on_completed
```

Combining observables

The operators listed here combine several source observables into a single observable. Some of them have already been covered in the previous chapters. They are the following:

Operator	Description	Chapter
combine_latest	Emits an item that is the combination of the source observable and the last item emitted from another observable	8
merge	Emits items from several observables as they arrive	3
start_with	Emits an item as the first item of the observable	8

The join operator

The `join` operator combines the items emitted by two observables when they are emitted within a specified time window. The `join` operator is very similar to the `combine_latest` operator, but with additional time constraints. The following figure shows the marble diagram of the `join` operator:

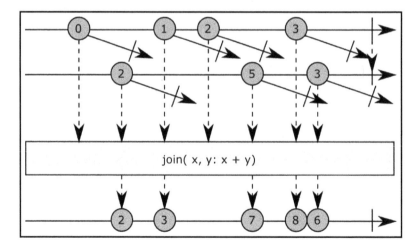

Figure 9.13: The join operator

Its prototype is the following:

```
Observable.join(self, right,
                left_duration_selector,
                right_duration_selector,
                result_selector)
```

Here, the `right` parameter is the second observable to combine (`self` is referred to as the left operator). The `left_duration_selector` parameter is a function that returns an observable whose lifetime corresponds to the validity time of the item emitted on the left observable. This function is called each time the left observable emits an item. The `right_duration_selector` parameter is a function that returns an observable whose lifetime corresponds to the validity time of the item emitted on the right observable. This function is called each time the right observable emits an item.

Here is an example of this operator:

```
numbers1 = Subject()
numbers2 = Subject()

numbers1.join(numbers2,
              lambda i: Observable.just(True).delay(200),
              lambda i: Observable.just(True).delay(300),
              lambda i, j: i + j) \
    .subscribe(
        on_next = lambda i: print("on_next {}".format(i)),
        on_error = lambda e: print("on_error: {}".format(e)),
        on_completed = lambda: print("on_completed")
)
numbers1.on_next(0)
numbers2.on_next(2)
numbers1.on_next(1)
time.sleep(0.4)
numbers1.on_next(2)
numbers2.on_next(5)
time.sleep(0.25)
numbers1.on_next(3)
numbers2.on_next(3)
```

The first parameter of the `join` operator is the `number2` observable. Then, two functions are provided. These function are called each time an item is emitted on `numbers1` and `numbers2`. They return an observable that emits only one item, but delayed. This allows us to control when the observable will complete. In practice, the first `lambda` returns an observable that completes after 200 milliseconds and the second `lambda` returns an observable that completes after 300 milliseconds. After that, items on both observables are emitted the same way as on the marble diagram of *Figure 9.13*.

This examples gives the following result:

```
on_next 2
on_next 3
on_next 7
on_next 8
on_next 6
```

This corresponds to the expected result, as shown in *Figure 9.13*.

The switch_latest operator

The `switch_latest` operator take a higher-order observable as input. Each time a new item is emitted on this source observable, a subscription is done on the child observable, and the existing subscription on the previous item is disposed of. The following figure shows the marble diagram of this operator:

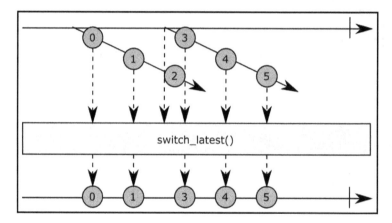

Figure 9.14: The switch_latest operator

Its prototype is the following:

```
Observable.switch_latest(self)
```

Here is an example of the `switch_latest` operator:

```
obs1 = Subject()
obs2 = Subject()
obs3 = Subject()
higher_order = Subject()

higher_order.switch_latest().subscribe(
    on_next = lambda i: print("on_next {}".format(i)),
    on_error = lambda e: print("on_error: {}".format(e)),
    on_completed = lambda: print("on_completed")
)

higher_order.on_next(obs1)
obs1.on_next("1: 1")
obs1.on_next("1: 2")
higher_order.on_next(obs2)
obs1.on_next("1: 3")
obs2.on_next("2: 1")
obs2.on_next("2: 2")
higher_order.on_next(obs3)
obs2.on_next("2: 3")
obs3.on_next("3: 1")
obs3.on_next("3: 2")
```

In this example, three observables are created as subjects, as well as a higher-order observable (also created as a subject). The higher-order observable is subscribed after the `switch_latest` operator. This higher-order observable emits the three other observables. Each of these observables emits three items, but with the emission of the next observable interleaved on the higher-order observable.

This example gives the following result:

```
on_next 1: 1
on_next 1: 2
on_next 2: 1
on_next 2: 2
on_next 3: 1
on_next 3: 2
```

Only the first two items of each observable are received. This is the expected result since the third item is always emitted after another observable is emitted on the higher-order observable. So, the `switch_latest` operator unsubscribes the corresponding observable before the third item is emitted.

The zip operator

The `zip` operator combines items emitted by several observables, one by one. Each time all the source observables emit one item, then these items are combined as another item emitted on the output observable. The following figure shows the marble diagram of this operator:

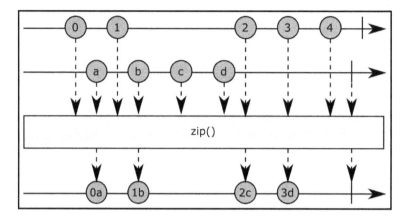

Figure 9.15: The zip operator

This operator can be used both as a method or a static method. Its prototype is the following:

```
Observable.zip(self, *args)
Observable.zip(cls, *args)
```

Here, several observables can be provided as `args`. The last parameter provided must be a function that combines the items of all the source observable items.

Here is an example of the `zip` operator:

```
numbers = Observable.from_([1, 2, 3, 4])
characters = Observable.from_(['a', 'b', 'c', 'd' ,'e'])

characters.zip(numbers, lambda c, n: "{}: {}".format(c, n)).subscribe(
    on_next = lambda i: print("on_next {}".format(i)),
    on_error = lambda e: print("on_error: {}".format(e)),
    on_completed = lambda: print("on_completed")
)
```

This example gives the following result:

```
on_next a: 1
on_next b: 2
on_next c: 3
on_next d: 4
on_completed
```

Each item is correctly combined, pairwise.

The zip_list operator

The `zip_list` operator behaves like the `zip` operator, but its output items are lists instead of a combination of the source items. Each list item contains all items emitted by the source observables. The following figure shows the marble diagram of the `zip_list` operator:

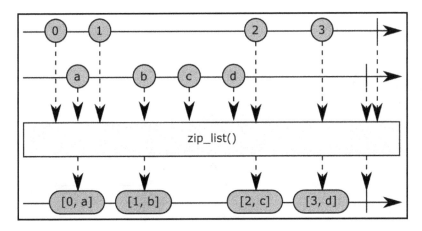

Figure 9.16: The zip_list operator

Its prototype is the following:

```
Observable.zip_list(cls, *args)
```

Here, all the observables to be combined are provided as arguments.

Here is an example of the `zip_list` operator:

```
numbers = Observable.from_([1, 2, 3, 4])
characters = Observable.from_(['a', 'b', 'c', 'd' ,'e'])

Observable.zip_list(characters, numbers).subscribe(
    on_next = lambda i: print("on_next {}".format(i)),
    on_error = lambda e: print("on_error: {}".format(e)),
    on_completed = lambda: print("on_completed")
)
```

This example gives the following result:

```
on_next ['a', 1]
on_next ['b', 2]
on_next ['c', 3]
on_next ['d', 4]
on_completed
```

Each item of the two source observables is combined pairwise, and returned in lists.

Utility operators

The operators listed here provide usual operations when working with observables. Some of them have already been covered in the previous chapters. They are the following ones:

Operator	Description	Chapter
observe_on	Changes the scheduler being used on the following operators	5
subscribe_on	Sets the scheduler being used by the root observable	5

The delay operator

The `delay` operator delays the emission of the source observable items by a specified time. The following figure shows the marble diagram of this operator:

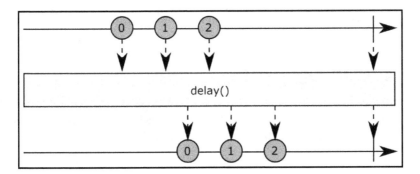

Figure 9.17: The delay operator

Its prototype is the following:

```
Observable.delay(self, duetime, scheduler=None)
```

Here, the `duetime` parameter is the delay to apply in milliseconds. The `scheduler` parameter can be used to specify a scheduler to use. If no scheduler is provided, then the timeout scheduler is used.

Here is an example of the delay operator:

```
numbers = Observable.just(1)

print("{}".format(datetime.datetime.now()))
numbers.delay(200).subscribe(
    on_next = lambda i: print("on_next {}: {}"
        .format(i, datetime.datetime.now())),
    on_error = lambda e: print("on_error: {}".format(e)),
    on_completed = lambda: print("on_completed")
)
time.sleep(0.5)
```

In this example, the `numbers` operator emits just one item, and its emission is delayed by 200 milliseconds.

This example gives the following result:

```
2018-08-15 23:43:39.426395
on_next 1: 2018-08-15 23:43:39.628009
on_completed
```

Here, the item is received 200 milliseconds after the subscription.

The do_action operator

The `do_action` operator allows us to execute a function each time an item is emitted on the source observable. This operator emits the same items as those received as input. The following figure shows the marble diagram of this operator:

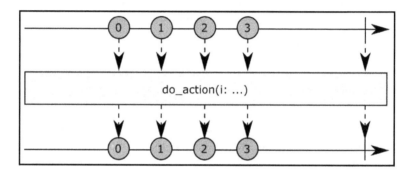

Figure 9.18: The do_action operator

Its prototype is the following:

```
Observable.do_action(self,
     on_next=None,
     on_error=None,
     on_completed=None,
     observer=None)
```

Here, `on_next`, `on_error`, and `on_completed` are functions called each time the following occur:

- An item is received from the source observable
- An error is received from the source observable
- The source observable completes

The `observer` parameter can be provided to forward all these events to `observer`.

Here is an example of the `do_action` operator:

```
numbers = Observable.from_([1, 2, 3])

numbers.do_action(lambda i: print("action")).subscribe(
    on_next = lambda i: print("on_next {}".format(i)),
    on_error = lambda e: print("on_error: {}".format(e)),
    on_completed = lambda: print("on_completed")
)
```

This example gives the following result:

```
action
on_next 1
action
on_next 2
action
on_next 3
on_completed
```

The materialize/dematerialize operators

The `materialize` and `dematerialize` operators allow us to serialize/deserialize an observable's events. The `on_next`, `on_completed`, and `on_error` events can be converted to items and back. The following figure shows the marble diagram of the `materialize` operator:

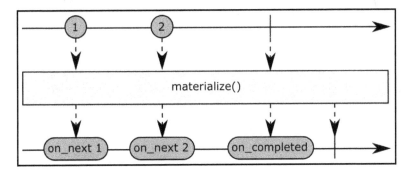

Figure 9.19: The materialize operator

The following figure shows the marble diagram of the `dematerialize` operator:

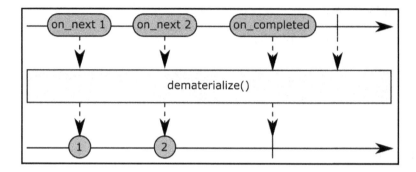

Figure 9.20: The dematerialize operator

The prototype of the `materialize` operator is the following:

```
Observable.materialize(self)
```

The prototype of the `dematerialize` operator is the following:

```
Observable.dematerialize(self)
```

Here is an example of the `materialize` operator:

```
numbers = Observable.from_([1, 2, 3, 4])

numbers.materialize().subscribe(
    on_next = lambda i: print("on_next {}".format(i)),
    on_error = lambda e: print("on_error: {}".format(e)),
    on_completed = lambda: print("on_completed")
)
```

This example gives the following result:

```
on_next OnNext(1)
on_next OnNext(2)
on_next OnNext(3)
on_next OnNext(4)
on_next OnCompleted()
on_completed
```

The four numbers are received wrapped in `OnNext` objects. Then, an `OnCompleted` item is received before the observable completes. So, all events of the observable have been received as items. These wrapped items are defined in the `rx.core.notification` module. They can then be used by the `dematerialize` operator this way:

```
from rx.core.notification import OnNext, OnCompleted

numbers = Observable.from_([OnNext(1), OnNext(2), OnNext(3), OnNext(4),
OnCompleted()])

numbers.dematerialize().subscribe(
    on_next = lambda i: print("on_next {}".format(i)),
    on_error = lambda e: print("on_error: {}".format(e)),
    on_completed = lambda: print("on_completed")
)
```

This gives the following result:

```
on_next 1
on_next 2
on_next 3
on_next 4
on_completed
```

The four numbers are received as items, and the `OnCompleted` item is transformed to a completion event.

The time_interval operator

The `time_interval` operator measures the time that has elapsed between two emissions of items. The following figure shows the marble diagram for this operator:

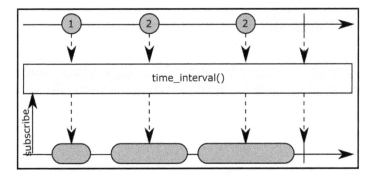

Figure 9.21: The time_interval operator

The prototype of this operator is the following:

```
Observable.time_interval(self, scheduler=None)
```

Here, `scheduler` is the scheduler to use to measure the interval. If no scheduler is provided, then the timeout scheduler is used. The `time_interval` operator emits items of type `TimeInterval`. They contain two properties:

- `value`, which contains the value of the source item
- `interval`, which contains a `datetime.timedelta` object

Here is an example of this operator:

```
numbers = Subject()

numbers.time_interval().subscribe(
    on_next = lambda i: print("on_next {}: {}".format(i.value,
i.interval)),
    on_error = lambda e: print("on_error: {}".format(e)),
    on_completed = lambda: print("on_completed")
)
numbers.on_next(1)
numbers.on_next(2)
time.sleep(0.1)
numbers.on_next(3)
time.sleep(0.2)
numbers.on_next(4)
```

The first two objects are emitted immediately. The third item is emitted after a delay of 100 milliseconds, and the fourth item after another delay of 200 milliseconds.

This example gives the following result:

```
on_next 1: 0:00:00.000155
on_next 2: 0:00:00.000305
on_next 3: 0:00:00.100798
on_next 4: 0:00:00.204477
```

This is the expected result: items 1 and 2 are received almost at the same time, item 3 is received 100 milliseconds after item 2, and item 4 is received 200 milliseconds after item 3.

The timeout operator

The `timeout` operator raises an error if no item is received on the source observable after some time has elapsed. The following figure shows the marble diagram of this operator:

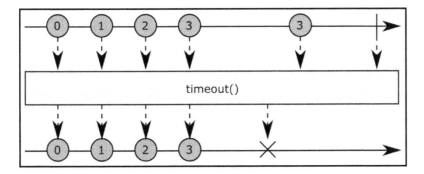

Figure 9.22: The timeout operator

Its prototype is the following:

```
Observable.timeout(self, duetime, other=None, scheduler=None)
```

The `duetime` parameter is the delay in milliseconds after an error is raised. The `other` parameter is an observable that must be emitted in the case of timeout. If the `other` observable is not provided, then a `Timeout` error is raised. The `scheduler` parameter allows us to provide a different scheduler from the default one. If this is not provided, then the timeout scheduler is used.

Here is an example of the `timeout` operator:

```
numbers = Subject()

numbers.timeout(300).subscribe(
    on_next = lambda i: print("on_next {}".format(i)),
    on_error = lambda e: print("on_error: {}".format(e)),
    on_completed = lambda: print("on_completed")
)
numbers.on_next(1)
numbers.on_next(2)
time.sleep(0.5)
numbers.on_next(3)
numbers.on_next(4)
```

The `timeout` operator is configured to 300 milliseconds, and a delay of 500 milliseconds is forced between the emission of items 2 and 3.

This example gives the following result:

```
on_next 1
on_next 2
on_error: Timeout
```

An error is effectively raised before item 3 is emitted.

The timestamp operator

The timestamp operator adds a timestamp to each item emitted. The following figure shows the marble diagram of this operator:

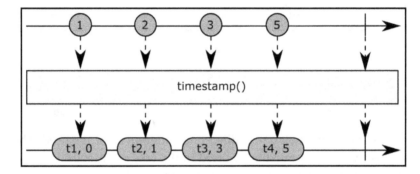

Figure 9.23: The timestamp operator

Its prototype is the following:

```
Observable.timestamp(self, scheduler=None)
```

An alternative scheduler can be provided with the scheduler parameter. If no scheduler parameter is provided, then the timeout scheduler is used.

Here is an example of the timestamp scheduler:

```
numbers = Subject()

numbers.timestamp().subscribe(
    on_next = lambda i: print("on_next {}: {}".format(i.value,
i.timestamp)),
    on_error = lambda e: print("on_error: {}".format(e)),
    on_completed = lambda: print("on_completed")
)
numbers.on_next(1)
time.sleep(0.1)
```

```
numbers.on_next(2)
time.sleep(0.1)
numbers.on_next(3)
time.sleep(0.1)
numbers.on_next(4)
```

This gives the following result:

```
on_next 1: 2018-08-15 21:53:18.642451
on_next 2: 2018-08-15 21:53:18.746261
on_next 3: 2018-08-15 21:53:18.847760
on_next 4: 2018-08-15 21:53:18.948793
```

The four items are received with a delay of 100 milliseconds between each.

The using operator

The `using` operator allows us to associate the lifetime of a resource with the lifetime of an observable. The following figure shows the marble diagram of this operator:

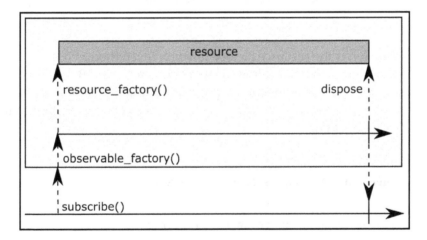

Figure 9.24: The using operator

When called, the `using` operator creates an observable and a `resource` object. The observable is created via a factory function. When the observable completes, then the `resource` object is automatically disposed of.

Its prototype is the following:

```
Observable.using(cls, resource_factory, observable_factory)
```

This operator is a factory operator; it creates an observable via the `observable_factory` parameter. `resource_factory` is a function that will be called to create the `resource` object. This function must return a disposable object so that the resource can be disposed of when the observable completes.

Here is an example of the `using` operator:

```
from rx.disposables import AnonymousDisposable

def resource():
    print("create resource at {}".format(datetime.datetime.now()))
    def dispose():
        print("dispose resource at {}".format(datetime.datetime.now()))
    return AnonymousDisposable(dispose)


Observable.using(resource,
                 lambda r: Observable.just(1).delay(200)).subscribe(
    on_next = lambda i: print("on_next {}".format(i)),
    on_error = lambda e: print("on_error: {}".format(e)),
    on_completed = lambda: print("on_completed")
)
time.sleep(500)
```

The `resource` function is the resource factory function (even though it does nothing useful here). The nested `dispose` function allows us to free this resource. It is returned as a disposable object. This `resource` function is provided as the first parameter of the `using` operator. The second parameter is `lambda`, which creates an observable that completes 200 milliseconds after its creation.

This example gives the following result:

```
create resource at 2018-08-16 00:04:24.491232
on_next 1
on_completed
dispose resource at 2018-08-16 00:04:24.694836
```

The `resource` function is called when the `using` operator is called, the observable completes 200 milliseconds afterward, and the `dispose` function is called.

The to_list operator

The `to_list` operator converts an observable sequence to a single item that contains all the items emitted by the source observable, wrapped in a list. The following figure shows the marble diagram of this operator:

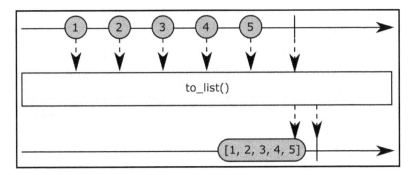

Figure 9.25: The to_list operator

Its prototype is the following:

```
numbers = Observable.from_([1, 2, 3, 4])

numbers.to_list().subscribe(
    on_next = lambda i: print("on_next {}".format(i)),
    on_error = lambda e: print("on_error: {}".format(e)),
    on_completed = lambda: print("on_completed")
)
```

This example gives the following result:

```
on_next [1, 2, 3, 4]
on_completed
```

Only one item is received, containing the source sequence as a list.

There are several variants of this operator:

- `to_set` converts a sequence to a set
- `to_dict` converts a sequence to a dictionary

Conditional operators

The operators listed here provide ways to apply conditions on observables or items emitted.

The all operator

The `all` operator indicates whether all items emitted in the source observable meet some criteria. The following figure shows the marble diagram of this operator:

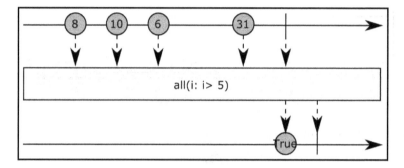

Figure 9.26: The all operator

Its prototype is the following:

```
Observable.all(self, predicate)
```

Here, the `predicate` parameter is a function called for each item emitted by the source observable. If the `predicate` function returns `True` for all items emitted on the source observable, then the operator emits a `True` item. Otherwise, it emits a `False` item.

Here is an example of the `all` operator:

```
numbers = Observable.from_([11, 12, 13, 14])

numbers.all(lambda i: i > 10).subscribe(
    on_next = lambda i: print("on_next {}".format(i)),
    on_error = lambda e: print("on_error: {}".format(e)),
    on_completed = lambda: print("on_completed")
)
```

The example gives the following result:

```
on_next True
on_completed
```

Since the values of all items emitted on the `numbers` observable are more than `10`, the `all` operator emits a `True` item.

The amb operator

The `amb` operator emits items from the first observable of two that emits an item first. The following figure shows the marble diagram of this operator:

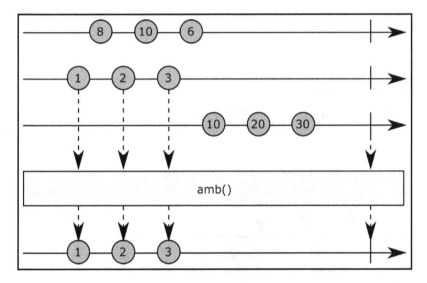

Figure 9.27: The amb operator

Its prototype is the following:

```
Observable.amb(self, right_source)
```

The `right_source` parameter is the second observable to watch.

Here is an example of the `amb` operator:

```
first = Subject()
second = Subject()

first.amb(second).subscribe(
```

```
    on_next = lambda i: print("on_next {}".format(i)),
    on_error = lambda e: print("on_error: {}".format(e)),
    on_completed = lambda: print("on_completed")
)
first.on_next(1)
second.on_next(2)
first.on_completed()
```

In this example, the `first` observable emits an item before the `second` observable.

This example gives the following result:

```
on_next 1
on_completed
```

The items emitted by the `amb` operator are those of the `first` observable because it is the first to emit an item.

The contains operator

The `contains` operator emits a `True` item if the source observable contains a specific item. Otherwise, it returns a `False` item. The following figure shows the marble diagram of this operator:

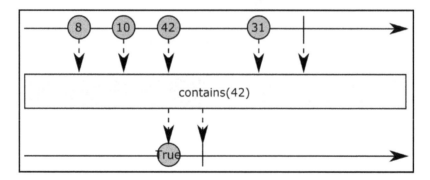

Figure 9.28: The contains operator

Its prototype is the following:

```
numbers = Observable.from_([1, 2, 3, 4])

numbers.contains(3).subscribe(
    on_next = lambda i: print("on_next {}".format(i)),
    on_error = lambda e: print("on_error: {}".format(e)),
```

```
    on_completed = lambda: print("on_completed")
)
```

This example gives the following result:

```
on_next True
on_completed
```

The default_if_empty operator

The `default_if_empty` operator emits an item if the source observable is empty. The following figure shows the marble diagram of this operator:

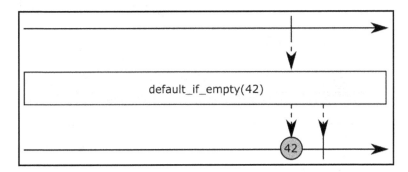

Figure 9.29: The default_if_empty operator

Its prototype is the following:

```
Observable.default_if_empty(self, default_value=None)
```

Here, `default_value` is the value to emit if the source observable is empty. If no value is provided, then an item with the `None` value is emitted when the source observable is empty.

Here is an example of this operator:

```
empty = Observable.empty()

empty.default_if_empty("default").subscribe(
    on_next = lambda i: print("on_next {}".format(i)),
    on_error = lambda e: print("on_error: {}".format(e)),
    on_completed = lambda: print("on_completed")
)
```

This example gives the following result:

```
on_next default
on_completed
```

The sequence_equal operator

The `sequence_equal` operator emits a `True` item if two observables' sequences are the same. Otherwise, it emits a `False` item. The following figure shows the marble diagram of this operator:

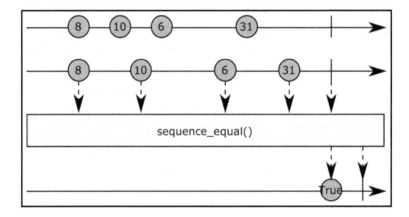

Figure 9.30: The sequence_equal operator

Its prototype is the following:

```
Observable.sequence_equal(self, second, comparer=None)
```

The `second` parameter contains the other observable to compare. The `comparer` parameter is a function being used to compare two items. Its default value is the equality operator.

Here is an example of this operator:

```
numbers = Observable.from_([1, 2, 3, 4])
compare = Observable.from_([1, 2, 3, 4])

numbers.sequence_equal(compare).subscribe(
    on_next = lambda i: print("on_next {}".format(i)),
    on_error = lambda e: print("on_error: {}".format(e)),
    on_completed = lambda: print("on_completed")
)
```

This example gives the following result:

```
on_next True
on_completed
```

The skip_until operator

The `skip_until` operator skips items emitted by a source observable until an item is emitted by another observable. The following figure shows the marble diagram of this operator:

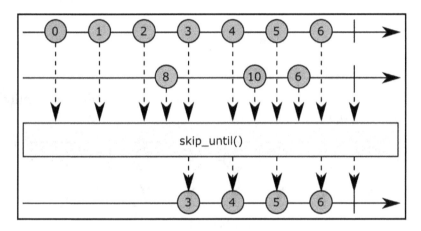

Figure 9.31: The skip_until operator

Its prototype is the following:

```
Observable.skip_until(self, other)
```

Here, `other` is an observable being used to stop skipping items from the source observable.

Here is an example of the `skip_until` operator:

```
numbers = Subject()
trigger = Subject()

numbers.skip_until(trigger).subscribe(
    on_next = lambda i: print("on_next {}".format(i)),
    on_error = lambda e: print("on_error: {}".format(e)),
    on_completed = lambda: print("on_completed")
)
numbers.on_next(1)
```

```
numbers.on_next(2)
trigger.on_next(True)
numbers.on_next(3)
numbers.on_next(4)
numbers.on_completed()
```

The `numbers` observable emits two items before the `trigger` observable emits an item. Then, the `numbers` observable emits items 3 and 4.

This example gives the following result:

```
on_next 3
on_next 4
on_completed
```

The skip_while operator

The `skip_while` operator skips items emitted from the source observable until the criteria are met. The following figure shows the marble diagram of this operator:

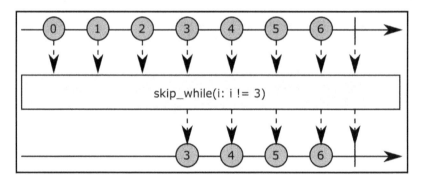

Figure 9.32: The skip_while operator

Its prototype is the following:

```
Observable.skip_while(self, predicate)
```

Here, `predicate` is a function being called each time an item is emitted from the source observable. When the `predicate` function returns `True`, then the `skip_while` operator starts emitting items of the source observable.

Here is an example of the `skip_while` operator:

```
numbers = Observable.from_([1, 2, 3, 4])

numbers.skip_while(lambda i: i < 2).subscribe(
    on_next = lambda i: print("on_next {}".format(i)),
    on_error = lambda e: print("on_error: {}".format(e)),
    on_completed = lambda: print("on_completed")
)
```

This example gives the following result:

```
on_next 2
on_next 3
on_next 4
on_completed
```

The take_until operator

The `take_until` operator emits items from its source observable until another observable emits an item. The following figure shows the marble diagram of this operator:

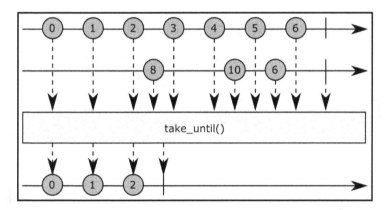

Figure 9.33: The take_until operator

Its prototype is the following:

```
Observable.take_until(self, other)
```

Here, `other` is an observable used to stop emitting items from the source observable.

Here is an example of the `take_until` operator:

```
numbers = Subject()
trigger = Subject()

numbers.take_until(trigger).subscribe(
    on_next = lambda i: print("on_next {}".format(i)),
    on_error = lambda e: print("on_error: {}".format(e)),
    on_completed = lambda: print("on_completed")
)
numbers.on_next(1)
numbers.on_next(2)
trigger.on_next(True)
numbers.on_next(3)
numbers.on_next(4)
numbers.on_completed()
```

This example gives the following result:

```
on_next 1
on_next 2
on_completed
```

The take_while operator

The `take_while` operator emits items from the source observable until a criterion is met. The following figure shows the marble diagram of this operator:

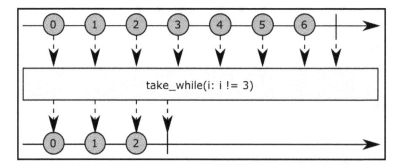

Figure 9.34: The take_while operator

Its prototype is the following:

```
Observable.take_while(self, predicate)
```

Here, `predicate` is a function called each time an item is emitted form the source observable. When the `predicate` function returns `True`, then the `take_while` operator stops emitting items of the source observable.

Here is an example of the `take_while` operator:

```
numbers = Observable.from_([1, 2, 3, 4])

numbers.take_while(lambda i: i < 2).subscribe(
    on_next = lambda i: print("on_next {}".format(i)),
    on_error = lambda e: print("on_error: {}".format(e)),
    on_completed = lambda: print("on_completed")
)
```

This example gives the following result:

```
on_next 1
on_completed
```

Mathematical operators

The operators listed here implement some basic mathematical operations, as well as being building blocks to implement any kind of computation on items.

The average operator

The `average` operator computes the average value of all items emitted on the source observable. The following figure shows the marble diagram of this operator:

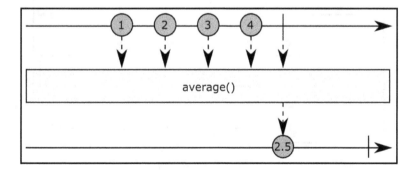

Figure 9.35: The average operator

Its prototype is the following:

```
Observable.average(self, key_selector=None)
```

Here, the `key_selector` argument is a transform function that returns the value to average from an item. If no `key_selector` is provided, then the item itself is used.

Here is an example of the `average` operator:

```
numbers = Observable.from_([1, 2, 3, 4])

numbers1.average().subscribe(
    on_next = lambda i: print("on_next {}".format(i)),
    on_error = lambda e: print("on_error: {}".format(e)),
    on_completed = lambda: print("on_completed")
)
```

This example gives the following result:

```
on_next 2.5
on_completed
```

The concat operator

The `concat` operator concatenates several observables. Each observable is concatenated to the previous one as soon as the previous observable completes. The following figure shows the marble diagram of this operator:

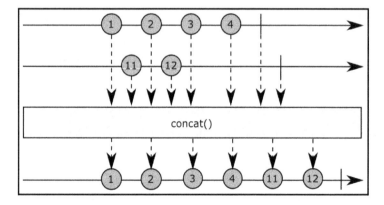

Figure 9.36: The concat operator

This operator can be used both as a class method and a static method. Its prototypes are the following ones:

```
Observable.concat(self, *args)
Observable.concat(cls, *args)
```

Here, `args` is either several observables to concatenate, or a list of observables.

Here is an example of the `concat` operator:

```
numbers1 = Observable.from_([1, 2, 3, 4])
numbers2 = Observable.from_([11, 12])

numbers1.concat(numbers2).subscribe(
    on_next = lambda i: print("on_next {}".format(i)),
    on_error = lambda e: print("on_error: {}".format(e)),
    on_completed = lambda: print("on_completed")
)
```

This example gives the following results:

```
on_next  1
on_next  2
on_next  3
on_next  4
on_next  11
on_next  12
on_completed
```

The count operator

The `count` operator counts the number of items in the source observable that meet some criteria. The following figure shows the marble diagram of this operator:

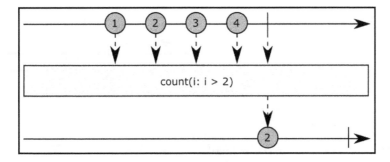

Figure 9.37: The count operator

Its prototype is the following:

```
Observable.count(self, predicate=None)
```

Here, the `predicate` argument is a function that returns `True` if the item must be counted, or `False` otherwise.

Here is an example of the `count` operator:

```
numbers = Observable.from_([1, 2, 3, 4])

numbers.count(lambda i: i > 2).subscribe(
    on_next = lambda i: print("on_next {}".format(i)),
    on_error = lambda e: print("on_error: {}".format(e)),
    on_completed = lambda: print("on_completed")
)
```

This example gives the following result:

```
on_next 2
on_completed
```

The max operator

The `max` operator emits the item of the source observable that contains the maximum value of the whole sequence. The following figure shows the marble diagram of this operator:

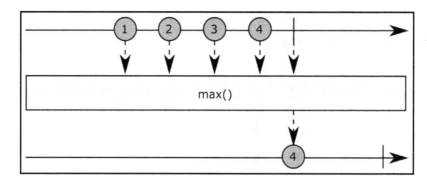

Figure 9.38: The max operator

Its prototype is the following:

```
Observable.max(self, comparer=None)
```

Here, the `comparer` parameter is a function being used to compare items. If no `comparer` is provided, then the equality operator is used.

Here is an example of the `max` operator:

```
numbers = Observable.from_([1, 2, 3, 4])

numbers.max().subscribe(
    on_next = lambda i: print("on_next {}".format(i)),
    on_error = lambda e: print("on_error: {}".format(e)),
    on_completed = lambda: print("on_completed")
)
```

This example gives the following result:

```
on_next 4
on_completed
```

The min operator

The `min` operator emits the item of the source observable that contains the minimum value of the whole sequence. The following figure shows the marble diagram of this operator:

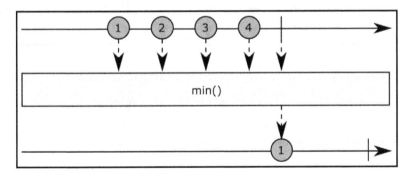

Figure 9.39: The min operator

Its prototype is the following:

```
Observable.min(self, comparer=None)
```

Here, the `comparer` parameter is a function being used to compare items. If no `comparer` is provided, then the equality operator is used.

Here is an example of the `min` operator:

```
numbers = Observable.from_([1, 2, 3, 4])

numbers.min().subscribe(
    on_next = lambda i: print("on_next {}".format(i)),
    on_error = lambda e: print("on_error: {}".format(e)),
    on_completed = lambda: print("on_completed")
)
```

This example gives the following result:

```
on_next 1
on_completed
```

The reduce operator

The `reduce` operator performs some computations over all the items of the source observable and emits a single item that contains the result of this computation. The following figure shows the marble diagram of this operator:

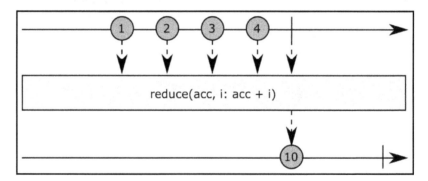

Figure 9.40: The reduce operator

Its prototype is the following:

```
Observable.reduce(self, accumulator, seed=None)
```

The `accumulator` parameter is a function that implements a computation on each item. This function takes two parameters: the accumulated (`acc`) value and the item (`i`). Its prototype is this one:

```
def accumulator(acc, i)
```

This function must return the new accumulated value.

The `seed` parameter allows us to set the initial value of `accumulator`. In cases where the source observable emits no items, then this value is also the one emitted by the `reduce` operator.

Here is an example of the `reduce` operator:

```
numbers = Observable.from_([1, 2, 3, 4])

numbers1.reduce(lambda acc, i: acc + i, seed=0).subscribe(
    on_next = lambda i: print("on_next {}".format(i)),
    on_error = lambda e: print("on_error: {}".format(e)),
    on_completed = lambda: print("on_completed")
)
```

The example gives the following result:

```
on_next 10
on_completed
```

Note that this operator is roughly equivalent to `scan().last()`.

The sum operator

The `sum` operator computes the sum of all items emitted by the source observable. The following figure shows the marble diagram of this operator:

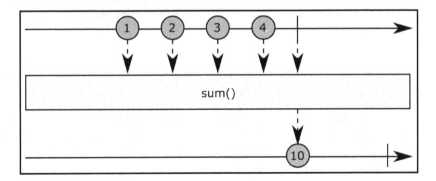

Figure 9.41: The sum operator

Its prototype is the following:

```
Observable.sum(self, key_selector=None)
```

Here, the `key_selector` argument is a transform function that returns the value to `sum` from an item. If no `key_selector` is provided, then the item itself is used.

Here is an example of the `sum` operator:

```
numbers = Observable.from_([1, 2, 3, 4])

numbers1.sum().subscribe(
    on_next = lambda i: print("on_next {}".format(i)),
    on_error = lambda e: print("on_error: {}".format(e)),
    on_completed = lambda: print("on_completed")
)
```

This example gives the following result:

```
on_next 10
on_completed
```

Summary

Here we are; with approximately 80 ReactiveX operators covered, you should now have all the keys to implement a reactive application by creating, combining, filtering, or implementing any logic.

Being at ease with all these operators is one of the difficult parts of ReactiveX. The framework contains many operators, sometimes with confusing names, and sometimes with similar names but different behaviors. Moreover, the 80 operators covered here are only half of all the available operators in RxPY! However, most of the remaining ones are variants of the ones described here.

This chapter can be used as a quick reference to find the operator adapted to each use case. Hopefully, for each operator, the example provided with the description should also help you to clearly understand how and when to use the operator.

Some operators can be difficult to comprehend. They are usually the ones that work on higher-order observables. If you do not understand them at first, do not give up on using RxPY. This is part of the ReactiveX learning curve, and you can come back to them once you are familiar with all the basic operators.

The next chapter will focus on another important area of any framework: testing and debugging. As you will see, if functional programming and ReactiveX help in writing testable code, it lacks facilities for debugging.

Questions

- How can you print something each time an item is emitted?
- How can you compute a value from all the items of an observable?
- How can you subscribe to the latest observable emitted by a higher-order observable?
- How can you combine the values of several observables, item-wise?
- How can you retrieve the first item of an observable?
- How can you classify the items of an observable, based on some criteria?
- How can you drop some elements of an observable, based on some criteria?
- How can you chain several observables, one after the other?

Further reading

The official ReactiveX documentation contains a list of all operators implemented for all supported programming languages. When you need an operator not listed here, refer to this documentation before trying to implement it: `http://reactivex.io/documentation/operators.html`.

10
Testing and Debugging

Testing has been mentioned a lot of times in previous chapters, especially while stating that ReactiveX and functional programming ease code testing. So, the time has come to see how to test RxPY code. This chapter is composed of three parts, each of which explain how to test and debug an RxPY application:

- The first part is dedicated to **testing**: what testing is, how to do it in Python, and how to apply it to RxPY and AsyncIO code
- The second part explains the importance of **logging**, and presents a possible way to implement it in a functional application
- Finally, the third part describes **debugging** an RxPY application and how to use the debug tools available in AsyncIO

Testing

Testing is a whole topic in itself and many books, blogs, and websites are dedicated to it. The testing field has changed a lot since the beginning of the century: the testing industry evolved from manual validation (sometimes with even no test plan), to a heavily automated process. Automation is great in testing because it allows us to execute many tests in very little time. So, automated tests can be executed more often (on each commit instead of each release, for example). As a consequence, bugs are detected more rapidly, and fixing them is easier. At the end, the product is better and the developer can spend more time implementing new features.

Testing can mean many different things because there are different kinds of test:

- Unit tests verify that each function of the application works as expected
- Integration tests verify that the application works correctly with the other components it depends on
- System tests verify that the application works when being deployed

This chapter is dedicated to unit tests, for three reasons:

- This is the first level in the testing chain. So it means that any bugs found in this step cost less to fix than in the other testing phases. The earlier, the better. So all bugs detected with unit tests save time and money.
- The Python standard library contains a module dedicated to this kind of testing.
- With functional programming, unit tests can cover a big part of the application logic. So a good code coverage with unit tests can sometimes detect bugs that would be seen in system tests with other programming paradigms. The following figure shows the bug cost curve depending on when bugs are detected:

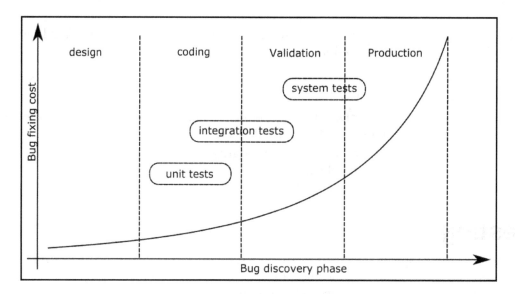

Figure 10.1: The cost curve of bug discovery

Unit tests are, by design, autonomous tests. So they can be executed easily by the developer during coding sessions, but also automatically in a continuous integration process. The five principles of unit tests are the following, abbreviated as **F.I.R.S.T**:

- **Fast**: Executing unit tests is fast. They must take, at most, a few seconds so that they can be executed during code development.
- **Independent**: Unit tests are independent of each other.
- **Reproducible**: Given the same code as input, a unit test always provides the same result.
- **Self-Validating**: A unit test indicates whether it passed or failed.

- **Timely**: Tests are written when appropriate, ideally before implementing the functionality. This principle comes from the TDD methodology, but is very accurate—writing a test before the feature allows us to check that the test fails when the feature does not work.

Introduction to Python unit testing

Python has built-in support for unit tests, with the `unittest` module of the standard library. This module contains all the features needed to easily write unit tests. However, running tests directly with this module is cumbersome. Some other tools allow us to simplify this step. In this chapter, the `nosetests` tool will be used. It is available in PyPI, and can be installed in the following way:

```
(venv-rx) $ pip3 install nose
```

Okay, now let's see how to write and execute a very simple test, before testing some ReactiveX code. First, the `TestCase` class must be imported:

```
from unittest import TestCase
```

A test case is a group of tests. The usual way to use them is to write one test case per class or feature. A new test case is defined by declaring a new class that will inherit from the `TestCase` class, as can be seen in the following example:

```
class MyTestCase(TestCase):

    def test_example(self):
        self.assertEqual(3, 1 + 1)
```

In this example, the `MyTestCase` test case is defined. It contains only one test: `test_example`. All tests must have their names prefixed with `test_`. Each `test_` method in a test case is the implementation of a test. A test case can have many checks in it. In this example, the `test_example` checks that 3 is equal to `1 + 1` (which is wrong).

Checking for a test result is done with assertions. In this example the `assertEqual` assertion is used. This assertion checks that the two parameters are equal. If they are equal, then the assertion passes; otherwise, the test fails. If all assertions of a test pass, then the test passes.

This example is available in the GitHub repository (https://github.com/PacktPublishing/Hands-On-Reactive-Programming-with-Python) of this book, in the `test_base.py` script.

Running this test is done as follows:

```
(venv-rx) $ nosetests test_base.py
```

It gives the following result:

```
F
========================================================================
FAIL: test_example (test_base.MyTestCase)
------------------------------------------------------------------------
Traceback (most recent call last):
  File "/xxx/Hands-On-Reactive-Programming-with-Python/ch10/test_base.py",
line 7, in test_example
    self.assertEqual(3, 1 + 1)
AssertionError: 3 != 2


------------------------------------------------------------------------

Ran 1 test in 0.001s

FAILED (failures=1)
```

The first F letter being printed means that a test has failed. When several tests are executed, then each passed test is printed with a dot. Then the reason for the failure is printed, with the line that caused the failure. In this case, the error is that 3 is different from 2. With the error being fixed, the test passes.

Using assertions allows us to create tests that are self-validating. Many assertions are available, covering all needs. The main ones are detailed here:

- `assertEqual(a, b)`/`assertNotEqual(a, b)`: Checks that two objects are equal or different, by using the equality operator
- `assertTrue(a)`/`assertFalse(a)`: Checks that the provided object is true or false
- `assertIs(a, b)`/`assertIsNot(a, b)`: Checks that object a is of type b, or not of type b
- `assertIsNone(a)`/`assertIsNotNone(a)`: Checks that the value of a is none, or not
- `assertIn(a, b)`/`assertNotIn(a, b)`: Checks that a is in b (with the Python In operator), or not in b
- `assertIsInstance(a, b)`/`assertNotIsInstance(a, b)`: Checks that a is an instance of b, or not an instance of b
- `assertRaises(exc, fun, *args, **kwds)`: Checks that the execution of fun with args and kwds as parameters raises the exc exception

Dependency injection versus mock

Another aspect that quickly appears in unit testing is how to manage dependencies. Let's consider the simple case of a **function** with an **input** and an **output**, as shown in the following figure:

Figure 10.2: A function data flow

Testing such a **function** is easy. It is very similar to the previous example. However, in many cases, a **function** (or a class method) has dependencies, as shown in the following figure:

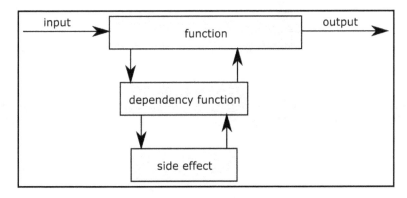

Figure 10.3: A function with dependencies

In this case, a seemingly simple questions appears: what should be tested? Only the **function**? Or also the **dependency function**? Then how do we deal with the **side effect**? There is no unique answer to these questions. It always depends on what should be tested versus what is supposed to work. However, most of the time, the test boundary is set on the code of the package being written. Everything else is considered to be working, or tested somewhere else. So, if the **dependency function** is in the application package, then maybe it should really be called when testing the **function**. Otherwise, the call to the **dependency function** may be avoided, and replaced by a fake **function**.

There are two ways to do this: either with **dependency injection** or with **mocks**.

Mocks are a type of smart stub: they are replacement functions for the original function, and they can return whatever you choose, for each call. The `unittest` module contains a dedicated sub-module to implement mocks in Python. Mocks can be a very powerful way to handle dependencies in unit testing, but the way they are implemented in Python (compared to most other testing frameworks) is not easy to comprehend, and sometimes they can be difficult to configure correctly.

Dependency injection takes the issue the other way: instead of directly calling a **dependency function**, the tested **function** should receive it as an **input** parameter. This is shown in the following figure:

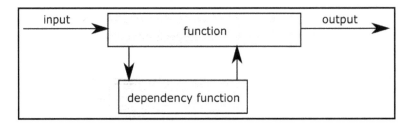

Figure 10.4: Dependency injection

The big advantage of testing such a pure code is the fact that the function now has the same signature as that on *Figure 10.2*. The drawback is that this can have a big impact on the design of the application.

Depending on the situation, dependency injection or mocks will be used to stub dependencies that must not be used in a test. However, when writing functional code, this situation occurs only with code external to the package. Moreover, splitting pure code and side-effects should further reduce the situations where dependency code should be stubbed.

Note that stubbing external code is not always necessary. As an example, stubbing the `json.loads` function to test the configuration parser of the audio transcoder would be overkill: it is a dependency, but there is no reason to stub it in any way.

Testing a custom operator

Now let's see how to test a custom operator. Consider the following code:

```
def integer_passthrough(numbers):
    def on_subscribe(observer):
        def on_next(i):
```

```
        if type(i) is int:
            observer.on_next(i)
        else:
            observer.on_error(TypeError("Item is not an integer"))

    disposable = numbers.subscribe(
        on_next=on_next,
        on_error= lambda e: observer.on_error(e),
        on_completed= lambda: observer.on_completed()
    )
    return disposable

    return Observable.create(on_subscribe)
```

The `integer_passthrough` function takes an observable of numbers as input and returns it directly. If a received item is not a number, then an error is raised. The nominal case can be tested in the following way:

```
def test_next(self):
    numbers = Observable.from_([1, 2, 3, 4])
    expected_numbers = [1, 2, 3, 4]
    expected_error = None
    actual_numbers = []
    actual_error = None

    def on_next(i):
        actual_numbers.append(i)

    def on_error(e):
        nonlocal actual_error
        actual_error = e

    integer_passthrough(numbers).subscribe(
        on_next=on_next,
        on_error=on_error
    )

    self.assertEqual(None, actual_error)
    self.assertEqual(expected_numbers, actual_numbers)
```

The callbacks provided to the `subscribe` call are used to keep track of all events that occurred: the emitted items, as well as the errors. The test simply compares the received values with the ones which are expected. Two asserts are used here:

- One to check that no error has been raised
- The other to check that the received numbers are the expected ones

Note that the `assertEqual` method compares two lists directly. This avoids comparing the list item per item.

Testing errors is done in a similar way:

```
def test_error_on_string(self):
    numbers = Observable.from_([1, 2, 'c', 4])
    expected_numbers = [1, 2]
    actual_numbers = []
    actual_error = None

    def on_next(i):
        actual_numbers.append(i)

    def on_error(e):
        nonlocal actual_error
        actual_error = e

    integer_passthrough(numbers).subscribe(
        on_next=on_next,
        on_error=on_error
    )

    self.assertEqual(None, actual_error)
    self.assertEqual(expected_numbers, actual_numbers)
```

Here, a character is provided in one item of the `numbers` observable. So it is expected that only the first two items are emitted. However, this version of the test does not check the error, so it fails. This can be seen in the following example:

```
(venv-rx)$ nosetests test_operator.py
F.
======================================================================
FAIL: test_error_on_string (test_operator.IntegerPassthroughTestCase)
----------------------------------------------------------------------
Traceback (most recent call last):
  File "/xxx/Hands-On-Reactive-Programming-with-
Python/ch10/test_operator.py", line 63, in test_error_on_string
    self.assertEqual(None, actual_error)
AssertionError: None != TypeError('Item is not an integer',)
-------------------- >> begin captured logging << --------------------
Rx: DEBUG: CurrentThreadScheduler.schedule(state=None)
Rx: DEBUG: CurrentThreadScheduler.schedule(state=None)
Rx: DEBUG: CurrentThreadScheduler.schedule(state=None)
Rx: DEBUG: CurrentThreadScheduler.schedule(state=None)
Rx: DEBUG: CurrentThreadScheduler.schedule(state=None)
--------------------- >> end captured logging << ---------------------
```

```
---------------------------------------------------------------
Ran 2 tests in 0.005s

FAILED (failures=1)
```

Fixing the test is done by replacing the first `assertEqual` statement with following line of code:

```
self.assertIsInstance(actual_error, TypeError)
```

Now, with the addition of the preceding line, the test passes:

```
(venv-rx) $ nosetests test_operator.py
..
---------------------------------------------------------------
Ran 2 tests in 0.004s

OK
```

Another test you can do on this operator is to check that it correctly forwards errors received on the source observable:

```
def test_forward_error(self):
    numbers = Observable.throw(ValueError())
    expected_numbers = []
    actual_numbers = []
    actual_error = None

    def on_next(i):
        actual_numbers.append(i)

    def on_error(e):
        nonlocal actual_error
        actual_error = e

    integer_passthrough(numbers).subscribe(
        on_next=on_next,
        on_error=on_error
    )

    self.assertIsInstance(actual_error, ValueError)
    self.assertEqual(expected_numbers, actual_numbers)
```

This test is very similar to the previous one, but this time the `numbers` observable directly throws an error.

This example is available in the GitHub repository (`https://github.com/PacktPublishing/Hands-On-Reactive-Programming-with-Python`) of this book, in the `test_operator.py` script.

Injecting asynchronous obervables

The previous example showed the principles of custom operator testing. However, in this example, the operator is working in a synchronous way. Fortunately, testing operators using several observables emitting items in an asynchronous way is also possible. The key is that the asynchronous part can be simulated, thanks to `Subject`.

The following example is a test for the `buffer` operator, where two observables are supposed to emit items in an asynchronous way. By using subjects, it is possible to simulate the order of arrival of each item on each observable:

```python
def test_nominal(self):
    numbers = Subject()
    windows = Subject()

    expected_numbers = [ [1, 2], [3, 4, 5]]
    expected_error = None
    actual_numbers = []
    actual_error = None

    def on_next(i):
        actual_numbers.append(i)

    def on_error(e):
        nonlocal actual_error
        actual_error = e

    numbers.buffer(windows).subscribe(
        on_next=on_next,
        on_error=on_error
    )

    numbers.on_next(1)
    numbers.on_next(2)
    windows.on_next(True)
    numbers.on_next(3)
    numbers.on_next(4)
    numbers.on_next(5)
```

```
        windows.on_next(True)

        self.assertEqual(None, actual_error)
        self.assertEqual(expected_numbers, actual_numbers)
```

Here, two items are first emitted on the `numbers` observable. Then the `windows` observable emits an item, which should complete a first buffer. Then three more items are emitted on the `numbers` observable, and another on the `windows` observable and complete a second buffer. Note that the test expects that two items are returned by the `buffer` operator to pass, which is the case here.

This example, completed with an error test, is available in the GitHub repository (`https://github.com/PacktPublishing/Hands-On-Reactive-Programming-with-Python`) of this book, in the `test_buffer.py` script.

Testing AsyncIO code

Python does not contain any specific features or modules to test asynchronous code. However, this is not really needed: it is possible to use the `unittest` module to test AsyncIO code quite easily. Each test can instantiate a new event loop, do the testing on it, and stop the event loop. Once the event loop is stopped, assertions can be done to check whether the test has passed or failed, as can be seen in the following example:

```
class AsyncIOTestCase(TestCase):
    def setUp(self):
        self.loop = asyncio.new_event_loop()
        asyncio.set_event_loop(self.loop)

    def tearDown(self):
        self.loop.stop()
        self.loop.close()

    def test_example(self):
        future = self.loop.create_future()

        expected_result = [42]
        expected_error = None
        actual_result = []
        actual_error = None

        def on_next(i):
            actual_result.append(i)

        def on_error(e):
```

```
            nonlocal actual_error
            actual_error = e

    def on_completed():
        self.loop.stop()

    Observable.from_future(future).subscribe(
        on_next=on_next,
        on_error=on_error,
        on_completed=on_completed
    )

    self.assertEqual([], actual_result)
    self.loop.call_soon(lambda: future.set_result(42))
    self.loop.run_forever()
    self.assertEqual(expected_result, actual_result)
```

The `setUp` and `tearDown` methods are called respectively before and after each test has been executed. The `setUp` method creates a new event loop. The `tearDown` method stops and closes the event loop. The event loop should already be stopped by the test at this step, but this is a safeguard to ensure that the event loop is stopped even if a test fails.

In this test, the event loop runs forever. It is, however, stopped as soon as the observable completes, which is an easy way to test that the `on_completed` event has been received. Before the event loop starts, a coroutine is scheduled from `lambda` wrapping `future`. When `future` completes, then the observable completes and the test can continue. Also, note the presence of a first assertion after the subscription: since nothing should have happened before `future` is completed, this assert checks that nothing has happened yet.

This example is available in the GitHub repository (`https://github.com/PacktPublishing/Hands-On-Reactive-Programming-with-Python`) of this book, in the `test_asyncio.py` script.

Logging

Logging is often an efficient way to start analyzing where an issue comes from. If most actions and errors can be logged easily in the application, then this can become a powerful tool to detect when errors occurred, and understand what happened.

However, for such a mechanism to be really useful, it has to rely on a real logging system, and not only debug traces that must be decommented manually. Fortunately, once again, Python comes with a complete logging system in the standard library. The `logging` module contains all the features needed to efficiently use logs:

- Configurable log levels
- Several logging namespaces
- The possibility to add new backends to process the logs

So, a good way to help find issues, both during testing and debugging, is to add logs to all important actions and all possible failures. The natural way to implement this is with a logging driver. Such a driver takes an observable of a log request as a sink, and uses the Python logging system to do the actual logging. Other drivers can use this logging driver by exposing another source observable that contains all the log requests. The following figure shows a reactivity diagram of this principle on the transcode driver:

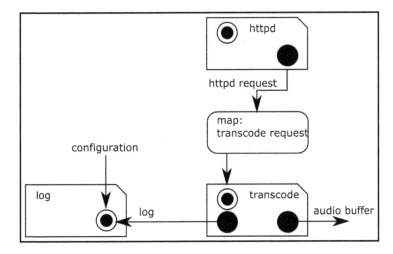

Figure 10.5: Logging via a dedicated driver

The **log** driver is a sink-only driver: it takes log requests as input, and does not return a source observable. The log driver also accepts **configuration** items as input: these items configure the level of each logger. The **transcode** driver now returns two source observables: the existing `response` observable, and a new `log` observable.

Using the Python logging module in this way has several benefits:

- The actual logging is independent of the configuration: each component that has to log some information just emits log requests.
- There is no overhead if nobody subscribed to the log sources (in this case the component does not emit any log request). This allows us to completely disable logging by not using the log driver.
- The configuration can be dynamic. Just like the transcode driver configuration is dynamic, it is possible to make the logging configuration dynamic. This allows us to change the debug level on-demand during production.

In practice, a log driver would accept items that look like this:

```
Log = namedtuple('Log', ['logger', 'level', 'message'])
```

In the previous example, `logger` is the name of the logger, `level` the level of the provided message, and `message` the information to the log. If components and drivers are written in dedicated modules, as was done in the audio transcode application, then the provided logger name can be just __name__, that is, the name of the module.

Emitting logs in the encode driver requires a few changes. First, a second `Source` observable is declared, as can be seen in the following example:

```
Source = namedtuple('Source', ['response', 'log'])
```

And this new `Source` is returned with two observables when the driver is called, as can be seen in the following code:

```
return Source(
    response=Observable.create(on_subscribe),
    log=Observable.create(on_log_subscribe)
)
```

The following code demonstrates how the `on_log_subscribe` function just stores the logs observer:

```
def encoder(sink):
    log_observer = None

    def on_log_subscribe(observer):
        nonlocal log_observer
        log_observer = observer
```

Then logs are created in the following way:

```
if log_observer is not None:
    log_observer.on_next(logging.Log(
        message="some information",
        level=DEBUG,
        logger=__name__
        ))
```

Not all parameters are needed (`level` and `logger` should be optional with default values), and this code block can be wrapped in a helper function so that it fits on one line. With these simple changes, an application can have dynamically configurable logs.

Debugging

ReactiveX is a great framework for writing asynchronous code, and unit tests. However, it also has an Achilles' heel, which is debugging. A common weakness of all ReactiveX implementations is debugging. This is basically an empty field, with no tool to easily help with tracking issues. This lack of debugging tools is also the reason why using a good logging system to help to track bugs is a good idea.

This will probably change in subsequent years. Several other frameworks based on streams or graphs include nice debugging tools. One example is the GStreamer tracing system, which allows us to track virtually every object moving in a graph. Another one is TensorFlow, where each operation can be named and graphs can be visualized, with great navigation features. But for now, the only option to track ReactiveX issues is to go back to the old basic trick: printing traces.

Adding traces

Debugging synchronous Python code is traditionally done with the Python debugger (`pdb` or `ipdb`). Unfortunately, this tool is almost useless in asynchronous code, and in reactive code. The reason is that in synchronous code when an exception is raised without being caught, the program stops. From that situation, using the debugger or just reading the printed stack trace allows going very quickly to the source of the error. However, with AsyncIO and ReactiveX the situation is different:

- On AsyncIO, an exception is propagated until the event loop. The event loop does not exit but interrupts the current task and prints the error. The rest of the application continues to run after that.

- On ReactiveX, an exception is transposed to an error event. So the observable completes on an error, and this error is propagated until an operator catches it.

In both cases, most of the time, the root of the error is not available when the call stack is finally dumped. So the debugger is of little help.

This is why adding traces is one of the few tools directly available in RxPY to see what is going on when debugging an issue. This can be done with the do_action operator, described in Chapter 9, *Operators in RxPY*. The first possible way to use it is by setting all three callbacks in each call, as can be seen in the following example:

```
.do_action(
    on_next=lambda i: print("trace: {}".format(i)),
    on_error=lambda e: print("trace: {}".format(e)),
    on_completed=lambda: print("trace: completed")
)
```

This snippet, which would be part of an observable chain, prints a trace for each event that occurs on the observable: next, error, and completed. However, using the do_action operator in this way quickly clutters the code, as the number of traces increases. Instead, a specific observer should be provided so that traces can be added in one line.

For this, a custom Observer class is first needed as can be seen in the following example:

```
from rx import Observer

class TraceObservable(Observer):
    def __init__(self, prefix):
        self.prefix = prefix

    def on_next(self, value):
        print("{} - on next: {}".format(self.prefix, value))

    def on_completed(self):
        print("{} - completed".format(self.prefix))

    def on_error(self, error):
        print("{} - on error: {}".format(self.prefix, error))
```

The previous example declares a new TraceObservable class that inherits from the Observer class. The base constructor of Observer is not called because it is an abstract base class, so it does not implement a constructor. The constructor takes a prefix as a input. This prefix is printed on each event received. The three methods (on_next, on_completed, on_error) implement the interface of Observer, by printing the received event.

This class can then be used in the following way:

```
import json

Observable.just('{ "foo": 2}') \
    .do_action(TraceObservable("trace 1")) \
    .map(lambda i: json.loads(i)) \
    .do_action(TraceObservable("trace 2")) \
    .subscribe(
        on_next=lambda i: print("on_next: {}".format(i)),
        on_error=lambda e: print("on_error {}".format(e)),
        on_completed=lambda: print("completed")
    )
```

In this example, an observable is created from a JSON string. This string is then decoded and the result is printed. Two traces are added: one before the `map` operator, and another one after. They are prefixed differently. This next example gives the following result:

```
trace 1 - on next: { "foo": 2}
trace 2 - on next: {'foo': 2}
on_next: {'foo': 2}
trace 1 - completed
trace 2 - completed
completed
```

As everything is fine, both trace points print the item received, and also the final subscription. Then they all complete.

The following example shows an error added to the JSON string with an extra double quote:

```
Observable.just('{ "foo": 2"}')
```

When we do this, parsing will fail. The example now gives the following result:

```
trace 1 - on next: { "foo": 2"}
trace 2 - on error: Expecting ',' delimiter: line 1 column 11 (char 10)
on_error Expecting ',' delimiter: line 1 column 11 (char 10)
```

`trace 1` prints the item to parse. Then `trace 2` catches the error raised by the `map` operator, and prints it. Since the final subscription also prints a error, they also display it.

The important point here is that, in a more complex example, the final subscription will probably not print the original error (at best, it is logged). It will rather catch it and do an action, or notify another error on another observable. So, without a tracing point, the original error is lost, and finding its origin can be very difficult.

In such cases, several trace points can be added in the application, so that the error can be found with a dichotomy search (yes, this is not a very fancy way to debug code in the 21st century).

Another thing that can be very useful in such situations is printing the call stack of the error, once again to more easily find where the issue comes from. When errors are raised from exceptions, the call stack is available. So it can be printed in the on_error method of the TraceObservable, as can be seen in the following example:

```
def on_error(self, error):

    if isinstance(error, Exception):
        print("{} - on error: {}, {}".format(
            self.prefix, error,
            traceback.print_tb(error.__traceback__)))
    else:
        print("{} - on error: {}".format(self.prefix, error))
```

With this new code, the error is printed in the following way:

```
trace 1 - on next: { "foo": 2"}
  File "/.../select.py", line 31, in on_next
    result = selector(value, count[0])
  File "/.../utils.py", line 57, in func_wrapped
    ret = fn(*args, **kw)
  File "/.../utils.py", line 46, in func1
    return func(arg1)
  File "rxpy_trace.py", line 26, in <lambda>
    .map(lambda i: json.loads(i)) \
  File "/.../json/__init__.py", line 354, in loads
    return _default_decoder.decode(s)
  File "/.../json/decoder.py", line 339, in decode
    obj, end = self.raw_decode(s, idx=_w(s, 0).end())
  File "/.../json/decoder.py", line 355, in raw_decode
    obj, end = self.scan_once(s, idx)
trace 2 - on error: Expecting ',' delimiter: line 1 column 11 (char 10),
None
on_error Expecting ',' delimiter: line 1 column 11 (char 10)
```

The full call stack is printed, and thus we can find where the exception has been raised, that is, in the file "rxpy_trace.py", line 26.

The full code of this example is available in the GitHub repository (https://github.com/PacktPublishing/Hands-On-Reactive-Programming-with-Python) of this book, in the rxpy_trace.py script.

Debugging AsyncIO

AsyncIO is easier to debug than ReactiveX. It comes with a simple, but very handy, debugging feature. Let's consider the following example:

```
import asyncio
import time

async def do_something():
    print("I do something")
    time.sleep(0.5)
    print("Done")

loop = asyncio.get_event_loop()
loop.run_until_complete(do_something())
loop.stop()
loop.close()
```

This example executes a coroutine that prints something, waits for 500 milliseconds, prints something else, and exits. Running the preceding example now gives the following result:

```
I do something
Done
```

Everything seems fine, but there is an issue in this code. The debug feature of AsyncIO traps it and prints it. Enabling debug is done for each event loop in the following way:

```
loop.set_debug(True)
```

With this line of code added before the event loop is started, the example gives the following result:

```
I do something
Done
Executing <Task finished coro=<do_something() done, defined at
asyncio_debug.py:5> result=None created at
/usr/local/Cellar/python/3.6.5/Frameworks/Python.framework/Versions/3.6/lib
/python3.6/asyncio/base_events.py:447> took 0.503 seconds
```

AsyncIO tells us that the `do_something` coroutine executed during 500 milliseconds, which is an eternity for the event loop. So it tells us that the blocking call to `time.sleep` must be replaced by something else. In this case, `sleep` can be replaced with its asynchronous equivalent:

```
await asyncio.sleep(0.5)
```

Now, the example with the debug being enabled does not print this warning again.

The full code for this example is available in the GitHub repository (`https://github.com/PacktPublishing/Hands-On-Reactive-Programming-with-Python`) of this book, in the `asyncio_debug.py` script.

 Instead of enabling the AsyncIO debug mode for each event loop, it is possible to enable it globally, by setting the `PYTHONASYNCIODEBUG` environment variable by using the following command:
`(venv-rx) $ PYTHONASYNCIODEBUG=1 python3 asyncio_debug.py`

The debug mode of AsyncIO monitors the following things:

- Coroutines that are defined but never awaited
- Calls to `call_soon` from a thread other than the event loop
- Execution time of callbacks and coroutines
- Resources that are not closed: transports and event loops

This mode is of great help when debugging an issue, and also in ensuring that the behavior is correct. So it is good practice to enable it when testing an application.

Summary

Having read this chapter, you should now be able to test your code, and debug it when issues are found.

This chapter described how testing can be done, in a way that is fully automated so that it can be integrated in continuous integration systems. The Python standard library is a solid foundation on which RxPY and asynchronous code can be tested rather easily. You should also understand why pure functions are easier to test than side-effects: they can be fully tested by using dependency injection, which is easier to use than stubs or mocks.

Logging is a subject in-between testing and debugging. It can be useful during the initial testing phases, or when regressions are detected. One major benefit of ReactiveX here is that, once a logging infrastructure is in place, then it becomes easy to configure it dynamically.

Finally, debugging is the dark side of ReactiveX, with no tools dedicated to this task. Using trace points is currently the only way to debug an application. Hopefully, this should change in the future. AsyncIO, on the other hand, provides a simple but efficient tool to detect issues on asynchronous code. Moreover, this tool can be enabled without any change in the application, just by setting an environment variable.

The next chapter will continue our tour of Docker, and explain how it can be used to deploy an application such as the audio transcoder. At the same time, it will revisit the solution used in `Chapter 7`, *Using Third-Party Services*, to handle CPU-bound operations.

Questions

- Why is it important to find defects as soon as possible?
- What are the different kinds of software testing?
- What is a test case in unit testing?
- Why should tests be written before the actual code?
- Why should logging be done on dedicated observables?
- Logging is a side-effect. Is this true or false?
- What operator can be used to add some traces in a chain of operator?
- What are the two ways to enable the debug mode of AsyncIO?

Further reading

The Python unit testing module contains very detailed documentation. It is available here: `https://docs.python.org/3/library/unittest.html#module-unittest`.

The `nosetests` tool supports many options and can also be set with a configuration file. Its documentation is available here: `https://nose.readthedocs.io/en/latest/man.html`.

The `logging` module documentation is also quite complete, and can be found here: `https://docs.python.org/3.6/howto/logging.html#logging-basic-tutorial`.

11
Deploying and Scaling Your Application

This chapter details a possible system architecture to deploy our audio transcoding application and scale it. The first part explains the principles of reverse proxies and load balancers, and why and when they are needed. A practical use is shown with Traefik, a modern load balancer. The second part explains how to package a Python application inside a Docker image. Finally, the last part goes into the details of enabling HTTPS on the audio transcoding service.

The following topics will be covered in this chapter:

- Introduction to Traefik
- Packaging a service with Docker Compose
- Adding TLS support with Let's Encrypt

Technical requirements

The use of Let's Encrypt requires that a server or a virtual machine is available with a public IP address and a registered DNS entry. Some information is provided in this chapter to set up such an environment.

Introduction to Traefik

Traefik is an open source reverse proxy and load balancer. Originally, these two features were handled by different components:

- Reverse proxies were implemented in HTTP servers such as Apache and NGINX
- Load balancers were implemented in dedicated products, whether software- or hardware-based

But quite recently, several open source projects emerged that implement both features in software. Traefik is one of these tools, and it leverages several new technologies:

- It is implemented in the Go language, a compiled language that offers high performance and ease of development
- It is highly integrated with the Docker ecosystem
- It has built-in support for Let's Encrypt, a free TLS certificate authority

Before looking at how to use Traefik, let's first explain what a reverse proxy is, what a load balancer is, and why these two components are of great importance when deploying web applications or microservices.

Reverse proxies and load balancers

Reverse proxies and load balancers are the two basic components used when deploying backend services. They provide solutions to routing HTTP APIs to the associated services, and scaling these services.

What is a reverse proxy?

Consider a typical design of a web application where some parts are running on the backend side, and some on the client side. This system is composed of the following:

- A web application running on a client device (a PC or a smartphone)
- Several features running on the backend side, and an HTTP server hosting static files

Depending on the complexity of the system, the backend part can be implemented either as a unique service or as several services. Using a unique service was the dominant design in the early 2000s. However in practice, splitting them into multiple independent services has many benefits. The main one is the fact that these components can be operated independently. They can also be written in different programming languages, using different technologies.

With the backend side of applications getting more and more complex, and the fact that most applications rely on much more than a few independent services, the split in multiple services is more and more popular. This split in many services is called a **microservice** architecture. It is a design where many small services are combined together, while being independent of each other as much as possible.

Splitting an application into many small services is fine, but this should not add complexity to the client side: All these services should be accessible as if they were a single service. More specifically, these services should be available via the same domain name. So, deciding on what service each HTTP request should be routed to has to be done via the URI of the request. In the case of an application running two services, one possibility is to do the following:

- Route all requests to /api/a to service A
- Route all requests to /api/b to service B
- Route all other requests to a web server to serve static files

This routing is the role of a reverse proxy. The use of a reverse proxy for this example application is shown in the following figure:

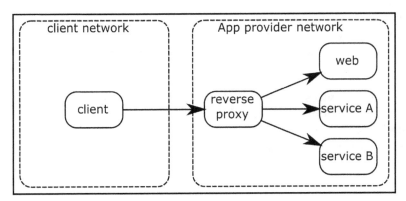

Figure 11.1: An HTTP reverse proxy

The reverse proxy is in between the client and the services. It receives all requests from the clients, and forwards them to each service, based on the information in the incoming HTTP requests. The routing decision can be done via different criteria:

- The path of the request
- The query part of the request
- The (sub) domain name being requested
- The headers present in the request
- The method of the request

So, a reverse proxy takes its name from the fact that it works in the opposite way to an HTTP proxy. The following figure shows how an HTTP proxy works:

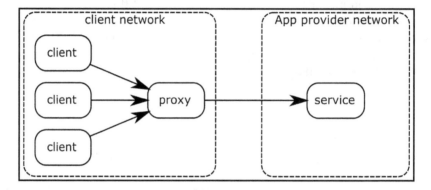

Figure 11.2: An HTTP proxy

A proxy filters outgoing requests from clients to websites/applications. It operates on the network of the client devices. A reverse proxy filters incoming requests from clients to the backend services. It operates on the network of the application provider.

So, a reverse proxy is a tool that simplifies the deployment of applications that are composed of several services running on the backend side. Originally, reverse proxies were used when several web domains or sub-domains were hosted on the same IP address. Using the criteria listed previously allows us to route each request correctly. Now, the same tools are used to route requests to web services.

What is a load balancer?

The other feature provided by Traefik is load balancing. Let's consider the system of the previous part, composed of two services and serving static files. If such a system is really deployed this way, then as soon as one service becomes unavailable, the application does not work anymore. Such a system is clearly not a reactive system as defined in `Chapter` `1`, *An Introduction to Reactive Programming*: it is not resilient and not elastic.

However, if the services are really implemented independently of each other, and in a stateless way, then it becomes possible to execute several instances of each service, and use any of the instances to serve incoming requests. This is shown in the following figure:

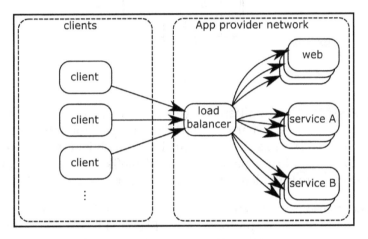

Figure 11.3: Running multiple instances of each service

In this new architecture, each service is instantiated multiple times. Each time an incoming request happens for one service, it then has to be routed to one of the instances of this service. This is the role of the load balancer: ensuring that requests are equally balanced between each instance of the services.

This new architecture is a step towards a reactive system; it is now more resilient, because if one instance of a service fails, then the other instances can handle the requests. It also provides a first step in elasticity by providing a way to adjust the number of running instances of each service.

Reverse proxies work exclusively on the HTTP protocol. However, load balancers can work on different protocols. The following figure lists the OSI model layers and the associated internet protocols:

OSI layers		
7	App	HTTP
6		
5		
4	Transport	TCP
3	Network	IP
2	Link	
1	Phy	

Figure 11.4: The OSI model

Load balancing is possible at two different layers of the OSI model: layers **4** and **7**. Some load balancers (being software or hardware) provide support for both levels. This is the case with the commercial *F5* products, the Linux kernel with its **Linux Virtual Server** (**LVS**) service, or HA Proxy. Other load balancers, such as Traefik, support only level **7** load balancing because they are fully dedicated to services running on HTTP.

HTTP load balancers also provide another feature: TLS termination. TLS, or SSL, is the protocol used to secure the HTTP protocol (aka HTTPS). TLS relies on certificates that allow the client to ensure that it talks to the correct server (and sometimes also to ensure that the client is allowed to connect to the server). These certificates are generated by providers called certificate authorities. They can generate certificates that will be recognized as trusted by all HTTP stacks (and so by web browsers).

Each HTTPS server needs a certificate to be present on the system. In an architecture where many services are present, managing these certificates can be a complex task. Some tools exist to deal with this, but an easy solution to this problem is to stop the TLS connection on the load balancer. Since the aim of TLS is to secure the connection up to the server of the application, this can end at the load balancer stage. After that, the load balancer forwards the requests using the HTTP protocol, without protection. However, since the load balancer and the services run on the network of the application provider, this can be considered a trusted environment. TLS termination on the load balancer is shown in the following figure:

Figure 11.5: TLS termination on the load balancer

Traefik principles

Traefik is both a reverse proxy and a load balancer. Its design is composed of four parts:

- Entry points, which are the listening connections with the outside world
- Frontends, which define routes with the backends
- Backends, which provide load balancing between several servers
- Servers, composed of Docker containers

Servers are the entities that are controlled by Traefik. The complete configuration of Traefik can be done via a TOML configuration file. Several parts of this configuration can also be set with Docker labels. Mixing both of them allows us to automatically configure Traefik when new server containers are started.

The functional principles of Traefik are shown in the following figure:

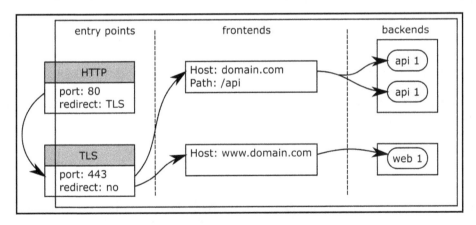

Figure 11.6: How Traefik works

The **entry points** can be configured by specifying a port, an optional SSL configuration, and an optional redirection to another entry point. The following is a configuration example:

```
[entryPoints]
  [entryPoints.http]
  address = ":80"
```

```
    [entryPoints.http.redirect]
    entryPoint = "https"
  [entryPoints.https]
  address = ":443"
    [entryPoints.https.tls]
      [[entryPoints.https.tls.certificates]]
      certFile = "./cert/traefik.crt"
      keyFile = "./cert/traefik.key"
```

This configuration defines two entry points:

- The first one is an HTTP entry point on port 80 that is redirected to the HTTPS entry point. In other words, it redirects all HTTP traffic to HTTPS.
- The second one is an HTTPS entry point on port 443. Its certificate and private key are configured with files.

The **frontends** support two kinds of configuration: modifiers and matchers. Modifiers are rules that change the original request (such as adding a prefix to the request path, or rewriting it). Matchers are rules that just match to the incoming request. Here are the most common matcher rules:

- **Headers**: Matches if the request contains the provided header/value pair
- **Host**: Matches if the request is for one of the provided hosts
- **Method**: Matches if the request has one of the provided HTTP methods
- **PathPrefix**: Matches if the path of the request starts with one of the provided paths
- **Query**: Matches if the request contains the provided query strings

Configuring frontends via labels allows us to automatically register them when a new Docker server is started. For example, for one container, the following section can be used in a docker-compose file:

```
labels:
  - "traefik.frontend.rule=PathPrefix:/api/transcode/v1"
```

This rule matches any request that starts with the path /api/transcode/v1.

Finally the backends support the following settings to configure load balancing:

- **Server weight**: This allows us to load-balance between several servers of different capacities. When different weights are set on the server instances, then each server receives a number of requests proportional to its weight.
- **The load balancing method per backend**: Two methods are supported–**Weighted Round Robin** (**WRR**; the default), and **Dynamic Round Robin** (**DRR**). The WRR method uses weights to distribute the requests on each server. The DRR method takes into account the performance of each server to increase or decrease its weight dynamically.
- **Circuit breaker**: This allows us to temporarily disable a server that is broken or behaves badly according to the provided metrics. Metrics can be provided based on latency, network error, and result errors.
- **Maximum number of connections**: This allows us to protect a server against heavy loads.

The Traefik documentation provides all the details on these settings, with some examples of how to use each of them.

Packaging a service with Docker Compose

Chapter 7, *Using Third-Party Services*, introduced Docker, an isolation framework based on containers. In that chapter, a single container was started directly with the Docker command line. This method is fine for starting a single container, but has several drawbacks:

- All parameters must be provided in the command line, which can be quite long
- If several containers must be started, then multiple commands must be used

One solution to these issues is to use shell scripts that contain all these commands with their parameters. The Docker framework provides a tool dedicated to this task, more generic than custom scripts: Docker Compose.

Introduction to Docker Compose

Docker Compose is a tool that simplifies the deployment of multicontainer applications. It relies on YAML configuration files to configure each container. Each container definition in the YAML file describes all parameters that can be provided as arguments to the Docker command. It also contains some additional parameters for additional features provided by Docker Compose. The following are the features of Docker Compose:

- **Run multicontainer applications on a single host**: Multiple containers can be defined in the configuration file. All these containers are started and stopped with a single command.
- **Save and restore volume bindings when containers are created**: If a container is updated, then its volume bindings are restored from the last version of the container. This allows us to keep data when upgrading containers.
- **Create containers only when their configuration has changed**: When a full stack is stopped and restarted, only the containers that changed are recreated. This allows us to restart a stack faster.
- **Environment variable substitution**: Some variables can be used in the configuration file so that different configurations can be used. These variables are defined in another dedicated configuration file.

With Docker Compose, deploying an application is much simpler than starting all services manually, and it is also easier to scale the services. The full stack of the audio transcoder application requires three containers: one for the reverse proxy, one for Minio, and one for the transcoder. The following figure shows this architecture:

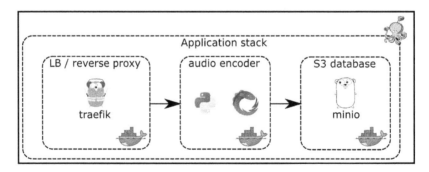

Figure 11.7: The audio transcoder application stack

Let's see how to create this setup.

Installing Docker Compose

This section describes the installation of Docker Compose on Linux. The Compose tool is already available in the installation packages for Docker for macOS and Docker for Windows, so this step is not necessary on these systems.

The installation of Docker Compose is done by directly downloading it:

```
$ sudo curl -L
https://github.com/docker/compose/releases/download/1.22.0/docker-compose-$
(uname -s)-$(uname -m) -o /usr/local/bin/docker-compose
```

The release number—1.22.0—should be updated with the latest version available. The latest release version is available on the GitHub release page (https://github.com/docker/compose/releases) of the project. This command downloads the Compose tool to the /usr/local/bin directory. Then, permissions must be changed so that all users can execute it:

```
$ sudo chmod +x /usr/local/bin/docker-compose
```

At that point, Docker Compose should be working:

```
$ docker-compose --version
docker-compose version 1.22.0, build f46880fe
```

Starting Traefik

The three services of the stack will be configured in the same configuration file, named docker-compose.yml. The first service to configure is Traefik. The first part with the definition of the reverse proxy is the following one:

```
version: '3'

services:
  reverse-proxy:
    image: traefik
    command: --api --docker
    ports:
      - "80:80"
      - "8080:8080"
    volumes:
      - /var/run/docker.sock:/var/run/docker.sock
```

The version number identifies the version of the configuration file specifications. Then, the services section contains the definition of all containers. For now, there is only one container named `reverse-proxy`. The content of this section is the actual specification of the container.

The `image` parameter is the name of the image to use. If the image is not available locally, then it is downloaded from the Docker hub.

The `command` parameter overrides the default command of the image. In this configuration, Traefik is started with its web interface enabled, and it listens to Docker events.

The `ports` parameter indicates the port bindings to use between the container and the host. Here, port `80` is used for the `reverse-proxy` feature, and port `8080` exposes the web interface.

Finally, the `volumes` parameter defines the volume bindings to use. The binding defined here is the Docker socket. This allows Traefik to connect on the Docker bus to communicate with other containers that will register to the load balancer later.

Traefik can be started with the following command:

```
$ docker-compose up -d reverse-proxy
```

Once started, a new Docker instance should be running:

```
$ docker ps
CONTAINER ID IMAGE COMMAND CREATED STATUS PORTS NAMES
65cbfc50c551 traefik "/traefik --api --do..." 11 seconds ago Up 10 seconds
0.0.0.0:80->80/tcp, 0.0.0.0:8080->8080/tcp audio-encode-server-1_reverse-
proxy_1
```

Packaging the audio transcoder

The next step is to put the audio encoding server in a container. Unlike the previous containers that have been used, this requires us to build a custom image. To build an image, its specifications must be declared in a file. A specification file contains a list of statements to execute so that files are added to the image. Here is the specification file of the encoding server:

```
FROM python:3.6

RUN apt-get update && apt-get install -y sox libsox-fmt-mp3

ENV config /opt/audio-encoder/config.json
```

```
WORKDIR /tmp/audio-encode-server
COPY ./ /tmp/audio-encode-server
RUN python setup.py install

CMD ["sh", "-c", "/usr/local/bin/audio-encode-server --config ${config}"]
```

The first line indicates that this image inherits from the `python:3.6` image. This image is based on the Debian distribution. Other Python images are available, based on Alpine. Alpine is a lightweight distribution, smaller than the Debian one. The `FROM` statement must always be the first one in a Docker file. See later for more details on how images are composed together.

The second statement adds the `sox` packages necessary for the audio transcoder.

Then, the `ENV` statement sets an environment variable for the configuration file. This variable is used later to specify the configuration file to use, and can be overloaded when the container is started. Using an environment variable is not strictly needed here because the configuration file can also be specified with a file binding.

The next block copies the Python package from the host to the image. First, the `WORKDIR` statement sets the current working directory inside the image being built. The `COPY` statement copies the content of the current directory on the host to `/tmp/audio_encode-server` on the image. Then, the `RUN` statement installs the package on the image via the setup tools.

Finally, a default command is configured to start the daemon when the container is started.

This configuration file should be saved in the source directory of the audio encoder, with the name `Dockerfile`. This name is the default one used to build an image. This file is available in the GitHub repository of this book (`https://github.com/PacktPublishing/Hands-On-Reactive-Programming-with-Python`).

Building the image is done with the `docker build` command:

```
$ docker build . -t audio-encoder
```

The dot (.) parameter indicates that the build is done from the current directory. The `t` parameter is the name of the image being generated.

From that point, the image is available locally:

```
$ docker images
REPOSITORY TAG IMAGE ID CREATED SIZE
audio-encoder latest fc8f6e605ef5 4 minutes ago 988MB
```

Note how big the image is. This is because it is based on Debian. If an application depends only on pure Python code, or on binary distributions of Python packages, then the use of the Alpine distribution allows us to create images of only a few megabytes instead of almost one gigabyte.

This container can be started manually in a similar way to Minio:

```
docker run -d -p 8000:8000 --name audio-encoder \
    -v /home/alice/config.json:/opt/audio-encoder/config.json \
    audio-encoder
```

This command starts the container with port 8000 exposed. This should match the one declared in the configuration file. The previous chapters used port 8080, but it is now used by the Traefik web interface. Here, a file binding is declared so that the configuration file is located on the host, but visible to the container.

All the required Docker images are now available to complete the definition of the application stack.

How images are composed together

Before running the full stack, let's talk a little bit about how images depend on each other. Docker is designed so that images can share common parts instead of duplicating them. This saves disk space, and avoids downloading the same files multiples times. It relies on a simple principle: an image is a filesystem packaged in a file. An image inherits from another image (or nothing, for root images); this means that a new image contains all the files of its parent image. New files are the only ones being stored in the new image. With this principle, only the differences from parent images must be stored on each image. Moreover, many different images can share the content of common parent images.

Technically, this is implemented on top of an overlay filesystem (also called an onion filesystem). The following figure shows the principles of an overlay filesystem:

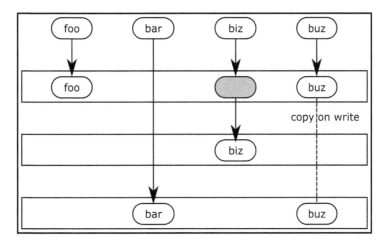

Figure 11.8: An overlay filesytem

An image is composed of the files present in several other layers. Each upper layer can add new files, replace existing ones, or mark files as deleted. In *Figure 11.6*, the base image contains the files `bar` and `buz`. The second layer image adds the `biz` file.

Finally, a third layer adds the `foo` file , removes the `biz` file, and modifies the `buz` file. A core principle of Docker images is that they are immutable: once they are created, they cannot be modified. Should this be the case, they cannot be shared between other images. So, when the `biz` file is removed, it cannot be removed from the second layer. Instead, a specific metadata file is written to indicate that this file does not exist. Also, due to the immutability property of an image, when the `buz` file is modified, nothing is done on the file of the first layer; instead, the file is copied to the third layer and then modified.

Finally, the final image exposes a filesystem with three files, where the `buz` file has been modified compared to the root image.

It is important to understand the immutability property of images. It implies that any file written in an image during the build process stays present in the image, even if it is deleted in another image. In fact, layers are not only created for each image, but for each RUN command. This means that credential files should never be manipulated when building Docker images, otherwise they will be present in one layer used by the final image.

Composing all services

The configuration file can now be completed so that Docker Compose not only starts Traefik, but also Minio and the encoding server. Let's start with the Minio service, by adding this block to the configuration file:

```
minio:
  image: minio/minio
  command: server /data
  ports:
    - "9000:9000"
  volumes:
    - ./data:/data
    - ./config:/root/.minio
  environment:
    MINIO_ACCESS_KEY: IU0645L6OOSV96GSEG72
    MINIO_SECRET_KEY: udTdXiaUh1equB7BE9Kn691a/DNGnMguIVEh0iyu
```

Two environment variables are provided here. They allow us to fix the credentials being used by this instance, instead of letting Minio generate them during the first start.

This container can be started with the following command:

```
$ docker-compose up -d minio
```

Then, a third service can be added for the audio encoder:

```
audio-encoder:
  image: audio-encoder
  depends_on:
    - reverse-proxy
    - minio
  expose:
    - 3000
  volumes:
    - ./config.json:/opt/audio-encoder/config.json
  labels:
    - "traefik.frontend.rule=PathPrefix:/api/transcode/v1"
    - "traefik.port=3000"
```

There are two new sections being used here. The depends-on section indicates that this container depends on the reverse-proxy and minio containers. When the audio-encoder container is started, Docker Compose first ensures that these two containers are started. If either of them has not started yet, then they are started automatically.

Next, two labels are provided:

- `frontend.rule` specifies the frontend rules to associate to this backend. Here, all requests with a path starting with `/api/transcode/v1` are routed to the `audio-encoder` backend.
- The `port` label indicates to Traefik which port should be used to route the traffic. This label is optional in this case because the container exposes only one port, so Traefik can determine this value automatically.

The `audio-encoder` container is started by using the following code:

```
$ docker-compose up -d audio-encoder
```

Now, the web interface of Traefik should display a frontend for audio encoding APIs and a backend composed of one server. The following screenshot shows the frontend part:

Figure 11.9: The audio encode server route via Traefik

Instead of starting each backend one by one, it is possible to start them all at once with the following command:

```
$ docker-compose up -d
```

The `d` option is similar to the option for the Docker `run` command: it tells Docker to detach from the container once it is started.

The whole stack can also be stopped with a single command:

```
$ docker-compose down
```

Using containers for horizontal scaling

`Chapter 5`, *Concurrency and Parallelism in RxPY*, detailed the use of multithreading to handle CPU-bound operations such as audio encoding. It also explained the limitations of this model with Python code, which was due to the limitations implied by the GIL. Python has never been good at multithreading, and will probably never be. However, in web applications or microservices, this is not necessarily an issue. Instead of using multithreading to deal with CPU bound operations, it is possible to use multiprocessing.

With multithreading, only one instance of the service is running, and this service uses multithreading to parallelize task executions. With multiprocessing, several single-threaded instances of the service are executed in parallel. However, this has some implications. The biggest one is that the service should be stateless; any request should be independent of other requests, or the internal state of the service. Since several instances of the service are running in parallel, there is usually no guarantee that some related requests will be served by the same instance (Traefik allows us to do this in some cases). Should the service be stateful, then the management of its state must be done by another service since it cannot be done in the context of the service instance (multiple processes do not share memory, so they cannot share their state directly).

With Docker Compose, starting new instances of the service is done with the `up` command and an additional parameter that indicates how many instances of the container must be running. For example, starting two more instances of the `audio-encoder` container is done the following way:

```
$ docker-compose up -d --scale audio-encoder=3
audio-encode-server-1_reverse-proxy_1 is up-to-date
audio-encode-server-1_minio_1 is up-to-date
Starting audio-encode-server-1_audio-encoder_1 ... done
Creating audio-encode-server-1_audio-encoder_2 ... done
Creating audio-encode-server-1_audio-encoder_3 ... done
```

Here, the existing services are kept as they are, and two new instances of the `audio-encoder` container are started. The `Starting` log on the existing instance is misleading; this instance is not stopped when executing this command, but it keeps running while the other instances are started.

Since Traefik monitors Docker instances, it sees that new instances are available and it adds them to the list of servers of the `audio-encoder` backend. Several instances are now running and the load balancer is now enabled. This can be seen in the web interface of Traefik.

Scaling down the audio-encode backend to one instance is done the same way:

```
$ docker-compose up -d --scale audio-encoder=1
audio-encode-server-1_reverse-proxy_1 is up-to-date
audio-encode-server-1_minio_1 is up-to-date
Stopping and removing audio-encode-server-1_audio-encoder_2 ... done
Stopping and removing audio-encode-server-1_audio-encoder_3 ... done
Starting audio-encode-server-1_audio-encoder_1 ... done
```

The two most recently added instances of the `audio-encoder` container are stopped, and only one instance remains. Here again, Traefik sees these changes and adjusts its configuration accordingly.

Adding TLS support with Let's Encrypt

Transport Layer Security (TLS), is the protocol used to secure HTTP traffic. This protocol is based on public key cryptography to authenticate peers in a connection, and on symmetric cryptography to cipher the content. The authentication relies on root certificate authorities that are known by HTTP client libraries. Historically, using a certificate recognized by web browsers and libraries was a paid-for service, like registering DNS domains.

However, since 2014, Let's Encrypt (`https://letsencrypt.org/`) allows us to get TLS certificates easily, automatically, and at no charge.

Introduction to Let's Encrypt

Let's Encrypt is a certificate authority that provides TLS certificates for free. Let's Encrypt is one of the most active services currently helping make web communications completely encrypted. This service relies on funds raised from various companies. In 2017, Let's Encrypt's operating costs were only 3 millions dollars, to serve almost 50 million active certificates! As a comparison, the same year, HADOPI, a French government service that aims to fight online media piracy, spent 7.5 million euros (about 8.6 million dollars) on sending about 2 million notification emails and 88 fees.

The success of Let's Encrypt is not only due to the fact that it is free, but also due to the tools provided to automate the retrieval and renewal of certificates. Nevertheless, Let's Encrypt is a very serious, official certificate authority. As such, in order to obtain a certificate, one has to prove that one owns the domain name for which the certificate is requested. There are two ways to prove this ownership:

- By adding a DNS record for the requested domain name
- By putting a resource file on an HTTP server running on the domain name

These operations can be done manually or automatically. The protocol used to issue the certificates is called the **Automated Certificate Management Environment (ACME)** protocol. Issued certificates are valid for 90 days. This is a period much shorter than the one usually used by other certificate authorities. This choice was driven by two aims:

- This limits the security impact in cases where private keys and certificates are stolen from a server. The stolen credentials are valid for at most 90 days.
- This encourages the use of automation for certificate renewal.

The tool provided by Let's Encrypt is called Certbot. This command-line tool allows us to request new certificates and renew them. Some additional tooling is necessary to use automatic renewal of certificates. A simple way to do this is via a cron job, or a `systemd` timer. Another even simpler way is to use a higher-level tool such as Traefik that implements the ACME protocol.

Deploying on a public server

So far, the audio encoder stack has been deployed on a local machine. However, in order to use an official TLS certificate with Let's Encrypt, a server with a public DNS entry is needed. Unless you have your own domain name already available on a server somewhere, it is not possible to use an official TLS certificate.

An easy way to get a machine with an associated DNS name is to rent a virtual machine from a cloud provider. These machines always have an associated DNS entry. It is often a purely technical name, composed of a key used as a subdomain of the provider hosting the service name, for example:

- On the Amazon Web Services EC2 service, it looks like the following: `ec2-12-345-678-789.eu-west-1.compute.amazonaws.com`
- On OVH, it looks like the following: `vps123456.ovh.net`

Pure cloud providers usually rent virtual machines per hour. This is nice for doing some short tests, but can rapidly become costly. Whenever a long hosting is needed, it is often more cost-effective to rent a virtual machine on a monthly or yearly basis. This can save a lot of money; a typical ratio is that cloud hosting per hour is five times more expensive than per month, and cloud hosting per month is almost 10 times more expensive than renting a VM per year!

The following section has been tested on a **Virtual Private Server** (**VPS**) from OVH. They are one of the most cost-efficient hosting solutions for small systems. This machine has been configured with a Debian distribution, Docker installed on it, and remote SSH access. Details on these steps are not provided here since it is beyond the scope of this book.

Enabling the ACME protocol

The configuration of the ACME protocol with an HTTP authentication is quite simple. For this, a custom Treafik configuration file is needed instead of the default one. First, the entry points are configured:

```
defaultEntryPoints = ["https","http"]

[entryPoints]
  [entryPoints.http]
  address = ":80"
    [entryPoints.http.redirect]
    entryPoint = "https"
  [entryPoints.https]
  address = ":443"
  [entryPoints.https.tls]
```

Two entry points are defined, one for HTTP and one for HTTPS. HTTP requests are redirected to the HTTPS entry point so that all traffic is secured.

Then, some other parts of Traefik are configured:

```
[retry]

[docker]
endpoint = "unix:///var/run/docker.sock"
domain = "vps123456.ovh.net"
watch = true
exposedbydefault = false
```

The retry setting enables request retries in the case of network errors. The default number of retries is the number of servers in the backend, minus 1. So if a backend is composed of only one server, no retry is done before replying with an error.

Then, the Docker configuration enables communication on the Docker bus with the endpoint and watch settings. It also sets the DNS name of the server. The exposedByDefault parameter indicates that containers are ignored by Traefik unless they have the traefik.enable label set to true. This setting must be added to the audio-encoder container configuration.

Finally, here is the Let's Encrypt configuration:

```
[acme]
#caServer = "https://acme-staging-v02.api.letsencrypt.org/directory"
email = "admin@vps123456.ovh.net"
storage = "acme.json"
entryPoint = "https"
OnHostRule = true
  [acme.httpChallenge]
  entryPoint = "http"
```

Ignore the caServer comment for now. An email associated to the domain name must be provided for notifications from Let's Encrypt. The storage setting indicates in what file the credentials are stored. The entryPoint setting indicate which entry point is associated to the ACME service. The OnHostRule setting allows us to automatically generate a certificate request when a new host rule is seen on the frontend. This allows us to automatically enable TLS when new server containers are started on a sub-domain. Finally, the ACME service is configured to use the http challenge.

This whole configuration file is available in the GitHub repository (https://github.com/PacktPublishing/Hands-On-Reactive-Programming-with-Python) of this book, in the audio-encode-server-2/traefik.toml sub-folder.

The Docker Compose file of the stack also requires some changes. First, the new files needed by Treafik must be added to the bound files of the reverse proxy container:

```
volumes:
  - /var/run/docker.sock:/var/run/docker.sock
  - ./traefik.toml:/traefik.toml
  - ./acme.json:/acme.json
```

The first additional binding replaces the default configuration file with the one enabling TLS via Let's Encrypt. The second one is the file where the Let's Encrypt credentials will be stored. This file must be present before starting the stack:

```
$ touch acme.json
$ chmod 600 acme.json
```

Then, the `audio-encoder` container must be exposed to Traefik:

```
labels:
  - "traefik.enable=true"
```

The two other containers should not be exposed as frontends to Traefik, so both Minio and Traefik itself must have the `enable` label set to `false`:

```
labels:
  - "traefik.enable=false"
```

Before the stack can be tested, the `audio-encoder` Docker image must be uploaded to the server. There are several ways to do this:

- The first option is to upload the application's code and generate the image directly on the server. The problem with this solution is that the server must have all tools needed by the application installed locally, which is precisely what Docker allows us to avoid!
- The second option is to upload the image file generated locally to the server. With this method, there is nothing new to install on the server.
- The third option is to use a public or private Docker registry and upload the `audio-encoder` image to it so that it can be retrieved on the server.

This last solution is fine if the image can be published publicly (for example on `https://hub.docker.com/`), or if a private registry is available in your company.

Let's use the second option, which is quite simple thanks to SSH:

```
docker save audio-encoder | bzip2 | pv | ssh user@host 'bunzip2 | docker
load'
```

With this single line, a local Docker image is uploaded to the `host` server, and loaded in its local registry. Replace `user` with the name of the SSH user that logs in if authentication is done via login/password. The `pv` tool prints a progress bar for the transfer. If this tool is not available on your system, you can omit it.

Now, the whole application stack can be started with a single command:

```
$ docker-compose up -d

curl -X POST --data-binary @../audio-dataset/banjo1.mp3
https://vps123456.ovh.net/api/transcode/v1/flac/banjo1
```

The audio transcode service is now available on the internet, ready to scale, and served from HTTPS!

Now that the service works, the web interface of Traefik should be disabled or secured to prevent anybody from configuring it. Also, the Minio web interface may not be exposed publicly. An easy way to secure them while still being able to use them is to bind them on the localhost interface, and use SSH forwarding to access them remotely.

For this, the Traefik web interface port must be defined this way:

– `"127.0.0.1:8080:8080"`

And the Minio port must be defined this way:

– `"127.0.0.1:9000:9000"`

Then, local port forwarding must be configured when connecting via SSH to the server:

```
$ ssh -L 8080:localhost:8080 -L 9000:localhost:9000 user@server
```

Once the SSH connection is established, web interfaces are accessible on a web browser on the localhost.

A last note on Let's Encrypt's configuration: when testing the initial configuration, the certificate request often does not work. Several trials may be needed to fix access or configuration issues. The problem with this is that certificate requests are limited to 50 per week per domain. If this limit is reached, then no other certificate can be delivered for several days.

A staging environment is available to test a configuration before requesting real certificates. This can be done simply by not commenting the `caSever` line in the Treafik configuration file. The staging environment has no rate limit, but it generates certificates that are not signed by root entities. As a consequence, they are not recognized as valid certificates by HTTP clients. Once the configuration works, comment this line again, and re-create an empty `acme.json` file so that a valid certificate is requested.

Also, during this initial configuration step, it might be useful to add debugging traces in Traefik logs. Debug logs are enabled the following way in the configuration file:

```
debug=true
```

Then, the logs are visible via Docker:

```
docker logs audio-encoder_reverse-proxy_1
```

Summary

This chapter was the conclusion of our journey from an initial echo example up to a realistic application being deployed on a cloud environment, which was scalable and secured with TLS.

Reverse proxies are some of the basic tools needed to deploy applications, especially when they are composed of several services. Reverse proxies that operate on layer 7 also often implement load balancing features. Load balancing allows us to distribute the load between several instances of a service. Some of these tools, such as Traefik, leverage the Docker ecosystem to make their configuration very easy and dynamic.

Docker Compose allows us to manage containers much more easily than directly using Docker. Using it simplifies the deployment of applications that use multiple containers. Moreover, it allows us to easily scale a container up or down by starting or stopping some instances very easily.

Let's Encrypt is a great tool for two main reasons: it is one of the only solutions providing valid certificates for free, and it allows us to fully automate the renewal of these certificates. So, this service solves two of the main issues that prevent many small websites and companies from protecting their traffic with TLS.

The next chapter will explore how to extend reactive programming and observables beyond a single process or application. It will propose ways to use observables to communicate between processes and systems, is an attempt to go a step further towards reactive systems.

Questions

- What is a proxy?
- What is a reverse proxy?
- What is a load balancer?
- What additional features are provided by Docker Compose compared to Docker?
- What is the purpose of a `Dockerfile`?
- What are the prerequisites to scale a service horizontally?
- What service is provided by Let's Encrypt?

Further reading

Information on the LVS load balancer is available here: `http://www.linuxvirtualserver.org/`.

The full syntax of a `Dockerfile` is available here: `https://docs.docker.com/engine/reference/builder/#usage`.

Traefik supports labels to dynamically configure many things. A list of all these labels is here: `https://docs.traefik.io/configuration/backends/docker/#labels-overriding-default-behavior`.

There are more and more application that natively support the ACME protocol. A list of these clients is available here: `https://letsencrypt.org/docs/client-options/`.

12
Reactive Streams for Remote Communication

This is the last chapter in which we'll increase your knowledge of ReactiveX. This chapter explains how observables can be extended outside a single application. The first part of this chapter explains what existing communication patterns there are and how they relate to observables. The second part details how multiplexing is designed and why all of its steps are necessary. The last part is an implementation of the publish/subscribe protocol.

The following topics will be covered in this chapter:

- Communication patterns and observables
- Observable multiplexing
- Implementing publish/subscribe

Communication patterns and observables

All the examples studied up to now were implemented as a single process. But software of a higher complexity, running either on the backend side or on the edge side, is usually split into multiple processes, and on multiple systems or devices. Communicating between processes and systems can be done in many different ways, and many solutions exist. For backend communication, one solution is to expose REST-oriented APIs, such as the audio transcoding service implemented throughout this book. The advantage of this solution is that it is easy to integrate with many existing tools. However, from a reactive point of view, it means that observables cannot be exposed outside the service: an HTTP request completes as soon as the first answer is sent, while an observable can send many items.

In cases where several services are implemented in a reactive way, then it would be nice to expose their APIs as observables so that they integrate more naturally together. Since ReactiveX and reactive programming libraries are available in many programming languages, this still allows us to implement components using different programming languages. Such a solution goes against the trend of isomorphic applications where both the backend and the frontend are implemented in the same programming languages. Isomorphic applications can be great in some cases, however there are many situations where this is not applicable:

- In practice, JavaScript is the only possible programming language for isomorphic web applications. Java may be a solution for other clients, as well as C++. This leaves out most available programming languages.
- Different programming languages are better suited for different kinds of task. So restricting the implementation to a single programming language can be more of a restriction than a simplification.

So, using observables to expose APIs allows us to extend the reactive pattern while still being able to use different programming languages for different parts. A typical use-case, where this architecture is interesting, is a machine learning algorithm being continuously fed by a web application:

- The frontend can be implemented in JavaScript with Cycle.js.
- The backend can be implemented in Python with AsyncIO and the machine learning framework used for the model (the commonality for almost all these frameworks is that they expose Python bindings).
- The communication between the frontend and the backend can be based on a WebSocket or HTTP2 connection.

In order to implement such a system, the network link between the peers needs to fulfill the following constraints:

- It must be persistent, so that many messages can be sent without closing the connection. The persistent connection allows us to maintain a context as long as the connection is open, and release resources when the connection is closed. So a state is shared between the two peers as long as the connection is open. This is a different design from stateless RESTful APIs.
- It must be bidirectional, so that peers can talk to each other.
- It must be reliable: the integrity of the messages sent on the network link must be guaranteed (transmission-wise, not cryptographically-wise).
- It must preserve message ordering: messages sent in one order must be delivered in the same order.

Using a network protocol that does not fulfill these constraints is possible, but adds complexity because the missing properties have to be implemented before a remote observable can be used on such a link.

Fortunately, these constraints are fulfilled in many transport protocols such as TCP, TLS over TCP, WebSockets, and HTTP/2. Before a first implementation tentative, let's first detail three of the most popular communication patterns and how they can be implemented as observables:

- Publish/subscribe
- Channel
- Request/response

Publish/subscribe

The publish/subscribe communication pattern involves one event producer and several consumers. This pattern is also often named the observer design pattern. This pattern consists of a unidirectional stream of communication, where one component is the source of events (the producer), and one, or several, components are sinks of these events (the consumers). The following figure shows how this pattern works:

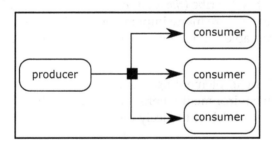

Figure 12.1: The publish/subscribe design pattern

The principle of this pattern is to decouple the producer from the consumers. The producer emits events with no knowledge of the existing consumers. The consumers register events to a producer, so that they receive events whenever they are available. Usually, an entity which lies between the producers and consumers allows us to provide this decoupling between both parts. This is the square in the middle of *Figure 12.1*. This entity can be as simple as a function or a class, or very complex, such as a broker composed of several nodes forming a cluster.

The publish/subscribe pattern is used on all kinds of communication:

- **Intra-process, via functions or classes**: Intra-process publish/subscribe is implemented via the classical observer design pattern. This pattern is very popular in object-oriented programming. It is heavily used in GUI environments because it is event-driven. All programming environments provide APIs to use this pattern. For example, Qt and GObject implement APIs for this pattern.
- **Inter-process, via IPC**: Inter-process publish/subscribe is also widely available. The implementation in this case relies on a message bus, with a central broker process where all publishers and subscribers register. The role of the broker is to route messages to their recipients. D-Bus, the IPC foundation of almost all Linux distributions, is a typical example of such an implementation.
- **On a network link**: Publish/subscribe over a network link is also very common. More than that, it is more common because usually it provides better performance and less latency than the request/response pattern. Most of the time, the network implementation relies on a broker. In these cases, the broker is a cluster. Distributing the load on several nodes allows us to process messages even if a node fails, and to scale the messaging system horizontally. Typical implementations are Kafka, MQTT, and ZeroMQ.

As already explained in Chapter 1, *An Introduction to Reactive Programming*, ReactiveX is an implementation of publish/subscribe (*the observer pattern done right*) for intra-process communication. Because there are many implementations of this pattern for remote communication, the observable abstraction can also be used over network links. There are two ways to do this:

- The first one is by implementing a driver on top of an existing technology. For example, in an environment where Kafka is used, then one just has to wrap a Kafka library into a driver to nicely integrate a ReactiveX application with Kafka streams.
- The second one, which is the subject of this chapter, consists of implementing this broker on top of a persistent connection, by leveraging the features of ReactiveX. On one side, this requires writing more code. But on the other side, existing brokers may not be available or suitable in the operating environment.

Let's look again at the observable contract to get an idea of how an observable can be represented on a network layer, that is, via messages being sent on a network link. The observable contract requires that the observable receives notifications from the observer via one of the following events: OnNext, OnCompleted, and OnError. The observable contract also requires that the observer communicate with the observables via two events: subscribe and unsubscribe.

These five events are the only events needed to implement an observable emitting items to an observer, with both entities being on two systems. The following figure shows a sequence diagram of a typical observable life cycle on a network link:

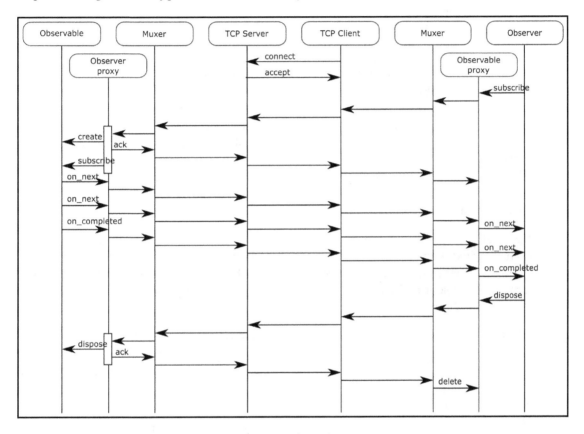

Figure 12.2: Publish/subscribe implemented as an observable

The principle is straightforward, but there are some key points. There are eight entities involved in this diagram:

- The **TCP Server** and the **TCP Client**. The network link in this example is a TCP connection. The client must first connect to the server before any communication is possible.
- The **Muxer** is instantiated both on the client side and on the server side. This component is in charge of transforming network messages to API calls, and vice versa. In practice, this entity implements both multiplexing and demultiplexing but is named **Muxer** for simplicity. This part will be detailed in a following sub-part.

- The **Observer proxy** and the **Observable proxy** are wrappers between their respective ReactiveX API and the **Muxer**.
- The **Observer** and the **Observable** are the end parties that communicate with each other.

As shown in *Figure 12.2*, most of the communication is a direct mapping of the **Observer/Observable** APIs on messages. However, there are some implications, due to the fact that the **Observer** and the **Observable** are on different systems. The first one is the fact that, when an **Observable proxy** is created, then nothing happens on the peer. The reason is that the creation of an **Observable** cannot fail with the RxPY API (this is also the case in many other implementations of ReactiveX). So, this request should be forwarded to the peer. There would be no means to notify an error in a similar way other than with a local observable. The first request that goes to the peer is the subscription request. The call to **subscribe** cannot return errors, but it is possible to notify an issue after this call. If something goes wrong during the subscription on the network side, then the **Observable proxy** can complete on error.

On the publisher side, when a subscription message is received, then the **Observable** is created and immediately subscribed. An additional acknowledgement message is sent to notify the subscriber that the subscription succeeded. If any error is raised on the producer side, then a nack is sent to the peer so that the subscriber can stop the subscription. Such an error sequence is shown in the following figure:

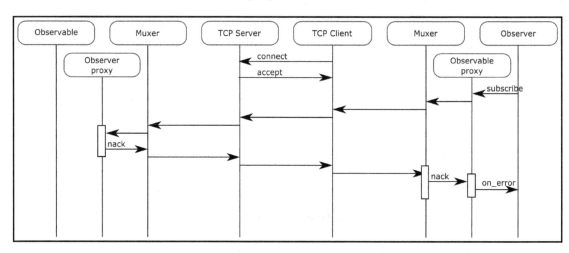

Figure 12.3: An error during subscription

The fact that the **Observable** creation is deferred until subscription has another consequence: any parameter provided to the **Observable** creation API has to be saved, and provided in the subscription message.

One last thing must be done with remote observables: hot observables should be shared after the observable proxy, that is, on the consumer side. The reason behind this is performance. If an **Observable** is made hot on the producer side and a client subscribes to it via several observers, then the associated messages will be duplicated as many times as there are observers. On the other hand, if the **Observable proxy** is made hot and observers subscribe to this hot observable, then the observable items of the producer are sent only once on the network. This is shown in the following figure:

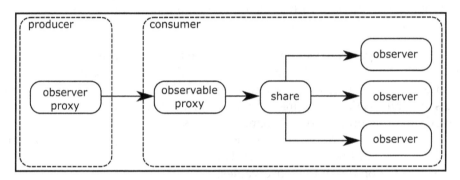

Figure 12.4: Hot observables must be subscribed on the consumer side

Channel

The channel communication pattern involves two peers. This pattern is a bidirectional communication: two nodes communicate with each other, sending messages without a strong relationship between each message. The following figure shows how this pattern works:

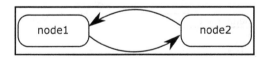

Figure 12.5: The channel communication pattern

Although this communication pattern can be used over all kinds of communication channel, it is mostly used in network communications.

The differences between intra-process, inter-process, and network channels are as follows:

- Intra-process channels are quite rare. These would involve recursive calls to inter-dependent functions. Not something to be used on a daily basis!
- Inter-process communication is also quite rare, although more natural to implement than intra-process channels. This pattern is possible with many IPC brokers. However there are not many use-cases where two components talk to each other with a loose coupling between each other's messages.
- Network channels, on the other hand, have a very popular use-case for this communication pattern: chat services. On such services, the messages emitted by each peer are not technically linked to the other messages. Hopefully these messages are semantically linked together, but only for the end-users who wrote the payload of these messages.

Despite its limited usages, the channel pattern can be used as a base for other communication patterns. So, implementing it is a requirement before dealing with more evolved patterns. Channel communication requires a bidirectional channel. However, observables are unidirectional channels. So how can a bidirectional channel be implemented on top of unidirectional channels? The solution is easy: by using two unidirectional channels communicating in the opposite direction, and linking them logically. This forms a bidirectional channel. The following figure shows the channel pattern implemented on top of two observables:

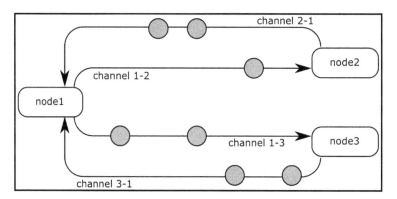

Figure 12.6: The channel communication pattern on top of observables

On this implementation, each node subscribes to an observable of the other node. The two observables must be logically linked so that a node can use several channels, either with the same peer, or with other peers: This ensures that a message is sent to the correct peer. The following figure shows a sequence diagram for the messages being sent on the network link to establish a channel:

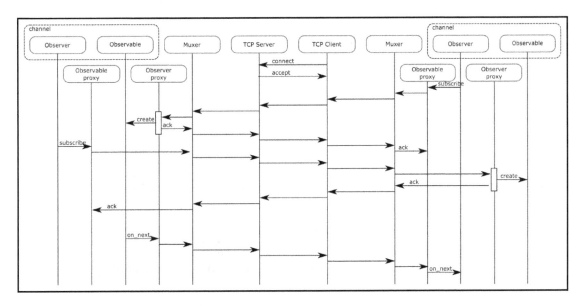

Figure 12.7: A channel as two observables on a network link

This sequence diagram is based on the one of the publish/subscribe patterns, but duplicated: each node subscribes to an observable of the remote node. However, this is done strictly sequentially so that the two observables are linked together.

The first step consists of both peers connecting together. One peer must be a **TCP Server** while the other must be a **TCP Client**. In this case, the choice of whether a node should be a server or a client is independent of the fact that the node is a producer or a receiver since it is both.

Then, one of the nodes initiates the creation of the channel. It does so by subscribing to the observable of the peer. This step is the same as for publish/subscribe. Once this observable is subscribed, the other node subscribes to the observable of the first node. At that point, the channel is available and both nodes can communicate with each other. Linking the two observables together is done on top of the publish/subscribe sequence described in the previous section. In practice, a channel component is in charge of this, via the composition of an observable and an observer.

Request/response

The request/response communication pattern involves two peers. This pattern is a bidirectional communication: a client asks for something from a service, and the service answers to this query. The following figure shows how this pattern works:

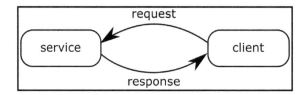

Figure 12.8: The request/response communication pattern

This communication pattern is probably the most used of all the available patterns. This is probably because it is the pattern used for human communication. Just like publish/subscribe, this pattern can be used on all kinds of communication: intra-process, inter-process, and on network links with **Remote Procedure Calls** (**RPCs**):

- Intra-process request/response is the pattern implemented by functions and methods of classes: a requester calls a function to request something, and the function answers this request. In this case, the function is the entity providing the service.
- Inter-process request/response is widely used on operating systems to make different daemons and applications communicate with each other. Usually, it is implemented in the same services as those providing publish/subscribe. However, in this case the communication on the message bus is between two peers, and no other client of the message bus can access these messages.
- Network request/response is available via many different protocols. From veterans such as CORBA, to universal protocols such as HTTP, all consortiums, and virtually all software companies, have implemented their own RPC protocol.

Request/response is quite different from publish/subscribe: the first protocol is bidirectional, while the latter is unidirectional. The first one is pull-based while the second one is push-based. This difference between pull and push communication is the key to understanding why observables can be used as a base tool to implement all communication patterns.

Pull-based communication is driven by the component which receives the information. This component actively requests information whenever it is needed. On the other hand, push-based communication is driven by the component that produces events. The receiver has no control over when this information will be available. So at first, it seems that these two modes are exclusive since some use cases can be implemented only in one or the other way (at least for an efficient implementation):

- Any request that can provide a different information at each request, or a request whose answer depends on the provided input, is inherently pull-based: a producer has no way of providing the correct information at the correct time without a query coming in from the requester.
- An event that can occur at any time, independently from any request, is inherently push-based: a consumer cannot just query the producer to know if something happened. To some extents, this is possible but it means that events must be buffered by the producer until all receivers have consumed them, and the consumers must constantly query the producer. This is usually known as polling, and when it is done in a very basic way, it is quite inefficient.

There are many examples where push-based communication has been implemented on top of a pull-based protocol. One of the most used ones is HTTP long polling, where the consumer sends an HTTP request, and the producer completes this query when an event is available. However, this is usually the beginning of trouble. In this example, if an event occurs between two HTTP requests, then the event is lost. One way to circumvent this issue is to use several HTTP connections so that one is always active, and no event is lost. **Bidirectional-streams Over Synchronous HTTP (BOSH)**, is one protocol using this trick to implement eventing on top of HTTP. Needless to say, such implementations are quite complex.

On the other hand, there are no widely known protocols implementing pull-based communication on top of push-based communication. MQTT 5 may become the first one, with request/response being implemented on top of the publish/subscribe pattern of MQTT. Let's see why implementing a pull communication on top of a push communication, while counterintuitive, is more simple, and probably more efficient than the other way.

The first requirement for pull communication is a bidirectional channel. The previous part showed how to implement this on top of two logically linked unidirectional channels. The second requirement is that one request must lead to one, and only one, answer (either a success with a value, or a failure). This description is a subset of the features provided by an observable. So, a response can be represented as an observable that emits a single item in the case of success, and completes on error in the case of failure. The following figure shows a possible request/response pattern implemented on top of observables:

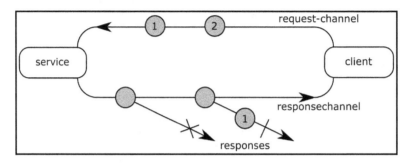

Figure 12.9: The request/response communication pattern on top of observables

The implementation relies on a bidirectional channel implemented on top of two observables, as explained previously. Each request is encoded as an item emitted on the request-channel observable. The response-channel observable is a higher-order observable, where each item is a `response` observable. A `response` observable emits, at most, one item containing the answer, before it completes. In the case of failure, the `response` observable completes on error without emitting any item. In *Figure 12.9*, the request **1** succeeds, while request **2** fails.

The problem with such an implementation is that many messages have to be exchanged on the network link: since each response is an observable, a new observable must be created, subscribed, and disposed for each answer. So, instead of the implementation shown in *Figure 12.9*, a more optimized one is shown in the following figure:

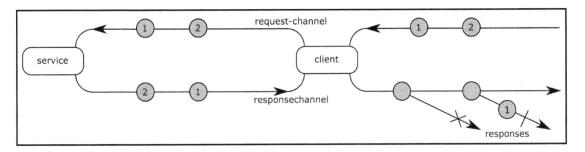

Figure 12.10: The request/response communication pattern, with one item per response

In this implementation, an answer is encoded as a single item on the network link. Then these items are exposed as observables on the client side. This allows us to still use observables as responses, but without any overhead on the network link.

The following figure shows a sequence diagram of one client sending a request to a service:

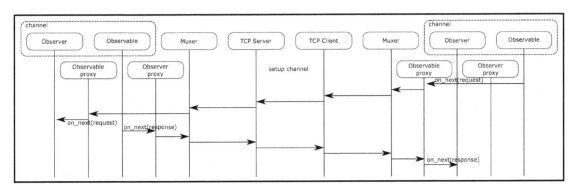

Figure 12.11: A request/response sequence diagram

The channel setup part is omitted here because it has already been detailed in *Figure 12.7*. Once the channel is established, each request is emitted as an `on_next` message on the network link, and the response is also emitted as an `on_next` message on the link. The request message must contain a request ID field, sent back in the response, so that the response can be associated to the correct request. Also, in the event of an error, then the error is emitted as an `on_next` message, not an error message. Otherwise this would close the channel, which is not the expected behavior.

Observable multiplexing

The three communication patterns studied in the previous part are certainly the most used ones in computer science. Other patterns exist, but most of the time they are variants of those. The sequence diagrams, as well as the figures showing how these pattern can be implemented on top of observables, should be clear enough so you can understand how they could be implemented. However, there are some important missing parts in these diagrams, things that must be handled so that the remote communication can work. The previous part described the network part, and how messages exchanged on it can be mapped to observables. But between these two parts, three other functional layers are needed:

- Framing
- Serialization
- Routing

The following figure shows these layers on a communication between two peers:

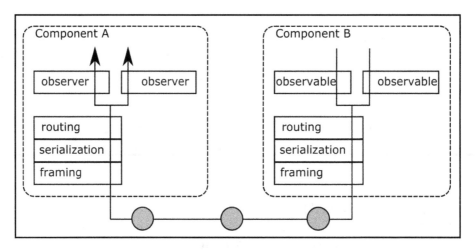

Figure 12.12: The functional layers of remote communication

Framing consists of composing complete messages from bytes received on the network link. **Serialization** consists of transforming messages received on the network link to objects (Python objects in our case). **Routing** consists of sending received objects to the correct recipient.

Let's detail each of these layers, before implementing the publish/subscribe pattern on a network link.

Framing

Framing is the first step to be done when network packets are received, and the last one when network messages are sent. In fact, the need for this step depends on the network protocol being used. Network protocols are classified in two categories:

- Datagram protocols
- Stream protocols

Datagram protocols operate on datagrams, that is, messages. Datagrams are the base unit sent on the network. So a producer writes a datagram on the network, and a receiver receives this same datagram, or nothing if an error occurred. UDP is an example of a datagram protocol.

Stream protocols operate on bytes. Bytes are the base units that are sent on the network. So, a producer writes bytes on the network link, and a receiver receives these bytes, but not necessarily split in the same way. For example, a producer may have sent ten bytes, and the receiver first reads five bytes, then three bytes, then the remaining two bytes. TCP is an example of a stream protocol.

Framing is a transformation that consists of transforming bytes to datagrams, and vice versa. This step is necessary because the upper layers operate on datagrams (messages), not bytes. So, when a datagram protocol is used, then the framing part is not needed because the network can send the datagram directly. However on a stream protocol, each datagram must be encoded (framed) before being sent as bytes, so that the receiver can decode (unframe) the received bytes to the original datagram. The following figure shows the principle of framing:

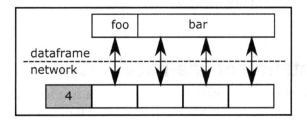

Figure 12.13: Framing

On the application side, a dataframe must be sent on the network link. This dataframe is composed of four bytes: one byte containing the `foo` information, and three bytes containing the `bar` information. When such a dataframe is framed, a header is first sent on the network. This header (one byte in this example) gives information about the data that will follow on the network. Then the dataframe payload is sent on the network link, eventually, byte after byte. When such a dataframe is received, the first byte to be received is the header. Then all of the four bytes are received, either all at once, or in parts (up to four parts consisting of one byte). In this case, the header contains the information needed to know when the dataframe is complete.

There are many possible ways to implement framing. They vary in complexity depending on the guarantees provided by the transport layer. The transport protocols considered here provide many guarantees (on data ordering and validity). So, simple framing algorithms can be used. Two framing algorithm families are widely used:

- Line-based framing
- Length-prefixed framing

Line-based framing is adapted to simple situations where dataframes are composed of text. This is typically the case when dataframes are JSON strings. With line-based framing, a new line character is used to split or recompose dataframes. So, this framing simply consists of adding a new line character on the network link at the end of each dataframe. The advantage of this framing is that it is very simple. The drawback is that it is limited to text data, and special care is needed if this data contains new lines.

Length-prefixed framing works with any kind of payload. With length-prefixed framing, a header is added before the dataframe. This header is a number containing the number of bytes present in the following dataframe. The advantage of this framing is that it works with text and binary data. However, it is a little bit more complex than line-based framing because the endianness of the header must be handled correctly so that it works with all CPU architectures (little and big-endian). Sometimes, a magic pattern is also added in the header to ensure that framing does not go out of sync in case of data loss on the network link.

An implementation of line-based framing

Let's see how line-based framing can be implemented via two lettable functions (functions that can be used with the `let` operator). The following is the code for the framing operator:

```
def frame(datagram):
    def on_subscribe(observer):
        def on_next(i):
```

```
        if '\n' in i:
            observer.on_error(ValueError('
            newline must be escaped'))
        observer.on_next(i + '\n')

    datagram.subscribe(
        on_next=on_next,
        on_error=observer.on_error,
        on_completed=observer.on_completed,
    )
    return Observable.create(on_subscribe)
```

It takes an observable of datagrams as input, and returns an observable of data that can be sent on the wire. The `frame` function follows the now classical pattern on input/output observable functions. The `datagram` observable is subscribed when `observer` subscribes to the output observable. Each time an item is received, then a newline character is added at the end. Note that this could have been done directly with the `map` operator, as in the following example:

```
def frame(datagram):
    return datagram.map(lambda i: i + '\n')
```

However, an additional check is done here to ensure that the incoming input does not contain a newline. If this is the case, then an error is notified.

The `unframe` operator is more complex, because, for each received item, it can emit zero, one, or several items. The following is its code:

```
def unframe(data):
    def on_subscribe(observer):
        acc = ''

        def on_next(i):
            nonlocal acc
            lines = i.split('\n')
            lines[0] = acc + lines[0]
            acc = lines[-1]
            datagrams = lines[0:-1]
            for datagram in datagrams:
                observer.on_next(datagram)

        data.subscribe(
            on_next=on_next,
            on_error=observer.on_error,
            on_completed=observer.on_completed,
        )
    return Observable.create(on_subscribe)
```

The pattern is still the same. The `acc` variable is an accumulator initialized to an empty string. This accumulator stores any remaining characters from the previous items, so that complete lines can be recomposed from multiple items. The `on_next` function splits the received string, based on the newline character. Depending on the way the data is received on the network, there can be zero, one, or more lines in the item. After splitting the item into multiple lines, the first line is prefixed with any remaining data from the previous item. Then the accumulator is updated with this as the content of the last partial line. Note that, if the received item ends with a newline character, then the last entry of the list returned by the `split` function is an empty string. Finally, all full lines are sent on the output observable.

Serialization

The next layer (from the bottom to the top on *Figure 12.12*) is serialization. Once a datagram is available, it has to be converted to a Python object. Like framing, many different serialization protocols exist. Some are text-based, and some are binary-based.

Text-based serialization is widely used because it is usually easy to implement. In some cases, a hand-made serialization algorithm based on key/values separated by a specific character can be enough. Typically, the **Comma-Separated Values (CSV)** format, widely used to store datasets, is the simplest form of text-based serialization. A consequence of this simplicity is that such simple algorithms have limitations. The main one is that they cannot handle complex types, that is, the values cannot be structured values, but only base types, such as integers and strings.

Some more evolved text-based algorithms exist to cope with these limitations. The most widely used one is probably **JavaScript Object Notation (JSON)**. JSON is widely used to encode information on the web, its syntax is simple, and it allows us to serialize complex types composed of lists or objects. Another advantage of JSON is that one object can be serialized on a string composed of only one line, which makes it a perfect combination with line-based framing. The main drawback of all text-based serialization algorithms is performance: parsing text is complex, so these algorithms can have a significant performance impact on high workloads.

Binary-based serialization is more complex to implement than text-based serialization. There are several reasons for this. The first one is that, since they encode objects in binary blobs, ensuring compatibility between multiple systems and programming languages is more complex. The second one is also why binary-based serialization is worth the effort: encoding data in a binary format allows for many optimizations, both on the size of encoding, and speed of encoding. So binary-based serialization is much more efficient than text-based encoding. Depending on the context, this can be an important criterion for the choice of the serialization algorithm in an application.

Among all the available algorithms, Google developed and open-sourced one of the most versatile ones: Protobuf. Protobuf allows us to serialize simple objects, up to very complex ones, that are large. Moreover, it supports a feature rarely supported by its competitors: management of evolution in the structures. This allows us to add or remove fields in objects to serialize, while ensuring that existing software will work with these changes (not in all cases, but in a lot). Google provides implementations of Protobuf for many languages, with code generated from a **Domain Specific Language** (**DSL**) which makes it very easy to use. But Protobuf is only one of the many available solutions. MessagePack is an alternative, also supporting many programming languages. MessagePack aims to be similar to JSON in its ease of use but with binary encoding, which makes it much more efficient than JSON. Other popular solutions are AVRO and Thrift, both developed by the Apache foundation.

Choosing between text-based serialization or binary-based serialization should be based on two main criteria: performance and ease of use. If serialization may become the performance bottleneck of the application (which is rarely the case), then binary-based serialization should be used. Otherwise the choice should be based on ease of use in the ecosystem. Special care is needed on that point for binary-based serialization: many algorithms are not supported in JavaScript running in a browser. So, such algorithms cannot be used to talk between a web frontend and a backend.

An implementation of JSON serialization

Implementation of the serialization layer is easier than framing because it always emits one item when one item is received. So any serialization algorithm can be used with the map operator. As for JSON, Python already provides serialization and deserialization functions for this. So the deserialization part is just an additional map in an operator chain, as can be seen in the following example:

```
.map(lambda i: json.loads(i))
```

The serialization part is also shown in the following example:

```
.map(lambda i: json.dumps(i))
```

Routing

The last layer of the stack is routing. When multiple remote observables are active at the same time, then, on the consumer side, their events must be routed to the correct observer, and, on the provider side, the events must be routed to the correct network link.

Unlike framing and serialization, routing is not really something that has widely used implementations. It is also a topic on which much research has been done, with many available algorithms, but usually this part ends up with a specific implementation in each framework or application.

Implementing publish/subscribe

Time has come for the last example of this book, once again using both AsyncIO and RxPY. This last example is an implementation of the publish/subscribe communication pattern on a TCP connection. Two applications will be implemented here: the publisher, implemented in a TCP server, and the subscriber, implemented in a TCP client.

The publisher emits either an observable of four numbers (1, 2, 3, 4), or an observable containing the `"let's go"` string, each time a remote observer subscribes to it. The observable being returned depends on a parameter provided by the subscriber. The publisher supports several clients connected at the same time, and routes the items to the corresponding client.

Both applications are implemented via Cyclotron. The boilerplate to set up the project is not detailed in this chapter, so that explanations of the code can focus on the multiplexing part. Also, the observable subscription is simplified, with the `ack` and `nack` parts being omitted. The complete code for this example is available in the GitHub repository of this book, in the `rmux` sub-folder.

The publisher

Let's start by implementing the publisher part. Starting the implementation with the publisher, hosted in a TCP server, will allow us to test it via telnet before implementing the subscriber.

Implementation of a TCP server

The AsyncIO module contains implementations of a TCP server and client. These are the implementations used in this project. These two components are implemented as drivers because they are side-effects. The TCP server operates on the following data types:

```
Sink = namedtuple('Sink', ['request'])
Source = namedtuple('Source', ['response'])

# Sink items
Listen = namedtuple('Listen', ['host', 'port'])
Write = namedtuple('Write', ['id', 'data'])

# Source items
Connection = namedtuple('Connection', ['id', 'observable'])
Data = namedtuple('Data', ['data'])
```

Sink and Source for the driver are composed of only one observable each: a request observable for Sink, and a response observable for Source.

Two Sink items are needed. The first one, named Listen, is the request to start the server. This item contains two fields: the host and port used to bind the server. The second sink item, named Write, is used for writing data on an established connection. Its contains two fields. The first one is the id of the connection where the data must be written, and the second one is the data filed to write on the network link.

Two Source items are emitted. The Connection item is emitted each time a new client connects to the server. This item contains two fields. The first one is an id identifying this connection. This id must be provided back in the Write items. The second field is observable, which emits items each time data is available on the TCP link. So the response observable is a higher-order observable emitting one item each time a new client connects to the server. The second source item, named Data, is the item emitted on the observable of the Connection item. The Data item contains a data field containing the bytes received on the network link.

The subscription callback for the response observable looks like this:

```
def on_subscribe(observer):
    async def listen(host, port, handler):
        try:
            await asyncio.start_server(
                handler, host, port, loop=loop)
        except Exception as e:
            loop.call_soon(observer.on_error(e))
```

```
async def write(writer, data):
    writer.write(data)

def on_next(i):
    if type(i) is Listen:
        asyncio.ensure_future(listen(
            i.host, i.port, client_connected))
    elif type(i) is Write:
        asyncio.ensure_future(write(i.id, i.data))

sink.request.subscribe(
    on_next=on_next,
    on_completed=observer.on_completed,
    on_error=observer.on_error
)
```

Starting from the end, the `request` observable is subscribed with the error and completion handler forwarding the events to the response observer. The `on_next` handler accepts the two sink items defined previously.

The `Listen` item schedules the execution of the `listen` coroutine. This coroutine starts a TCP server bound on the host and port provided in the listen item. The handler of this server is the `client_connected` coroutine, which will be detailed later.

The `Write` item schedules the execution of the `write` coroutine. Wrapping the `write` call of `writer` is necessary because it is not a coroutine. However, this `write` method (`write` is an object of the `StreamWriter` class) is not blocking: it is buffering the data to send it asynchronously. So the data is not necessarily sent when the `write` method returns. The `id` field used in the `Write` item is a `StreamWriter` object.

Finally let's see the `client_connected` handler, called each time a client connects to the server. It is implemented as a nested function of `on_subscribe`, as follows:

```
async def client_connected(reader, writer):
    def on_connection_subscribe(observer, reader, writer):
        async def handle_connection(observer, reader, writer):
            while True:
                try:
                    data = await reader.read(100)
                    if data == b'':
                        break
                    loop.call_soon(observer.on_next, Data(data=data))
                except Exception as e:
                    loop.call_soon(observer.on_error(e))
                    break
```

```
            loop.call_soon(observer.on_completed)
            writer.close()

        asyncio.ensure_future(handle_connection(
            observer, reader, writer))

    connection = Observable.create(
        lambda o: on_connection_subscribe(o, reader, writer))
    observer.on_next(Connection(
        id=writer,
        observable=connection))
```

Let's start reading the code from the last block. First, an observable is created. Its subscription function is called with a reference to the context as the second argument. Then a `Connection` item is emitted on `observer` of the `response` observable.

The `on_connection_subscribe` function just schedules the execution of the `handle_connection` coroutine. This coroutine reads data on the connection infinitely, until the connection is closed by the client (in this case the read call returns no data). Each time some data is received, this data is emitted on the data observable of the connection. When the connection is closed, the data observable is completed and `writer` is closed.

Implementation of the publisher

The publisher is implemented as a Cyclotron component, being the entry point of the application. This component implements the three layers of remote stream multiplexing in fewer than 30 lines of code, thanks to the ReactiveX operators. This component uses only one driver, the TCP server implemented in the previous example. Here is the function implementing this component:

```
def rmux_server(sources):
    tcp_listen = Observable.just(tcp_server.Listen(
        host='127.0.0.1', port='8080'
    ))

    beat = (
        sources.tcp_server.response
        .flat_map(lambda connection: connection.observable
            .map(lambda i: i.data.decode('utf-8'))
            .let(unframe)
            .map(lambda i: json.loads(i))
            .flat_map(lambda subscription: create_observable[
                    subscription['name']]()
                .materialize()
                .map(lambda i: materialize_repr(i, subscription['id']))
```

```
            )
            .map(lambda i: json.dumps(i))
            .let(frame)
            .map(lambda j: tcp_server.Write(
                id=connection.id, data=j.encode()))
        )
    )

    tcp_sink = Observable.merge(tcp_listen, beat)
    return Sink(
        tcp_server=tcp_server.Sink(request=tcp_sink),
    )
```

Let's start with the first and last blocks of the function. First, the `tcp_listen` observable allows us to start the TCP server on a `localhost` and port `8080`. At the end of the function, this observable is merged with the `publish` observable, and the result is provided as the `request` field of the TCP server `Sink` object.

The publish observable is the implementation of the three steps (in both ways) of the multiplexing layers. It is composed of two nested `flat_map` operators. Each level of `flat_map` allows us to save some context information.

The first `flat_map` layer maps each connection item to its data observable. All the operations on a connection are done inside this operator. This allows direct access to the `connection` item, which is necessary to send back data on the correct connection.

Then the incoming data is decoded as a UTF-8 string. This step is necessary because the data received from the TCP server contains bytes. This data must be decoded to a string before it can be parsed as a JSON string. The next operator unframes the incoming data, by using the `unframe` function implemented in the previous part. After this `map` operator, a complete JSON line is emitted. So it can be deserialized with the Python JSON module.

Then comes the routing layer. The routing in this case is implemented with the `flat_map` operator. Each time a subscription item is received, then an observable is returned, depending on the `name` field provided in the `subscription` object. The `create_observable` variable is a dictionary containing an `Observable` factory for each supported name value, as can be seen in the following example:

```
def one_two_three_four():
    return Observable.from_(['1', '2', '3', '4'])

def lets_go():
    return Observable.just("let's go")

create_observable = {
```

```
        '1234': one_two_three_four,
        'heyho': lets_go,
    }
```

After this step, the observable must be serialized so that its items are sent on the TCP connection. Three types of event have to be sent: next, error, and completed, corresponding to the life cycle of an observable. The materialize operator just does this. So it is used to translate the observable to items representing the observable. An additional step is required to translate the object created by the materialize operator to something that can be serialized to a JSON string. This is done in the `materialize_repr` function. This function just maps RxPY notification objects to dictionaries, as can be seen in the following example:

```
def materialize_repr(notification, id):
    if type(notification) is OnNext:
        return {
            'what': 'on_next',
            'item': notification.value,
            'id': id,
        }
    elif type(notification) is OnError:
        return {
            'what': 'on_error',
            'error': str(notification.exception),
            'id': id,
        }
    elif type(notification) is OnCompleted:
        return {
            'what': 'on_completed',
            'id': id,
        }
```

Once this step is done, there is no more need to use the subscription item, so the next step is done outside the second `flat_map` level. In the next step, serialization is done, always with the Python JSON module. After that, framing is done, again with the function implemented in the previous part. Finally, the resulting item is mapped to a write request, using the connection id available via the first `flat_map` level.

To test this publisher implementation, install and start the server from a Terminal, as follows:

```
(venv-rx) $ python3 setup.py install
(venv-rx) $ rmux_server
```

Then, from another Terminal, connect to it via telnet, and send a subscribe JSON request, as follows:

```
$ telnet localhost 8080
Trying 127.0.0.1...
Connected to localhost.
Escape character is '^]'.
{"what":"subscribe", "id":"42", "name":"1234"}
```

The server should answer with five messages, representing the received observable, as per the following example:

```
{"what": "on_next", "item": "1", "id": "42"}
{"what": "on_next", "item": "2", "id": "42"}
{"what": "on_next", "item": "3", "id": "42"}
{"what": "on_next", "item": "4", "id": "42"}
{"what": "on_completed", "id": "42"}
```

You can also try using the `"heyho"` name to check that it also works, and verify, with several telnet connections at the same time, whether answers are sent to the client that requested the observable and not the others.

The subscriber

The subscriber is implemented in a similar way to the producer, but on top of a TCP client.

Implementation of a TCP client

The TCP client is also implemented as a Cyclotron driver. Its behavior is similar to that of the server: it takes the similar `Sink` observables as input and returns similar `Source` observables. The following example shows the types used by this driver:

```
Sink = namedtuple('Sink', ['request'])
Source = namedtuple('Source', ['response'])

# Sink items
Connect = namedtuple('Connect', ['host', 'port'])
Write = namedtuple('Write', ['id', 'data'])

# Source items
Connection = namedtuple('Connection', ['id', 'observable'])
Data = namedtuple('Data', ['data'])
```

The only difference is the `Listen` sink item that is replaced with a `Connect` item, taking the same arguments. The meaning however is different: the `Listen` item on the TCP server is a request to bind a server to the provided host and port, while the `Connect` item of the client is a request to connect to the provided host and port.

The subscription to the `Source` observable is the following code, also very similar to the server driver:

```
def on_subscribe(observer):
    async def tcp_client(host, port):
        try:
            reader, writer = await asyncio.open_connection(
                host, port, loop=loop)
            connection = Observable.create(
                lambda o: on_connection_subscribe(o, reader, writer))
            observer.on_next(Connection(
                id=writer,
                observable=connection))
        except Exception as e:
            loop.call_soon(observer.on_error(e))

    async def write(writer, data):
        writer.write(data)

    def on_next(i):
        if type(i) is Connect:
            asyncio.ensure_future(tcp_client(i.host, i.port))
        elif type(i) is Write:
            asyncio.ensure_future(write(i.id, i.data))

    sink.request.subscribe(
        on_next=on_next,
        on_completed=observer.on_completed,
        on_error=observer.on_error
    )
```

The handling of the `Write` item is exactly the same: a coroutine is scheduled to write data on the `writer` of the connection.

The Listen item schedules the execution of the tcp_client coroutine. The implementation of this coroutine is also similar to the client_connection coroutine of the server. It first tries to connect to the host and port provided in the Connect item. In the event of an error, the response observable is completed (in this case, the application will terminate but, for a client application, this behavior is usual). In the event of success, a Connection item is emitted on the response observable, with a new data observable in the observable field. The subscription function of this latter observable is a function that reads the data on the network link, as can be seen in the following example:

```python
def on_connection_subscribe(observer, context):
    async def handle_connection(observer, context):
        while True:
            try:
                data = await context.reader.read(100)
                if data == b'':
                    break
                loop.call_soon(observer.on_next, Data(data=data))
            except Exception as e:
                loop.call_soon(observer.on_error(e))
                break

        loop.call_soon(observer.on_completed)
        context.writer.close()

    asyncio.ensure_future(handle_connection(observer, context))
```

This function schedules a coroutine that reads data on the link until the connection is interrupted. Each time some data is available, then a Data item is emitted on the data observable of the connection. Once again, this is very similar to the behavior of the TCP server driver.

Implementation of the subscriber

The subscriber is implemented as a component. It uses two drivers: the tcp_client and stdout. Its implementation is as follows:

```python
def rmux_client(sources):
    response = sources.tcp_client.response.share()
    tcp_connect = Observable.just(tcp_client.Connect(
        host='127.0.0.1', port='8080'
    ))

    create_observable = (
        response
```

```
        .flat_map(lambda connection:
            Observable.just({
                'what': 'subscribe',
                'id':42,
                'name': '1234'})
            .map(lambda i: json.dumps(i))
            .let(frame)
            .map(lambda j: tcp_client.Write(
                id=connection.id, data=j.encode()))
        )
    )

    console = (
        response
        .flat_map(lambda connection: connection.observable
            .map(lambda i: i.data.decode('utf-8'))
            .let(unframe)
            .map(lambda i: json.loads(i))
            .group_by(lambda i: i['id'])
            .flat_map(lambda subscription: subscription
                .map(notification)
                .dematerialize()
            )
        )
        .map(lambda i: "item: {}\n".format(i))
    )

    tcp_sink = Observable.merge(tcp_connect, create_observable)
    return Sink(
        tcp_client=tcp_client.Sink(request=tcp_sink),
        stdout=stdout.Sink(data=console),
    )
```

Let's start reading it from the first and last blocks. The first step transforms the `response` observable to a hot observable, so that it can be subscribed for two purposes, without triggering new subscriptions on the driver. Then a `Connect` item is emitted in a dedicated observable.

On the last block, two observables are merged to form the TCP client `request` observable: `tcp_connect` contains the connection request, and `create_observable` contains the subscription requests. Finally, `Sink` is returned with observables for both drivers.

The `create_observable` observable emits items containing subscription requests for remote observables. It is driven by incoming `Connection` items on the `response` observable. In the previous code example, only one item is emitted on the `response` observable, leading to the emission of one subscription request. First, the `flat_map` operator is used to save the connection context. Then a subscription dictionary is created. The last three steps correspond to the multiplexing stack, and are used as on the producer: serialization on a JSON string, framing, and sending a Write item to the TCP driver.

The console observable is the handler of incoming messages. In this subscriber implementation, received items are just printed on the console. The first three operators are now familiar: saving the connection context with `flat_map`, decoding bytes to a UTF-8 string, unframing, and deserialization from JSON to a Python dictionary. Then the `group_by` operator is used, with the observable `id` as a key: this allows us to group all messages of the same observables in dedicated observables. In other words, messages are demultiplexed from a single observable to several observables. Using this operator in combination with the following `flat_map` allows us to operate on items of a single observable instead of dealing with items of several observables. So, inside the `flat_map` observable, all received items are for a single observable. These items can be converted into RxPY notification objects (`OnNext`, `OnCompleted`, and `OnError`) as can be seen in the following example:

```
def notification(obj):
    if obj['what'] == 'on_next':
        return OnNext(obj['item'])
    elif obj['what'] == 'on_completed':
        return OnCompleted()
    elif obj['what'] == 'on_error':
        return OnError(obj['error'])
```

From that point, the dematerialize operator is used to recreate an observable from these messages.

After all these steps, the end of the first `flat_map` operator contains the items of an observable which has been carried over the network link. In this implementation, received items are simply printed, one per line.

This client can now be used instead of telnet, as shown in the following example:

```
(venv-rx) $ rmux_client
item: 1
item: 2
item: 3
item: 4
```

The whole code of the publisher and the subscriber is available in the GitHub repository (`https://github.com/PacktPublishing/Hands-On-Reactive-Programming-with-Python`) for this book, in the sub-folder `rmux`.

Summary

This chapter set out to demonstrate that observables can be shared between services and applications, and do not have to be restricted inside an application.

Almost all communication protocols rely on three base patterns: publish/subscribe, channel, and request/response. Since all these protocols can be implemented on top of push-based communication, it means that observables can be used to implement all these protocols.

The three layers of the multiplexing stack are mandatory steps, each one serving a specific purpose. None can be omitted without breaking the functioning of a remote communication. These three layers are steps that must be taken when receiving and sending some messages.

The publish/subscribe implementation was relatively simple, thanks once again to AsyncIO and RxPY. This implementation requires additional features to be usable in production: more error handling, and control flow. However, considering this implementation is possible with very little code, remote observables can be considered as a valid way to communicate between components, eventually on top of existing protocols such as Kafka and MQTT.

The next (and final) chapter is a reminder of the best practices to follow when writing ReactiveX code, to avoid falling into common traps.

Questions

- What communication pattern is implemented by ReactiveX?
- What are the three widely used communication patterns?
- What is the difference between pull and push communication?
- Give examples of pull- and push-based protocols.
- What is framing?
- What is serialization?
- What is routing?
- What types of messages are needed to send an observable over a network link?

Further reading

The observable contract is the specifications of APIs exposed by observables and observers. Each of these APIs must be mapped to a message to expose an observable on a network link: `http://reactivex.io/documentation/contract.html`.

The Bosh XEP (XMPP Extension Protocol) is an example of how a pull protocol can be used to implement push. It is available here: `https://xmpp.org/extensions/xep-0124.html`.

At the time of writing this book, the MQTT 5 specifications are not yet published. The current draft is available here: `https://www.oasis-open.org/committees/documents.php?wg_abbrev=mqttshow_descriptions=yes`.

Once the specifications are complete, they will be available here: `http://mqtt.org/documentation`.

13
A Checklist of Best Practices

To conclude this journey in functional and reactive programming, this last chapter contains some advice on how to use ReactiveX more efficiently, or avoid some issues. The first part helps you choose the operator adapted to each use case. The second part is a reminder of the reason why side-effects should contain as little code as possible. The third part indicates how to deal with situations where nothing happens. Finally, the last part contains recommendations, based on the way ReactiveX observables and observers are specified.

The following topics will be covered in this chapter:

- The observable creation decision tree
- Keep side-effects as small as possible
- What to do when nothing happens
- Miscellaneous recommendations

The observable creation decision tree

This book contains the documentation of about 80 operators. The RxPY implementation contains about 130 operators. One of the most difficult parts of ReactiveX is using the most suitable operator for a given task. The following list will help you find which operator to use at that time:

To create an observable:

- That emits a single item: `just`
- That emits a single item returned from a function: `Start`
- That emits a sequence from an iterable or a generator: `from_`
- That emits a single item after a specified delay: `timer`
- That emits a single item from future: `from_future`
- That emits a sequence of items repeatedly: `repeat`

- From custom logic: `create`
- That emits a sequence of consecutive integers: `range` or `from_` (in combination with the Python range function)
- That emits a sequence of items at particular intervals of time: `interval`
- That completes without emitting items: `empty`
- That does nothing and never completes: `never`
- That drops all items of an observable and mimics its completion: `ignore_elements`

To create an observable from other observables:

- That emits all of the items from the other observables in whatever order they are received: `merge`
- That emits all of the items from the other observables, sequentially, one observable at a time: `concat`
- That combines the items from several observables sequentially, emitting new items each time all of the observables emit an item: `zip`
- That emits a composed item whenever any of the observables emits an item: `combine_latest`
- That emits an item when one observable emits an item within a window defined by an item emitted on another observable: `join`
- That emits the items from only the most recently emitted of those observables: `switch`
- That emits items from the first observable that emits an item: `amb`

To emit items from an observable after a transformation:

- One item at a time with a function: `map`
- By emitting all of the items emitted by observables created from each received item: `flat_map`
- Based on all of the items that preceded them: `scan` and `reduce`
- By attaching a timestamp to them: `timestamp`
- By emitting the amount of time that elapsed before the emission of the item: `time_interval`
- By delaying the items emitted by an observable before re-emitting them: `delay`

To serialize and deserialize an observable:

- Wrapping them in notification objects: `materialize`
- Unwrapping them from notification objects: `dematerialize`

To prefix items:

- To an observable: `start_with`
- Only if its sequence is empty: `default_if_empty`

To group items emitted by an observable:

- By collecting items from an observable and re-emitting them as buffers of items: `buffer`
- By splitting one observable into multiple observables: `window`
- So that similar items are emitted on the same observable: `group_by`

To re-emit only some items from an observable:

- By dropping those that do not match some predicate: `filter`
- Only the first item: `first`
- Only the first items: `take`
- Only the last item: `last`
- Only one item at the specified index: `element_at`
- Only the items after the first items:
    - After the first *n* items: `skip`
    - Until one of those items matches a predicate: `skip_while`
    - After a second observable emits an item: `skip_until`
- Some items except the last item:
    - Except the last *n* items: `skip_last`
    - Until one of those items matches a predicate: `take_while`
    - Except items emitted after a second observable emits an item: `take_until`
- By sampling the observable periodically: `sample`
- By only emitting items that are not followed by other items within some duration: `debounce`
- By suppressing items that are duplicates of already-emitted items: `distinct`:
    - Only when two consecutive items are duplicates: `distinct_until_changed`

To evaluate the entire sequence of items emitted by an observable:

- And emit a single Boolean indicating whether all of the items pass some test: `all`
- And emit a single Boolean indicating whether the observable emitted any item that matches a predicate: `contains`
- And emit a single Boolean indicating whether the observable emitted no items: `is_empty`
- And emit a single Boolean indicating whether the sequence is identical to one emitted by a second observable: `sequence_equal`
- And emit the average of all of their values: `average`
- And emit the sum of all of their values: `sum`
- And emit a number indicating how many items were in the sequence: `count`
- And emit the item with the maximum value: `max`
- And emit the item with the minimum value: `min`
- By applying an aggregation function to each item in turn and emitting the result: `scan` and `reduce`

To convert the entire sequence of items emitted by an observable into a single item, being a list: `to_list`
To make an operator chain:

- Operate on a particular scheduler: `subscribe_on`
- And change it inside an operator chain: `observe_on`

To invoke a particular action when certain events occur: `do_action`
To notify observers:

- Of an error: `throw`
- If a specified period of time elapses without it emitting an item: `timeout`

To recover gracefully from errors:

- From a timeout by switching to a backup observable: `timeout`
- From an upstream error notification: `catch`
- By attempting to resubscribe to the upstream observable: `retry`

To create a resource that has the same lifespan as the observable: `using`

To transform a cold observable to a hot observable: `share`

Keeping side-effects as small as possible

In functional and reactive applications, side-effects must be present only in drivers. For debugging purposes, traces can be added in the pure code with the `do_action` operator.

The code in drivers should be as small as possible, limited to the part that is the side-effect. If a driver contains a side-effect and additional logic, then the additional logic should be moved out of the driver into some pure code. This has several benefits:

- The driver is easier to test, since it does fewer things. This is good because testing side-effects is more complex than testing pure functions.
- The resulting logic is now independent of the driver. It means that is can be used with other drivers, implementing similar side-effects but in a different way or with different technologies. When this additional logic is a full protocol, then it becomes a sans-I/O implementation, a protocol implementation independent of the I/O part.

The features provided by a driver should almost always use one sink observable and one source observable. The source observable may be a higher order observable if several sequences must be emitted by the driver.

Moreover, for operational purposes, other source observables can be exposed:

- Logging should be exposed via a dedicated observable. As explained in `Chapter 10`, *Operators in RxPY*, this allows us to make logging dynamic, and independent of the items emitted for the feature provided by the driver.
- Following the same logic, a dedicated monitoring observable should be exposed. This observable should also be independent of the two other ones (the response and logging observables).

With these three kinds of observable, an application can be tracked easily in production. The monitoring part allows us to continuously check the health of the system, while the logging part can be used to look for reasons for issues detected while monitoring. If the logging configuration can be enabled dynamically, then issues can even be analyzed without restarting the service.

What to do when nothing happens

One of the most common issues when starting developing with ReactiveX is the issue that "nothing happens". There are several ways to avoid this, mostly by following the same development principles as any other piece of code:

- Write small parts of code and test them with unit tests. Whenever possible, follow **test-driven development (TDD)**. It feels like a waste of time in the beginning, but from my experience it saves time as soon as the first development release is delivered.
- Develop the application step-by-step, with something that executes as early as possible. The initial implementation will be full of stubs, but they are already doing something. With each feature being implemented one after an other, finding an issue is easier.

Following these simple principles, you may still not make any progress. In this case, using the do_action operator is the only way to find the cause of the issue. Most of the time, the cause is an error that is not correctly handled or propagated. Typical culprits for these mistakes are the following:

- A missing on_error handler
- An exception being thrown in a function called by an operator (for instance, the function provided to the map operator)
- A missing scheduler

So, the first step is to read code changes for such potential errors. If no obvious mistake is found, then the do_action operator can be used to process a dichotomy search for the issue: add a trace handler (such as the one implemented in Chapter 10, *Operators in RxPY*) somewhere in the middle of the data flow. If no error is found, then go further into the data flow until the error is printed. If the error is found, then go backward between the current location and the preceding location in the data flow. This will lead to the origin of the error quite rapidly. It is important in this step to use a trace observer that logs all events: items, errors, and completion. This allows us to spot anything that is not normal behavior, either an error being raised, a malformed item, or an early completion.

Miscellaneous recommendations

As a final note, the following are various recommendations on how to use ReactiveX and avoid some more traps.

Favor composition of existing operators

ReactiveX contains many operators. Many new operators can be written by combining several of them together. In such cases, it is preferable to use these existing operators and combine them in a lettable function rather than rewriting the whole logic from scratch. A lettable function is a function that takes an observable as input (with additional arguments if needed), and returns an observable. Such a function can be used as a custom operator with the `let` operator.

Always specify a scheduler

When using an AsyncIO event loop, it is very important to schedule items explicitly from the AsyncIO scheduler. Otherwise, depending on the way the operator chain is built, items may be emitted before the event loop is started (especially with observable cycles). This might lead to situations where items are lost, because they have been emitted before one of its observers subscribed to the associated observable. This is another possible reason why nothing happens when the application starts.

Subscriptions should not throw exceptions

When observables are composed together, subscription can happen at any time when the program runs. For example, the `concat` operator subscribes to each observable when the preceding observable completes. In such cases, if the subscription of one observable throws an exception, then the whole program stops. To avoid this, the subscription callback of a custom observable should call the `on_error` callback of the observer instead of throwing an exception in the case of an error. This allows the subscriber to gracefully handle the error.

Disposal should not throw exceptions

Disposal functions should not throw an exception, for the same reason that subscriptions should not throw exceptions: Since disposal may happen at any time during runtime, if a disposal function throws an exception, then the whole program stops. Unfortunately, unlike subscriptions, it is not possible to notify an error during disposal; the observer is already unsubscribed when the disposal function is called, and the disposal function does not return a value. So, the error can be silently handled in these cases, preferably logged to avoid losing it.

Be clear on hot and cold observables

Being aware of the type of each observable is of key importance. By default, observables in ReactiveX are cold. Following this convention will avoid surprises for people reading the code. Making cold observables hot only on purpose makes it obvious when reading the code. However, there are cases where an observable has to be implemented as a hot one. In such cases, make this information clear in the documentation of the observable factory.

Misusing a cold observable as a hot observable provokes the opposite effect from the "nothing happens" symptom: actions are executed multiple times instead of only once. This is also usually easy to detect, but finding the root cause can once again be more tricky. The dichotomy search with a trace observer is also valid in this case to find the root cause of the issue.

Summary

From the early code snippets of the first chapter up to these final recommendations on the behavior of subscriptions and disposal, you now have all the keys you need to implement functional and reactive applications that are readable, extensible, and robust.

The creation decision tree (list) is very useful when you are not fully at ease with all the available operators. Even after some time, it is a good idea to go through it again to avoid the tendency of always using the same operators even when more appropriate ones could be used.

It has been explained previously in this book but it is worth reminding you here: side-effects should be isolated from pure code, and their footprint should be reduced to the strict minimum. This often mean splitting some existing code into several parts, but this additional work is usually rewarded quickly with code that is easier to test. This also paves the way for sans-I/O protocols whose implementations can be reused on other transport layers.

The method provided here to debug applications that do not behave as expected is a reminder of Chapter 9, *Operators in RxPY*, but it is currently the only way to track down issues.

Finally, the last recommendations are things that you should know, but that are easy to forget when you are focused on developing or debugging an application. Never forget the base principles of observables and observers, and your code will behave the way you want!

By now you know (almost) everything on ReactiveX and RxPY, and you have all the knowledge necessary to write reactive AsyncIO applications. Experiment, play with, and use ReactiveX in your applications; the effort is worth it, and you will be surprised how easy it is to implement complex behaviors with it.

Questions

- Explain why side-effects must be as small as possible (in terms of code size)
- What is the advantage of a protocol implemented without I/O?
- What is the purpose of splitting logging and monitoring from features?
- Cite three reasons why an application does not behave as expected
- How can a trace observer be used to debug an application where nothing happens?
- What issue can occur when creating an observable without specifying a scheduler?
- What issue can occur when a cold observable is subscribed to several times?

Further reading

The sans-I/O principles, as well as a list of available protocol implementations, is documented here: `https://sans-io.readthedocs.io`.

The GitHub page of RxPY contains some links to additional material: `https://github.com/ReactiveX/RxPY`.

Assessments

Chapter 1

Is event-driven programming only possible with some programming languages?

Event-driven programming and reactive programming can be used with virtually any programming language and any programming paradigm. However, not all programming languages are equal in their ability to write event-driven code. Usually, the more low-level the programming language, the most difficult it is to write event-driven code in it. The term low-level is used here to describe the functionalities supported by the programming languages, not the fact that it is designed for system programming rather than applicative programming. A language with no support for closures, anonymous functions, and generators will lead to event-driven code that's hard to write, read, and maintain.

What are the differences between reactive programming and reactive systems?

Reactive programming is a way to structure code that reacts to events. A reactive system is not related to the way an application is programmed, but how it behaves. A reactive system is an application or an ensemble of applications that is responsive, resilient, and elastic, based on a message-driven architecture. Reactive programming is one tool that can be used to write a reactive system.

What is an observable?

An observable is an entity that emits zero or more items. An observable has an explicit lifetime, and it can end either successfully or with an error. Once an observable is completed, it cannot send other items.

What is an observer?

An observer is an entity that receives the events emitted by an observable.

Are observables pull-based or push-based?

Observables are push-based. This is different from iterables, which are pull-based.

What makes reactivity diagrams different from activity diagrams?

UML activity diagrams are used to document a code flow, while reactivity diagrams are used to document a data flow. An activity diagram is executed only when some code calls the function or method that implements this code flow. On the other hand, when the function implementing a reactivity diagram is called, only the connection between all operators is established. The execution of each operation occurs each time a new item is emitted on an input observable.

How do you create an observable emitting integers from 0 to 10,000?

Since the `from_` operator takes an iterable as an input, we can use it with any function from the Python standard library that returns a list. In this case, we can use the `range` function to create an observable:

```
Observable.from_(range(10001)) \
    .subscribe(lambda i: print(i))
```

This example prints numbers from 0 to 10,000.

How do you create an observable from another observable where all items are multiplied by 3?

If we have an observable of integers:

```
items = Observable.from_([1, 2, 3, 4])
```

Then, creating another observable emitting these items multiplied by 3 is done with the `map` operator:

```
three_times = items.map(lambda i: i*3)
```

Chapter 2

Why is asynchronous programming more efficient at handling I/O concurrency than multiple processes/threads?

Asynchronous programming is a very effective solution when dealing with I/O concurrency because it allows us to multiplex I/O actions without memory or computing overhead. Alternative solutions that are based on multithreading or multiprocesses require either more CPU either more memory, or even both.

Multithreading hits a limit when 1,000 threads are running concurrently. On heavy workloads, this puts some pressure on the OS scheduler and ends up wasting a lot of CPU resources due to contention.

Multiprocess solutions face the same problem, but also require more memory because the address space of the program is allocated for each instance of the program. Some of this memory is shared between these instances (such as the code sections), but a big part has to be replicated.

Why is asynchronous programming not a solution to improve performances on CPU-bound tasks?

Asynchronous programming cannot improve performance on CPU-bound tasks because it executes on a single core of the CPU. To improve the performance of a CPU-bound task, you have to parallelize the execution of this task on multiple cores. This is the situation that multithreading or multiprocess solutions are ideal for.

Why does multithreading not perform as well on Python as on other programming languages?

The Python interpreter (CPython) is implemented with a lock that prevents the execution of Python code from several threads in the same process. This lock is called the Giant Interpreter Lock. The consequence of this is the fact that several threads in a process cannot execute concurrently, even on a processor that has several cores. There are two ways to deal with this constraint:

- Use multiprocess instead of multithreading. Python code in two processes can execute simultaneously because they run in two different instances of the interpreter.
- Execute native code from Python. Many libraries are native libraries (that is, libraries implemented in C or C++ for example) with Python bindings. Native code from these libraries can run concurrently because the GIL is released when the interpreter runs native code.

What is the benefit of a generator compared to an iterator?

A generator is a simpler way to write an iterator. The main benefit of using a generator is the possibility of generating a very long, or even an infinite, sequence without loading it all in memory.

Why does a generator help with writing asynchronous code?

A generator helps with writing asynchronous code that looks like synchronous code, that is, code where logical operations follow each other instead of being spread throughout multiple locations in the program. This is possible thanks to a very special property of generators: they can be interrupted at a location and be resumed later to that location, with the execution context being saved and restored. In practice, this allows us to interrupt the execution of a function when waiting for an asynchronous operation to complete, and resume the execution of this function when the operation has completed.

What is the difference between a calling the next function and calling the send method of a generator object?

The `next` function resumes the operator from its last `yield` point. The `send` method allows us to additionally send back a value to the generator. The value passed as an argument of the `send` method can be retrieved as the return value of the `yield` expression. The combination of the `yield` expression and the `send` method allows a generator and its clients to communicate together in a bidirectional way. The generator can send values to its client when yielding, and the client can send values to the generator by using the `send` method.

How is a coroutine declared?

The correct way to declare a coroutine is by using the `async` keyword. However, this has only been available since Python 3.5:

```
async def foo():
    await something()
    print("foo")
```

It is also possible to declare a coroutine as a generator, and decorate it with `@asyncio.coroutine`:

```
@asyncio.couroutine
def foo():
    yield something()
    print("foo")
```

This last notation works for all versions of Python (with support for AsyncIO), but should be avoided whenever possible.

How can a coroutine call another coroutine?

A coroutine calls another coroutine by using the `await` expression. The `await` expression suspends the execution of the coroutine until the awaited coroutine completes. The result of the awaited coroutine is returned as the result of the `await` expression when the initial coroutine is resumed.

What is the role of the event loop?

The event loop schedules the execution of tasks and suspends the main thread activity when no task is active.

Chapter 3

What is a pure function?

A pure function is a function whose output depends only on its input parameters. A pure function has a deterministic behavior. This means that if it is called several times with the same values as input, then it will returns the same results. This deterministic behavior is called **referential transparency** in functional programming.

What is a higher-order function?

A higher-order function is a function that takes a function as an input parameter, and/or returns a function as an output. Higher-order functions are very useful for implementing abstractions or generic behaviors.

Why should side-effects be as small as possible?

Side-effects are parts of code that are not deterministic. This implies that this code is more difficult to test than pure code. So, making the footprint of side-effects as small as possible makes the whole application easier to test.

What is an observable cycle?

An observable cycle is the fact that several observables are inter-dependent. When an observable cycle is present, at some point an observable needs a reference to an observable that may not be yet available. This is a very common situation. An easy way to deal with it is to use subjects.

How can you wait in a coroutine until a item is received on an observable?

Coroutines can only wait for coroutines or futures to complete, via the await keyword. So, the easiest way to resume a coroutine when an item is emitted on a stream is to make this item emission complete a future. This is done by calling the `set_result` method of a future in the `on_next` callback of the observer.

How can you combine two observables into a single one?

There are several operators that allow us to combine several observables. One of the most commonly used ones is the `merge` operator. The `merge` operator combines several observables and returns an observable that contains all the items emitted by its source observables.

Would you implement some code that writes pixels to a screen as a component or as a driver? Why?

Writing pixels on a screen is an I/O operation (and, more specifically, a write operation). Any code that handles I/O operations should be written as a driver because it is a side-effect. Side-effects must be implemented as drivers. Components only contain pure code.

Chapter 4

How do you create an observable that emits only one value?

The operator just emits a single item and then completes. The following code snippet returns an observable that emits a string item and then completes:

```
single_item = Observable.just("a single item")
```

How do you create an observable that emits one item from each line of a text file?

This requires an observable with some specific code logic in it, so it must be implemented with the `create` operator. A possible implementation of this observable is as follows:

```
def create_line_observable(filename):
    def on_subscribe(observer):
        with open('filename') as f:
            lines = f.readlines()
            for line in lines:
                observer.on_next(line)
        observer.on_completed()

    return Observable.create(on_subscribe)
```

On subscription, this observable opens the file and reads it completely. Then it outputs one item per line, and finally it completes. Each subscription to the observable lead to a full read of the file. Since `lines` is a generator, it is possible to use it directly to return the lines of the file:

```
def create_line_observable(filename):
    def on_subscribe(observer):
        with open('filename') as f:
            lines = f.readlines()
            observer.from_(lines)

    return Observable.create(on_subscribe)
```

Does the just operator return a cold or a hot observable?

The `just` operator returns a single item for each subscription. This is the behavior of a cold observable.

What operator can you use to convert a cold observable to a hot observable, and start emitting items when the first observer subscribes to it?

Converting a cold observable to a hot observable is done with the `publish` and `connect` operators. The default behavior of the `publish` operator is to wait until the `connect` operator is called before emitting items. When there is a need to start emitting items as soon as the first subscription occurs, then reference counting can be used, as well as the `share` operator:

```
cold_numbers = Observable.from_([1, 2, 3, 4])
hot_numbers = cold_numbers.share()
```

Why is it important that observers handle errors?

Any exception that occurs in an operator is caught by RxPY and propagated as an error on the observable. If an observer does not handle errors, then these exceptions will be silently dropped, but the observable that raised the error stops emitting items. This can make debugging difficult because it seems that there has been no error, but the application stops working. So, it is important to implement the `on_error` callback on all observers to ensure that errors are correctly handled, or at least logged somewhere.

How can you convert an observable error to an observable item?

In some cases, it is useful to catch an error and convert it to an item. This can be done directly in the operator chain with the `catch` operator:

```
# obs is an observable that can raise an error
obs.catch(lambda e: "everything is fine") \
    .subscribe(lambda i: print(i))
```

Why should subscriptions be disposed?

When a subscription is created, it allocates some resources. The `subscribe` call returns a disposable object that implements a `dispose` method. Calling this method allows to release any resources that have been allocated during the subscription:

```
numbers = Observable.from_([1, 2, 3, 4])
disposable = numbers.subscribe(lambda i: print(i))
disposable.dispose()
```

Chapter 5

Why is using a blocking function a problem in an asynchronous application?

When a blocking function is called, the event loop is also blocked. This means that during the whole execution of the blocking function, no other action can occur in the application. Blocking calls are often I/O-based operations that can be very long (up to several seconds sometimes). If the application is stalled for such a long period, at best the user experience is degraded, and at worst some important messages will have been lost.

Why is using a CPU-intensive task a problem in an asynchronous application?

Using a CPU-bound task leads to the same issue as using a blocking call: the event loop is blocked for a long time, and it is just a matter of time before this breaks the functioning of the application.

What is the aim of a scheduler?

A scheduler is one of the ReactiveX components that allows us to integrate with asynchronous frameworks. The default behavior of ReactiveX is to be purely synchronous. This can seem counter-intuitive, but it is this property that allows us to integrate ReactiveX code easily with asynchronous frameworks such as AsyncIO. A scheduler only has to change the current execution context, with no other changes to the rest of the code. A scheduler changes the default synchronous behavior of subscriptions and makes them asynchronous, either running on an event loop or running on a worker thread. Several schedulers are available in RxPY to use different multithreading concurrency patterns, such as thread pooling.

What are the two possible ways to select the scheduler of a source observable?

The selection of a scheduler associated to a source observable can be done either at creation time or in the operators chain. Most factory operators accept a `scheduler` parameter that allows us to set the scheduler. In cases where the code creating the observable does not know which scheduler to use, the `subscribe_on` operator can be used once anywhere in the chain.

How is it possible to change the execution context inside a chain of operators?

Inside a chain of operators, it is possible to change the execution context of the operators by using the `observe_on` operator. The `observe_on` operator changes the execution context for all the operators that are after it in the chain.

Why is it very important to use AsyncIOScheduler in an AsyncIO reactive application?

If an observable is created without a scheduler, then all its associated chain will be processed during the call to `subscribe`. In this case, the subscription has completed before the event loop has started, which is probably not the intended behavior.

Chapter 6

What are the benefits of using named tuples instead of dictionaries to define operators item types?

There are three benefits of using named tuples compared to dictionaries:

- The first is the fact that the named tuples fields can be accessed with a dot notation instead of a dictionary square-bracket-style notation. The dot notation is easier to read and write than the square bracket notation. This makes the code easier to follow.

- The second is the fact that named tuples are more efficient than dictionaries at accessing their fields. This may have a beneficial impact on performance in an application that uses such objects widely.
- The last is the fact that named tuples are immutable. Object immutability is one of the principles used in functional programming. This property allows us to follow this functional programming principle when writing a reactive application.

What is the difference between a component and a driver in Cyclotron?

A component should only contain pure functions, while a driver contains side-effects. However, there is no enforcement of this behavior in Cyclotron. It is up to the programmer to follow these principles.

How is it possible to use a function (almost) like a custom operator?

When a function takes an observable as input and returns an observable, then it makes sense to use it directly in the chain of operators instead of having to break the chain to call it. The `let` operator allows us to do this by wrapping the function and forwarding keyword arguments to it.

What is the type of object returned by the function provided to the flat_map operator?

The function provided to the `flat_map` operator returns an observable. This is different than the `map` operator, whose parameter function returns an item. The items emitted by the `flat_map` operator are then merged in the observable returned by the `flat_map` operator.

Why is it better to parse the JSON configuration file with the loads function rather than the load function?

The `loads` function parses some JSON data provided as a string parameter. This allows us to implement the JSON parsing function as a pure function. On the other hand, the `load` function takes a file object as input. This means that a function using the `json.load` function is a side-effect. Using the loads function instead of load allows us to separate pure code from the side-effects when reading the file.

Why is the fact that sox works directly on files an issue?

Reading and writing to files are side-effects. So, the `sox` functions that are used to convert audio contain two kinds of code: access to the files and audio manipulation. If the audio manipulation part takes buffers as input and output, it could have been implemented as a pure function. The fact that `sox` works directly on files makes any function using it a side-effect. This is why is has to be implemented in a driver.

Another consequence is that file access cannot occur in an asynchronous way. This means that the `sox` library can block the whole application if an I/O access attempt is blocked for any reason. This is why such a library should not be used in a real asynchronous application.

Find another problem in the current implementation of audio transcoding.

The current implementation of the transcoding function does not handles errors. If for any reason the encoding fails (because the provided audio cannot be decoded, for example), then the server will crash. It should instead handle the error and return an HTTP error to the client.

Chapter 7

What are the existing software isolation technologies?

Three major isolation technologies exist:

- Emulators
- Virtual machines
- Containers

Emulators provide the strongest isolation, at the expense of performance. Virtual machines are more efficient than emulators but can only execute software with the same CPU architecture as the host, and provide fewer isolation guarantees. Finally, containers are the most efficient solution, but with fewer guarantees on isolation, at least in theory.

What is Docker?

Docker is a set of tools that ease the management of Linux containers.

On what kind of system does Docker software run?

A Docker image can run only on a Linux operating system. Moreover, most images are build for an x86-64 processor. It is, however, possible to generate images for ARM 64 processors.

What is the difference between a Docker image and a Docker instance?

A Docker image represents a filesystem hierarchy, as set of files containing a distribution packed in a single file. A Docker instance is an image that's currently being executed. Several instances of the same image can run at the same time on a system.

What kind of service is provided by S3?

S3 provides a key/value store. In S3, the key is a UTF-8 string, and the value is a binary blob. S3 objects are stored in buckets in a flat hierarchy.

How do you search for an object in an S3 bucket?

It is not possible to search for an object in an S3 bucket. So, you either have to know the key in advance or list the whole content of the bucket to retrieve the object in question.

How can CPU-bound operations be managed with RxPY?

Some RxPY schedulers can be used to execute some parts of an operator chain on another thread than the AsyncIO event loop. This allows us to easily move a CPU-bound task outside of the AsyncIO event loop.

Chapter 8

What is the purpose of the inotify feature?

Inotify is a feature provided by the Linux kernel. It allows us to monitor changes and access to files and directories. Using inotify allows us to monitor files changes without having to poll periodically for changes.

What is the feature provided by the debounce operator?

The `debounce` operator emits items only when no item has been received by the source observable since a defined time. It allows us to avoid flooding items by limiting their emissions.

Which operator can be used to remove duplicate items in an observable?

The `distinct_until_changed` operator emits items from the source observable but removes consecutive items with the same values. This operator can be used to create an observable that emits items without duplicates in consecutive items.

What is the difference between the take and skip operators?

The `take` operator emits the first items emitted by the source observable and drops the following ones. The `skip` operator drops the first items emitted by the source observable and emits the following ones.

What is a higher-order observable?

A higher-order observable is an observable that emits items that are themselves observables.

Why, in this application, is throwing an error on the observable chain not a good way to handle errors?

Directly throwing an error on the observable chain will cause the chain to stop (it will complete on error). So, no other request will be handled after that. Instead, an error must be gracefully handled by returning an HTTP error on the request that failed. This allows us to continue processing new requests.

Chapter 9

How can you print something each time an item is emitted?

It is possible to implement a side-effect without changing the items emitted on an operator chain by using the `do_action` operator. This operator allows us to call a function on each event type received from its source observable.

How can you compute a value from all the items of an observable?

Two operators can be used to compute a value from all items emitted on an observable: the scan and the reduce operators. Both operators call a function for each item, with an accumulator as input (on top of the item itself). This function must return the updated value of the accumulator.

The difference between scan and reduce is that scan emits the value of the accumulator for each item, while reduce only emits the value when the source observable completes.

How can you subscribe to the latest observable emitted by a higher-order observable?

When an observable emits items that are themselves observables, it is possible to subscribe only to the most recent child observable with the `switch_latest` operator.

How can you combine values of several observables, item by item?

The `zip` operator makes an item-by-item computation from several observables. Each time all source observables emit an item, a combined item is computed from these items.

How can you retrieve the first item of an observable?

Retrieving the first item of an observable is implemented by the `first` operator. Similarly, the last item can be retrieved with the `last` operator.

How can you classify items of an observable, based on some criteria?

The `group_by` operator takes a single observable and returns a higher-order observable. This higher-order observable contains one observable per class in the source observable.

How can you drop some elements of an observable based on some criteria?

The `skip_while` operator drops all items from its source observable until a criterion is fulfilled on the received items.

How can you chain several observable, one after the other?

You can chain several observables with the `concat` operator. The `concat` operator differs from the `merge` operator in the following way: the `merge` operator emits the items of all its source observables as they arrive (the items are interleaved), while the `concat` operator keeps the sequence of each observable (the items of one observable are emitted once the previous observable completed).

Chapter 10

Why is it important to find defects as quickly as possible?

Issues are fixed more easily and quickly when they are detected early. The cost of fixing an issue increases exponentially with the time elapsed since the associated code was written. So, finding defects as soon as possible makes the code more stable, faster, and cheaper than when they are detected late in the software development process.

What are the different kinds of software testing?

There are three big categories of software testing:

- Unit tests, which test functions
- Integration tests, which test the integration with dependent components
- System tests, which are end-to-end tests of the entire application

What is a test case in unit testing?

A test case is a group of tests. A test case allows us to group all tests of the same feature.

Why should tests be written before the actual code?

Writing tests before the code they test allows us to check that the test really fails when the feature is buggy. When tests are written after the code, they tend to be less complete. There are even cases where unit tests written after the code do not fail when the tested feature does not work!

Why should logging be done on dedicated observables?

Implementing logging as a specific feature, with a dedicated path in the observable graph, has several benefits:

- The logging information is independent from the feature provided by the component/driver.
- The logging feature is completely disabled if nobody subscribes to this observable.

Logging is a side-effect. Is this true or false?

In the example provided in this chapter, logging is a side-effect because the logs are printed on the console. However, another possible design is to write a logging handler that outputs the logs to another observable. This observable would then be routed to a console driver, or a file driver. In this case, the logging feature becomes pure code, and the side-effect is limited to the storing part of the logs.

Which operator can be used to add some traces in a chain of operator?

The do_action operator can be used to perform any action when events are received on an observable, independently of the chain of operators.

What are the two ways to enable the debug mode of AsyncIO?

The first way is to enable it per loop:

```
loop.set_debug(True)
```

The second way is to start the Python interpreter with an environment variable being set:

```
(venv-rx) $ PYTHONASYNCIODEBUG=1 python3
```

Chapter 11

What is a proxy?

A proxy is network equipment or software that filters all HTTP requests coming from clients inside a local network. Proxies can be used for several purposes:

- Restricting internet access
- Analyzing traffic to avoid viruses and attacks
- Caching content retrieved by a lot of people to speed up access

What is a reverse proxy?

A reverse proxy is network equipment or software present on the backend. Its role is to route incoming HTTP requests to the service that handles it. A reverse proxy allows us to hide the fact that multiple servers are used behind a single IP address.

What is a load balancer?

A load balancer allows us to easily scale a service. When several instances of a service are running, a load balancer distributes incoming request to these instances. Depending on the load-balancing strategy and the capacity of each instance, the distribution of the requests to the services may or may not be balanced.

What additional features are provided by Docker Compose compared to Docker?

Docker Compose provides the following facilities:

- Start and stop multiple containers in a single command
- Configure containers via a configuration file instead of many command-line arguments
- Scale the number of instances of a container

What is the purpose of a Dockerfile?

A `Dockerfile` is a configuration file that describes all the steps needed to build a Docker image. This configuration file is used by the `docker build` command to actually create a Docker image.

What are the prerequisites to scale a service horizontally?

A service can be scaled horizontally without any modifications if it is fully stateless. If a service is not stateless, then other components must be used to manage this state before the service can be scaled horizontally. This can be either by relying on another service or by implementing some communication between each service instance so that they form a cluster.

What service is provided by Let's Encrypt?

Let's Encrypt is a TLS certificate authority. They provide certificates that can be validated by HTTP clients such as web browsers without having to import the certificate on the server.

Chapter 12

What communication pattern is implemented by ReactiveX?

ReactiveX is an implementation of the publish/subscribe communication pattern.

What are the three most widely used communication patterns?

The three most widely used communication patterns are as follows:

- Publish/subscribe
- Request/response
- Channel

What is the difference between pull and push communication?

With pull-based communication, an observer actively requests information from an emitter each time it needs some data.

With push-based communication, an observer first registers itself to an emitter. Then the observer is notified each time the emitter emits an event.

Give examples of pull- and push-based protocols.

The following protocols are based on pull communication:

- HTTP
- Corba

The following protocols are based on push communication:

- MQTT
- Kafka

What is framing?

Framing is the fact that some data is packaged into a container that supports fragmentation. Once a data blob has been framed, it can be split into several parts before being transmitted on a communication channel. The receiver of these parts is then able to unframe them and recompose the original data blob.

What is serialization?

A serialization operation consists of encoding an object to another representation. The typical use case of serialization is to encode native objects to a representation that can be sent on a communication channel. Serialization is also a way to make information interoperable between several systems and/or programming languages.

What is routing?

The routing of events is the action of delivering each event to its recipient. This step is necessary when implementing event multiplexing, because the items of several observables are emitted on the same communication channel but in destination of different observers.

What type of message are needed to send an observable over a network link?

First, some messages are needed to handle the life cycle of the observable:

- `subscribe` messages, emitted to atomically create and subscribe to an observable
- `dispose` messages, emitted to unsubscribe from an observable

These two messages should have associated acknowledgement messages to confirm the success or failure of the request.

Then, one message type per observable event is needed:

- `item` messages, emitted for each item
- `error` messages, emitted when an observable completes on error
- `complete` messages, emitted when an observable completes on success

Chapter 13

Explain why side-effects must be as small as possible (in terms of code size).

In principle, side-effects should contain only the part of code that is a side-effect. However, when using existing libraries, the side-effect part often contains additional logic. This means that more code has to be tested, probably by using mocks. Since testing side-effects is more difficult than testing pure code, they should be stripped to the bare minimum.

What is the advantage of a protocol implemented without I/O?

A protocol implemented without I/O can be implemented only as pure code. As a consequence, such an implementation can be tested more easily and it can be reused on top of transport layers other than the original one intended.

What is the purpose of splitting logging and monitoring from features?

A feature, logging things that happen when providing this feature, and monitoring the health of this feature, are three distinct things. So, they each deserve a dedicated observable. This allows us to implement each part (feature, logging, and monitoring) without affecting the other parts.

Cite three reasons why an application is not behaving as expected.

When an application does not behave as expected, three frequent reasons are as follows:

- A missing error handler in a subscription
- An exception being raised by an operator (indirectly, via a function called by this operator)
- An missing scheduler

How can a trace observer be used to debug an application where nothing happens?

Trace observers, used with the `do_action` operator, allow us to track where an issue came from. They can by used at different locations in the operator chains to find the operator that provokes the unexpected behavior.

What issue can occur when creating an observable without specifying an scheduler?

In applications with cycles, where cycles are handled with subjects, it is possible that a subject subscribes to an observable, but drops the received items because no observer has yet subscribed to it. One way to fix this issue is to use a scheduler so that root observable items are scheduled on the event loop.

What issue can occur when a cold observable is subscribed to several times?

A cold observable emits a new sequence of items at each subscription. So, the consequence is that as many sequences are emitted as there are subscribers. This usually leads to situations where something happens several times instead of only once.

Other Books You May Enjoy

If you enjoyed this book, you may be interested in these other books by Packt:

Mastering Python Design Patterns
Sakis Kasampalis

ISBN: 978-1-78398-932-4

- Explore Factory Method and Abstract Factory for object creation
- Clone objects using the Prototype pattern
- Make incompatible interfaces compatible using the Adapter pattern
- Secure an interface using the Proxy pattern
- Choose an algorithm dynamically using the Strategy pattern
- Extend an object without subclassing using the Decorator pattern
- Keep the logic decoupled from the UI using the MVC pattern

Functional Python Programming
Steven Lott

ISBN: 978-1-78439-699-2

Use Python's generator functions and generator expressions to work with collections in a non-strict (or lazy) manner

- Utilize Python library modules including itertools, functools, multiprocessing, and concurrent.futures for efficient functional programs
- Use Python strings using object-oriented suffix notation and prefix notation
- Avoid stateful classes with families of tuples
- Design and implement decorators to create composite functions
- Use functions like max(), min(), map(), filter(), and sorted()
- Write higher-order functions

Leave a review - let other readers know what you think

Please share your thoughts on this book with others by leaving a review on the site that you bought it from. If you purchased the book from Amazon, please leave us an honest review on this book's Amazon page. This is vital so that other potential readers can see and use your unbiased opinion to make purchasing decisions, we can understand what our customers think about our products, and our authors can see your feedback on the title that they have worked with Packt to create. It will only take a few minutes of your time, but is valuable to other potential customers, our authors, and Packt. Thank you!

Index

Z

zip operator

www.ingramcontent.com/pod-product-compliance
Lightning Source LLC
Chambersburg PA
CBHW060649060326
40690CB00020B/4576